Wild Wild Guru

Wild Wild Guru

An insider reveals the true story behind
the Netflix documentary Wild Wild Country

SUBHUTI ANAND WAIGHT

CORONET

First published in Great Britain in 2019 by Coronet
An Imprint of Hodder & Stoughton
An Hachette UK company

1

Copyright © Subhuti Anand Waight 2019

A CIP catalogue record for this title is available from the British Library

Hardback ISBN 9781529345278
Trade Paperback ISBN 9781529345469
eBook ISBN 9781529345476

Typeset in Bembo by Hewer Text UK Ltd, Edinburgh
Printed and bound in Great Britain by Clays Ltd, Elcograf S.p.A.

Hodder & Stoughton policy is to use papers that are natural, renewable
and recyclable products and made from wood grown in sustainable forests.
The logging and manufacturing processes are expected to conform
to the environmental regulations of the country of origin.

Hodder & Stoughton Ltd
Carmelite House
50 Victoria Embankment
London EC4Y 0DZ

www.hodder.co.uk

To Lady Gaga

Her hair shimmering in saffron and green, the colours of India's national flag, Lady Gaga greeted the media with a traditional Namaste, then sat on a purple throne to answer questions.

"I feel so blessed. I never would have imagined years ago that I would be able to come to India and perform," she explained. "The sights in India are beautiful but the most beautiful sights are the people."

Lady Gaga had flown to New Delhi to give a concert at the Formula One Grand Prix. During her press conference, America's most flamboyant performer surprised her audience by revealing her affection for Osho, the controversial Indian mystic.

"Oh yes, Osho," she said. "I read a lot of Osho's books and I have been reading a lot about [Osho's views on] rebellion, which is my favourite so far. And how creativity is the greatest form of rebellion in life."

A comment that provoked many young Gaga fans to start googling "Osho" to find out who their favourite songbird was talking about. A few months later, she sent a tweet to her 18 million Twitter followers: "thinking about an OSHO tattoo". This was followed by several tweeted Osho quotes.

Lady Gaga is a gifted artist and a gutsy young woman who's not afraid to take risks. But still, I have to say to her: reading Osho's views on rebellion is one thing; living through the experience of rebellion with him is a different ballgame.

I can't help noticing Lady G has kept very quiet about Osho since Netflix released the documentary series *Wild Wild Country* in the spring of last year, showing the conflict that exploded in

Oregon when Bhagwan Shree Rajneesh – as Osho was then called – arrived from India with thousands of his followers.

I don't blame her for it. The Netflix series focused on crime and controversy – that was its formula for success – and I rather suspect Lady Gaga didn't have a clue about any of this turbulent history while she was reading Osho's books.

Lady G is from a new generation that missed Osho's physical presence here on Planet Earth. But I didn't. I was there. I lived with him for 14 years. I went the whole nine yards with him. I witnessed those events first hand, and I know they were far more mysterious and intriguing than *Wild Wild Country* could ever hope to show.

So, for Stefani Germanotta, and for all those interested in Osho, here is the story of my journey with a rebel, my dance with a madman, my adventures with a wild wild guru.

Contents

PART ONE

Call of the East

Hungry for Power

Steve Jobs and I never met, but we have one thing in common: we both took LSD and discovered, as Jobs put it, that "there's another side to the coin". In other words, we used the drug to open up our minds and came to realise there's more to life than getting an education, starting a career, setting up home with a wife and kids, and working 9-to-5 to pay the bills.

Jobs went on to create Apple computers, became extremely rich, then died of pancreatic cancer. I went on to discover meditation, became extremely poor and, at the time of writing this book, am still alive.

This is how it happened:

In the early 1970s, while working as a seemingly "straight" political reporter in the Houses of Parliament, I was doubling as a weekend hippie. As soon as Friday evening rolled around, I would jump in my car with a few unemployed, long-haired, macrobiotic-eating friends and, leaving London far behind, drive long into the night, heading for a cosy little cottage deep in the Cornish countryside.

We would arrive in the early hours, take several deep breaths of pure country air, then unroll our sleeping bags on the bungalow floor and crash out. Waking up the next morning, we would breakfast on whole grain porridge, consume a small tab of "California Sunshine" and spend the rest of the day lying naked on a beach in some sheltered Cornish cove, watching the emerald-green waves crashing along the shoreline, with hovering seagulls eyeing us curiously from above. Or going on other adventures, like riding horses through forests while stoned out of our minds.

I had some interesting moments, such as holding an intimate conversation with the Hindu god Vishnu, who suddenly appeared on a hillside across the valley from my cottage in the form of a giant

3

serpent. I know, the purists will tell you it is Shiva who is associated with snakes, wearing a cobra around his neck, but it was after all my vision, not theirs.

Even though I always managed to get my exhausted body and over-stretched mind back to London in time for Commons Question Time on Monday afternoon, it was clear that I couldn't maintain this dual lifestyle for long. It also became obvious that drugs, while offering a glimpse of altered states, could not deliver a permanently enhanced level of consciousness.

True, my LSD trips had helped me rediscover innocence, love of nature and simplicity of being – precious human qualities I'd tasted as a child but which I'd somehow sidelined as irrelevant when entering the world of adults. But, alas, these wonders were soon lost again, this time amid a labyrinth of drug-induced mind-games. The distinction between genuine personal experience and hallucinogenic fantasy was constantly being blurred. I'm told Charlie Manson had a similar problem.

There was a deeper issue nagging me: what was I looking for in my drug trips? What was I expecting to see, or understand? A few years earlier, the Beatles had captured the rebellious spirit of a generation by taking LSD, smoking dope, and in 1967 producing the seminal album *Sgt. Pepper's Lonely Hearts Club Band*, with songs explicitly describing drug experiences, like "A Day in the Life" and "Lucy in the Sky with Diamonds" – both banned by the BBC. Many other pop, rock and folk artists were pumping out songs with similar themes. As Bob Dylan noted, the times certainly were a-changing and the spirit of the era seemed promising, but promising . . . what? Social revolution? Free love? Peace on earth? A brotherhood of man? It sounded good, but integrating those ideals into daily life seemed challenging.

I remember one evening, in our Cornish bungalow, we decided to play Monopoly and became so caught up in the struggle to defeat each other that any feelings of togetherness and harmony drifted out the window with the smoke from our joints. Suddenly, it wasn't about brotherhood. It was about who would be king of the castle. On the surface, we tried to keep our cool, but it was a pretence. As the game intensified and neared its climax, I could feel our combined, unexpressed hostility pulsating in the room. In the end I was the winner, bankrupting the others with my hotels on Bond Street, Oxford Street and Regent Street, but the price I paid was my hippie idealism.

As John Lennon once cryptically observed: "I love humanity, it's the individual human beings I can't stand."

Meanwhile, back in London, my up-close-and-personal view of British politics was presenting me with some interesting insights. One lunchtime, I strolled into the House of Commons Chamber, which was empty except for a small group of tourists being shown the long rows of green leather seats by their guide.

As political correspondent for the *Birmingham Post* I had a Lobby pass, and the two policemen on duty knew me, so I had free access any time – except, of course, when the Commons was in session, when I had to be either up in the Press Gallery or outside the Chamber, in the Lobby.

On impulse, I wandered over to the government front bench and sat down where the Prime Minister usually sits. After a while, I just naturally seemed to slide down in the seat, lift my legs and rest my boot heels on the wooden edge of the table that stands between the government and opposition benches, the home of the two despatch boxes.

So, this is what it feels like, I thought.

At that moment, the guide spotted me, stalked over and said: "Excuse me, young man, but if you want to do that you need to get elected by the British voters, then be chosen as head of your party, and then be invited by Her Majesty the Queen to form a government."

I stood up, spread my hands in a gesture of *fait accompli*, and smiled. "Well," I replied, "Now I've done it. Just think of all the trouble I've saved myself."

If looks could kill, I'd have been the first journalist to have his career terminated on the House of Commons floor.

Some time later, I was attending a press briefing in 10 Downing Street. Normally, such briefings were held in a room at the top of one of the Palace of Westminster's modest towers. But this was summer recess, when the venue switched to Number 10. As the briefing ended, I loitered behind, inventing a supplementary question to keep a government official talking to me until the rest of the Lobby correspondents had departed. Then, when he'd finished, I strolled out of the door of Number 10 on my own.

It was summertime, so there was a big crowd on the other side of the road – this was before the entire road was blocked off to thwart terrorist attacks – and all eyes focused on me.

"Who is he? Who is that man?" I heard them say to each other as I strolled casually down the street in my trendy Village Gate suit.

These two experiences capture the essence of political ambition as I have observed it in a succession of British Prime Ministers and American Presidents over the years. They may proclaim lofty ideals about "wanting to do good" and "serving the people". They may even believe what they're saying is true. But, in almost every case, these good intentions conceal an underlying motivation: the longing for attention and the driving need to be seen as "somebody" in the eyes of others. Power makes you feel bigger than you really are and, when it's taken away, it makes you shrink – sometimes literally.

For example, in modern times, one of Britain's shortest Prime Ministers – in height, not duration – was Labour politician Harold Wilson. Officially listed as five feet eight inches, Wilson was actually well below it, but the strange thing was I never paid much attention to his height until he resigned as Prime Minister. A few months later, when I happened to see him, walking along the corridors in Westminster, I was astonished: he looked as diminutive as Bilbo Baggins in the Hobbit. It left me wondering: did his height really diminish, or was it the absence of power that made him look so dwarfish?

On the other side of the Atlantic, we all came to know about President Jimmy Carter's famous smile, which, when he was campaigning as a candidate, seemed as wide as the Atlantic itself. After his election in 1977, however, Carter was hit by several crises that destroyed his popularity, the most notable being his inability to rescue American Embassy staff held captive in Tehran after the Iranian Revolution. Carter slowly morphed from a very cheerful candidate into a very serious president. His smile shrank at the same rate as his unpopularity grew, and the media delighted in counting how many of Carter's teeth remained visible.

George W. Bush avoided combat service in the Vietnam War and was accused of cowardice because of it. But then as president he himself started a war, invading Iraq. Why? Some of us would say that it was to prove he could "finish the job" his father failed to complete in the Middle East. He was eager to be hailed as a "war president" and, indeed, American voters willingly supported Bush's heroic self-image.

Pay any kind of personal compliment to Margaret Thatcher – her hairstyle, her perfume – and the Iron Lady, also known as "Attila the Hen", would immediately dissolve into a shy, embarrassed, grateful little girl.

These people's dependence for self-esteem on the approval of those around them was a big eye-opener for me. In our great democracies, we have seemingly created a system that invites the walking wounded to run for office, using the power given by others to cover up their own sense of inferiority.

As for me, if I'm honest I was drawn to politics for a similar reason, wishing to be seen as "somebody" in the eyes of society, and, as a young man, had briefly toyed with the idea of entering the political fray. But then I realised journalism offered an easier, more painless route to Westminster. Why bother to campaign for votes and battle an election? Way too much effort! Easier to sell my writing talent to an editor and get a job in the Press Gallery, from which elevated position I could look down upon the politicians squabbling in the Chamber below and write sarcastic, witty articles about their antics.

However, my fascination with power didn't last long and Westminster soon became boring. Although there were moments of high political drama – including the expulsion of Russian spies, the struggle to join the European Community and, for light entertainment, the occasional sex scandal – there were long periods of routine legislative business. Increasingly, I came to view the House of Commons as a rubber stamp machine for either a Labour government or a Conservative government, depending who was in power at the time.

After a few years as a political journalist, I arrived at the unremarkable conclusion that, if, indeed, there was any meaning to be found in life, it probably lay somewhere other than in the Palace of Westminster.

No career in political journalism. No alternative, hippie band of brothers. What was left? Looking East, I began to hear the distant sound of *Ommmmmmmmmm*.

In Search of the Miraculous

"Take off that wig, Pete, it's grossing me out!"

I could understand my friend's complaint, but I wasn't about to oblige him. This was my first cross-dressing party and I was enjoying the strange and wonderful feeling of being a woman. I wore a brunette wig, with hair falling down to my shoulders, and as in those days I was clean shaven, using lipstick, powder and make-up on my face was no problem. My boobs, of course, were padded, but the dress covering my body felt silky-soft and sensual. Nylon tights hid my hairy legs.

I wasn't the only gender-bender at the party. The whole scene was like that: men dressed as women, women dressed as men. My friend couldn't handle it and left, but the man lying beside me on the couch was paying me lots of flattering attention.

Really, "he" was a "she", a lovely German from Berlin, whom I'd met during the meditation training we'd just completed. The chemistry between us was playful and the fact that we had exchanged gender roles made our attraction to each other seem very exotic.

"What's your name, honey?" he asked.

"Heloise," I said, allowing him to caress my cheek. "What's yours?"

"Freddie," he replied. Well, that made sense, because "his" real name was Frederika, making it an easy transition.

In this mating dance, it felt so nice to be the one who didn't have to make the moves, but to allow the "man" do the work. Ah, the joys of being a woman! We ended up in bed for the night, where the roles shifted to something akin to normal. Next day, I was back to my job as a meditation trainer.

But let me back up and explain how I got here:

In 1968, when the Beatles returned from India talking about meditation, I had realised they were on to something. I'm afraid it didn't do their music much good. Their *White Album*, composed mostly during their stay in Rishikesh, was a hotchpotch of tunes with no central theme, and failed to turn me on the way *Sgt. Pepper* had done. But I intuitively felt they were right about India. It had secrets to share. Maybe meditation would provide the answer to my ongoing, restless questioning of my purpose in life.

The Beatles' spiritual guide, Maharishi Mahesh Yogi, affectionately known to the British press as "the giggling guru", had opened the door to the West with Transcendental Meditation. In his wake, all kinds of gurus soon followed: Swami Prabhupada and his chanting Hare Krishna devotees; the little boy wonder, 13-year-old Guru Maharaji and his Divine Light mission; Yogi Bhajan, with his Kundalini Yoga and 3HO – happy, healthy and holy followers. These and many more came flying West, as demand for Indian spirituality almost outstripped supply.

But, for me, there was a problem. I was allergic to gurus. The idea of bowing down to one of these spiritual-looking guys gave me the creeps. It seemed to imply a degree of reverence and respect that I was unwilling to give them. So, deliberately turning away from what India was offering – at least for the time being – I decided instead to explore the Human Potential Movement that was growing in London around the same time. This felt more comfortable, perhaps because it was an extension of conventional Western psychology rather than imported Indian spirituality, and was investigating more rational ways to expand our ideas about ourselves.

In the autumn of 1970, I joined an alternative network based in North London, called People Not Psychiatry, which explored the notion – fashionable at the time – that to solve our psychological problems all we needed was more human contact and more honesty in our relating. I wasn't too sure about that, but I liked the guy who ran the PNP network, Michael, who struck me as refreshingly down-to-earth and intelligent in his quest for personal growth.

It seemed we were moving along parallel lines, especially when, in 1974, we both signed on for a 40-day holistic training offered by a new self-help outfit, freshly arrived from New York and called "Arica".

For my part, this required me to give up my job at Westminster, which was a scary step, but somehow inevitable if I was to devote myself to the challenge of self-exploration. Over the next couple of years, I financed myself first by living on savings, then on unemployment benefit and lastly through a brief and utterly boring stint as a UK government employee, writing pro-British press releases for overseas media.

Arica pulled me out of the mainstream. It had a leader, a Bolivian mystic called Oscar Ichazo, and in him I met a teacher with the right attitude: a man who was saying that gurus were unnecessary. Yes! Just my cup of tea. As an alternative, Ichazo was offering a series of practical exercises and techniques that would raise consciousness, causing the ego, the "I" – our separate sense of self – to collapse and be replaced with a state of pure enlightenment.

Ichazo's esoteric knowledge seemed boundless and his Arica Training consisted of an eclectic cocktail of methods and meditations, gleaned from various spiritual traditions, including Sufi, Tibetan Buddhist and Hindu sources.

Where did he get it all from? Ichazo didn't say, but some seasoned seekers, who'd studied the life of the Armenian mystic George Gurdjieff, were convinced that Ichazo was in contact with the fabled "Sarmoun Brotherhood" whom Gurdjieff considered to be the ultimate source of all wisdom. This secret sect was supposed to be living in a remote monastery, somewhere in the Hindu Kush Mountains of Afghanistan.

It was all very exciting and exotic. We chanted mantras, gazed at elaborate yantras and mandalas that colourfully symbolised spiritual powers, explored pranayama yogic breathing, tuned into baraka divine energy, learned about the body's seven energy centres, called chakras, did fitness exercises called psycho-calisthenics, and generally got high as kites.

Meanwhile, Ichazo had assured us that collapse of the ego would happen through understanding the "Enneagram", an ancient system dating back thousands of years to the Chaldeans in Mesopotamia, who apparently had a thing about numbers. The Enneagram symbol had already been introduced into the West by Gurdjieff, who claimed it could explain the laws of the universe, but I believe Ichazo may have been the first to apply it to human psychology.

The Enneagram described nine types of personality. Once we discovered our type and could see our own repetitive thought patterns, the ego would vanish, or so we were informed. I found it to be a brilliant system for understanding my own psychology but, for better or worse, useless for enlightenment.

Admittedly my ideas about "enlightenment" were decidedly fuzzy, presuming it to be a state of oneness with all things, in which I'd be communing with the divine, radiating light and feeling 24-hour cosmic bliss. But, whatever it was, the ego seemed to be in the way and, according to Ichazo, the Enneagram should have been able to take care of this minor obstacle.

Ichazo, however, had seriously under-estimated the ability of the human ego to survive any kind of assault on its Teflon-coated defences. Rather than becoming enlightened, we in Arica eagerly jumped on our Enneagram numbers and turned them into a new form of entertainment.

"Hey, I'm a Number Seven, what are you? Seven, too? Wow, that's so cool! What number is your girlfriend? A Three? Really? She looks more like a Two!" It became a mind-game, not an ego endgame.

Still, I was sufficiently impressed with Arica to become a trainer and was pleasantly surprised to find that this new role greatly improved my sex life. At the end of my first training as a teacher, I made love with three of the most beautiful women in the group, including the lovely Frederika. This was how I learned, at first hand, that women tend to be attracted to men in positions of authority, especially, so it seemed, spiritual authority, and the days when taking advantage of this would, rightly, be considered an abuse of power were still far into the future.

For me, it marked the end of a sexual drought that had lasted several years. It might be hard to explain, but up until then, first as a university student, then as a journalist, I had focused my energy on developing and sharpening my intellect. In the process of acquiring a degree and starting work as a reporter, I'd become sceptical, witty, sarcastic and cynical, distancing myself in order to become an observer of life, rather than a participant. But I wasn't exactly a nerdy-looking guy. In a puzzling paradox, I was aware some women found me attractive, but I couldn't allow myself to act on it. Finding myself face to face with a willing woman, I typified the hesitant, reserved, polite Englishman who couldn't quite bring himself to utter the magic words "Shall we spend the night together?"

As a result, my sex life had suffered, until this recent upsurge of female interest. Nothing had changed in me to justify the new situation. I somehow knew that. No, it was my role as the cool-looking, all-knowing meditation trainer that had upped my desirability to the point of overriding my English reserve.

Slowly, I came to understand a deeper truth about myself: I wasn't a sexy guy, in the sense of actually enjoying sex. I had other priorities, which had more to do with my self-image than sensual satisfaction. For example, it was essential for me to be seen by others as a man capable of attracting good-looking women. It was also important to be regarded as a competent lover who knew how to satisfy a sexual partner.

But, as for enjoying sex itself? Yes, I could make love and none of my partners complained, but what was I getting out of it? It seemed more like a carefully rehearsed routine than genuine sensual pleasure.

Perhaps that was why, at the cross-dressing party, I found new excitement in the gender reversal game. I was beginning to look for variety as a way of maintaining my interest in sex. This could have easily led me to explore a wider field, such as London's drag queen scene, or the gay scene . . . I could feel these horizons opening up as ways of keeping myself stimulated.

If Arica had succeeded in its stated aim of expanding into a popular, global force for human awakening, I might have gone along for the ride, content to womanise my way towards enlightenment.

But Ichazo's school never took off as a mass movement. The London teaching house closed, the PNP guy disappeared and "Freddie" returned to Berlin. Soon, I found myself back to square one in the self-exploration game, feeling bored and scouting around the New Age scene for something new.

Where, I wondered, was the real deal?

Orange Arrivals

In the autumn of 1975, Michael – the guy I'd met in the PNP network – suddenly reappeared in London, dressed in a blazing orange robe, with a necklace of wooden beads that ended in a locket containing the photo of a bearded guru. He'd just come back from India.

"If life is a movie, then I have met a man who lives outside the cinema," Michael informed me. His spiritual metaphor didn't impress me, but the meditation method he brought with him certainly did. In fact, to be honest, it frightened the life out of me.

About a dozen of us were invited down into Michael's basement, where we stripped naked and listened to instructions for "Dynamic Meditation":

Ten minutes deep, fast, chaotic breathing through the nose, empha-sising the exhale.

Ten minutes catharsis: scream, shout, cry, laugh . . . go crazy.

Ten minutes jumping up and down, arms raised, shouting the mantra "Hoo! Hoo! Hoo!"

Then a voice will say "STOP!" Don't move. Freeze.

Fifteen minutes silence.

Fifteen minutes dancing softly to music.

Instructions completed, a gong sounded, loud drumming rhythms started to play, and we were off. Immediately, people around me were breathing fast and furious, like a bunch of steam trains puffing madly along parallel railway tracks.

I think what frightened me, on that first occasion, was that I couldn't seem to breathe deep enough, or fast enough, to keep up with everyone else. Moreover, I was afraid that if I did breathe so fast, I would lose control . . . and then what? I needn't have worried. Loss of control happened anyway – at least to others. A second gong sounded for the next stage and everyone began screaming and shouting, banging pillows, punching the air, rolling on the floor, crying, sobbing and moaning . . . it was a madhouse.

In fact, that's exactly what it was intended to be. Later on, I came to appreciate how Dynamic Meditation encourages the release of pent-up feelings, prior to going into silence, whereas with ordinary, traditional, sitting meditations you just "sit on your shit", so to speak.

But, that first time, I was merely hoping to survive without someone attacking me. They didn't, of course, but having been brought up as a polite Englishman it was simply shocking to find myself drowning in a sea of uninhibited, deafening, emotional release.

The jumping phase followed and I did my best, but had to stop several times, taking extensive breaks, while those around me shouted "Hoo! Hoo! Hoo!" and jumped so high they practically touched the basement ceiling.

"STOP!"

Thank God. I had survived the three active phases of Dynamic. Sweat began trickling down my neck and back. The room felt dark and damp. Nobody moved a muscle. The silence became intense, deeper than any kind of silence I'd experienced before. I could feel the thumping of my heart. I could hear my mind, chattering away in the background, more distant than usual.

A soft flute heralded the music phase and we danced, more or less where we were, each in his or her own place, not moving around the room. This kind of dancing, it seemed, was intended to be an internal experience. We still had our eyes closed, yet we were moving our bodies freely, as we wished, with no one looking on, until finally the music faded and disappeared.

The meditation was over, but something new was beginning. In spite of being freaked out by Dynamic, I could recognise the power of the method and the intelligence of the man who'd created it. Guru or no guru, I had to go and meet him at his ashram in Pune, India, where he was based.

After introducing us to Dynamic Meditation, Michael served us tea and, as I relaxed on his sofa, he played an audiotape of his guru giving a discourse. I cannot remember a word of what the man said, but I was surprised at how touched I felt by his voice. It was so gentle, so soft and, above all, so peaceful. Such a contrast to the screaming in Dynamic. So different from the speeches in Westminster. So unlike my own voice, which by comparison seemed filled with stress and strain. This was the sound of a man at ease with himself.

"I would give anything to have that kind of peace in my life," I remember thinking.

Further encouragement for the India trip came from Frederika, who, to my surprise, also returned from Pune in orange. She came to London to see me and shared my bed, and I noticed a delightful difference when making love with her. She was more relaxed, more at home in herself. In close, intimate embrace, her body felt the same, but her energy seemed more expanded, more available and inviting. Melting into her, in sexual union, it seemed like we were swimming together in a warm, dark, tropical ocean, with no clear idea where the shoreline had gone.

But it was her long, lingering kisses that really got me. They had an orgasmic quality that hadn't been there, before her trip to India. They seemed sweeter, deeper, richer . . . in a word, they contained more "energy" and I seemed to be drinking it from her lovely mouth. Neither of us wanted to stop. I swear that if she hadn't needed to get up, pack her bag and head for Gatwick Airport, we'd have been kissing still.

"Greetings to Bhagwan," murmured Frederika, as she leaned out of the train window at Victoria Station, offering me one last kiss before her departure. She knew I'd been hooked and would soon be on my way to Pune.

These two experiences, with Frederika and Michael, made something clear to me. What I was looking for, in my quest, wasn't so much about finding new and more exotic forms of spiritual experience, although this remained a possibility. It was really about squeezing more juice, more energy, out of what was already available, here and now.

So, now it was my turn to leave London, heading at last for the Mystic East.

Before continuing my tale, however, I do have to say a final word about Steve Jobs, whose interest in LSD I mentioned in the beginning of this book. One of his most famous sayings, as I'm sure you recall, was his assessment of the meaning of life: "We're here to put a dent in the universe."

Mr Jobs, I don't think so. Based on my own experience, we're not here to dent the universe. We're here to dance with it.

PART TWO

Ashram in Pune

Energy Ball

As soon as I got off the plane in Mumbai, something in me relaxed. I don't know why. Maybe it was the chaos I encountered at the baggage reclaim: a single belt, upon which several white-clad porters, all wearing *dhotis* and Gandhi caps, clambered freely, grabbing hold of bags, while the rest of us waited patiently in the crowded little hall.

In March 1976, Mumbai airport was small and bare-bones basic, so very different from the massive edifice that stands there today. The cramped space and endemic chaos could have frustrated me, but instead, rather surprisingly, it soothed me. It was as if, entering such an alien world, my usual attitudes were put on hold, replaced by innocent wonder.

I wasn't allowed to carry my own bag. One of the porters seized it, pushed his way aggressively out of the airport and brought me to a beaten-up, yellow-and-black taxi. In exchange for a few rupees, the porter, who'd strategically refused to let go of my bag until he'd been paid, gave me his blessings and my taxi sped away through densely crowded streets towards the nearest train station.

The ride was a revelation. On the way, we skirted Dharavi, which even then probably ranked as the world's biggest slum – certainly, it was the only slum I'd ever seen – and we weaved our way through hordes of bicyclists and pedestrians, not to mention cows, goats, dogs, beggars, bullock carts and rows of tiny shops so filled with goods they seemed to spill out onto the street.

I was impressed by the traffic rules. There weren't any.

I was impressed by the heat inside the cab. There was no AC.

I was impressed by my relaxed, unquestioning acceptance of everything that was happening. It made me wonder, entering this alien world where reincarnation was taken for granted, whether I'd lived in India before. Maybe it was just jet-lag. But then, during subsequent years, I heard reports from many Westerners, arriving in India for the first time, who, amid the chaos, experienced similar feelings of a cosy sense of "coming home". Maybe we were all old souls returning to this holy land for one more crack at enlightenment.

But there was something more, which was entirely unexpected and only gradually became clear to me. I felt awed by an overwhelming sense of anonymity, knowing I could disappear in this country, melt into this seething mass of people, and nobody would know or care. All the welfare safety nets we take for granted in the West – insurance, social security, unemployment benefit, health care – meant nothing here. There was something very appealing in it.

As my train rumbled slowly out of Mumbai and began to cross open fields, I was curious to see many half-naked men, squatting close to the railway tracks. I wondered if they were meditating, then I realised they were shitting. We were passing through their bathroom.

Soon, we were climbing slowly up a long grade, rising from India's coastal plain to the Deccan Plateau, our passage keenly observed by groups of small monkeys, sitting by the tracks, hoping for idly thrown handouts. Hawkers muscled their way continuously along the central aisle of my compartment, offering small, espresso-like shots of sugary sweet chai, peanut bars called "chikki" and dubious-looking omelette sandwiches. I stuck to the chai.

"Chai . . . chai . . . chai wallah . . ." The eternal call sign of Indian National Railways.

At journey's end, my bag was seized once more and, following the porter, I made my way out of the station to a line of motorised rickshaws, a popular method of public transport that vaguely resemble a motorbike, only with three wheels, a double-wide passenger seat and a covering plastic hood.

"Rajneesh Ashram?" I asked a driver, standing by the first rickshaw. He wiggled his head from side to side, which, of course, is the classic Indian gesture for "yes", but which I mistakenly took to be "no".

"Rajneesh Ashram?" I asked, turning to the second driver.

"Yes," he said, so I got in. The first driver didn't object. Foreigners are such odd people, he must have thought.

We bounced our way on roughly surfaced streets out of the city towards a sleepy, once-elegant suburb called Koregaon Park. Filled with large bungalows and houses – some nearly the size of mansions – the park had originally been built for British army officers and had, after independence, passed into the hands of impoverished Indian princes, thereby falling slowly into genteel decay.

The ashram was a complex of two or three of these bungalows, purchased and lumped together, covering about one and a half acres of land. There were no walls around the property, just a half-fallen barbed wire fence and a badly fitting gate. When I stepped out of my rickshaw, a large, bearded, grandly turbaned Sikh gentleman in an orange robe let me in, assured me he'd take care of my bag, and pointed towards the office.

There, I met Laxmi, Bhagwan's secretary, a small woman sitting in a large chair behind a big desk, flanked on her left by a secretary of her own. Laxmi had pale brown skin, a dazzling, white-toothed smile and deep, dark, fierce-looking eyes. Wearing a reddish-orange robe and matching headscarf, she exuded a natural sense of authority and spoke about everything with absolute certainty.

Laxmi was talking to a middle-aged German couple, so I sat down and listened, waiting my turn. I can't remember how the conversation went, but I do recall that after a while I began to realise that the questions being asked by the couple were somehow missing the point. I don't think I articulated it, even to myself, but it was clear that their questions were superficial and intellectual – mostly, as I recall, concerning differences between Christian and Hindu beliefs. They arose out of a desire to learn, not from a thirst to experience. But Laxmi was patient, responding to each question as best she could, until finally the couple stood up, thanked her and left.

Laxmi waited until they were out of earshot, then flicked one of her hands in a gesture of dismissal. "Pah!" she exclaimed, addressing an assistant who sat beside her. "They are head people."

She swivelled her chair and looked directly into my eyes. "Now Peter here is a heart person."

Boom! An invisible ball of energy, warm and soft, shot across the desk and hit my heart with a resounding thump. There was no resistance on my part, because it happened so fast and took me completely by surprise. Besides, my heart welcomed it, receiving this unexpected gift like some long-forgotten nourishment.

It was an astonishing experience, completely outside my frame of reference. I didn't know what to do with it, so I focused instead on Laxmi's words. She had taken charge of the conversation, somehow having seen through me, or into me, and I couldn't believe what I'd just heard.

Me? A heart person? Me, the sarcastic political journalist? Me, the cynical, aloof observer whom no charlatan – politician or guru – could ever hope to deceive?

"I'd like to see Bhagwan," I explained, trying to stay on track.

"Yes, tonight!" Laxmi turned to her assistant. "Put his name down for darshan."

"Darshan", I understood, was the name given to evening meetings with Bhagwan, where visitors could meet him face to face, and ask questions.

The assistant looked up quizzically. "Is he taking sannyas?" she asked.

"Sannyas", I already knew, was the term Bhagwan used to offer "initiation" into discipleship. This idea came out of a long Indian tradition of spiritual seekers, men and women alike, who chose to "renounce the world" and don orange clothes as a sign of their religious status, becoming "sannyasins".

Before I could open my mouth, Laxmi had the answer. "Of course he's taking sannyas!" she replied. Again, there was no resistance from me, because, even from an intellectual viewpoint, she was right. After all, I hadn't flown halfway round the world in order *not* to take sannyas.

Not that I had any real idea what Bhagwan's version of "sannyas" was, except that I would need to wear orange clothes and a wooden-beaded necklace, called a mala, with a locket hanging from it containing the mystic's portrait. But I did understand that this gesture, or ritual, or ceremony, would establish in some mysterious way a connection between me and him.

Henceforth, I would be Bhagwan's disciple and he would be my spiritual master, whatever that might mean. I would have to try it, in order to know it. Like dropping acid, I intuitively understood, it was one of those things you had to dive into first and think about afterwards.

So, that was that. Before I'd even met Bhagwan, the essential, existential message had been delivered by Laxmi. What made this meeting remarkable, apart from the mystical physics involved in hurling a ball of energy across an office desk without even trying, was that it gave me a taste of a new quality – a quality I can only describe as self-love.

That's what it felt like after the energy ball hit my chest, and for three days afterwards. It wasn't love for Laxmi and it wasn't love for Bhagwan, even though it appeared to be something coming from them. It was, in my experience, love for myself. And this, I believe, is the sign of a true mystic: you don't end up loving him, or her. You end up loving yourself.

Which might explain a very strange statement I would hear Bhagwan say, several weeks later: "My work is to take away that which you don't have, and give you what you already have."

Doesn't make sense? Well, that's a promising start to this book, because, in the end, nothing about my story is likely to make sense. When you put it all together, embrace all the paradoxes, the only logical conclusion is a headache.

With that in mind, let us continue . . .

Meeting the Man

It was seven o'clock in the evening and already dark as we rounded the corner at the back of his house. Bhagwan was sitting in a chair on a white marble platform in what had formerly been a car porch. As we approached, I fancied I could see an aura of orange light, glowing softly around his head and shoulders . . . but it could have been the ceiling lamps.

Bhagwan welcomed us with a big smile and gestured for us to sit around him on the floor. He had a wispy, greyish-black beard, a bald head and long, thinning hair at the sides and back. He talked with each of us individually – there were a dozen of us present. His deep brown eyes seemed to look right into your soul, which would have been scary if they hadn't also been sparkling with laughter. He was 44 years old, or ageless, or child-like, or all three rolled into one.

When it was my turn to scoot forwards on my bum and sit directly in front of him, he smiled and asked, "How long are you going to stay?"

"Forever," I heard myself reply, which seemed a very odd thing to say and not at all what I'd planned. But I figured it was okay, because if he was the real deal, there wasn't any point in looking anywhere else. Besides, I did not feel constrained by my answer. For me, it was an expression of how I felt in that moment, not a binding vow for eternity. It wasn't like taking monastic orders, disappearing into a monastery and never coming out again.

On the contrary, throughout my time with Bhagwan, I would feel that freedom was the highest value, both for him and for me. I could have walked out of his door any moment and it wouldn't have been a problem. But still, it was an acknowledgement from my side that I needed a spiritual guide and was ready to commit myself to a master–disciple relationship with him.

Bhagwan laughed at my reply, murmured "very good" and then initiated me into sannyas, telling me to sit silently with eyes closed, while he wrote my new name on a piece of headed notepaper.

"Listen to the bird," he told me, referring to a little night song, uttered by an invisible bird, hidden in the darkness of the surrounding garden. In the silent pool of energy that seemed to engulf us on the car porch, the song stood out clearly and its notes seemed to dance in a vast space, although whether this sense of space was inside or outside me was difficult to tell.

My mind didn't put up with the silence for long.

"Damn the bird, damn Bhagwan!" I heard myself thinking. It was shocking, but not all that surprising. I already knew that my mind had a life of its own, was impossible to control and loved to make cynical observations at inappropriate moments – the journalist in me wasn't going to give way to the sannyasin so easily.

Bhagwan put a necklace of wooden beads around my neck and touched me delicately with his thumb, in between my eyebrows, which I knew was the location of my so-called "third eye", considered in India to be a doorway to inner space, or consciousness. I wasn't sure I believed in this mysterious energy centre, but of course I wasn't about to object to Bhagwan's method of initiating me. I don't recall any special experience arising from his touch. On the other hand, the whole ceremony seemed pretty exotic.

But I was already wearing orange clothes, so that part was already done. Then he gave me the name "Swami Anand Subhuti".

"Anand means bliss," he explained. "Subhuti was the name of Buddha's chief disciple. The literal meaning is: someone who is well known . . . famous, hmm?"

Looking back on it, I reckon Bhagwan must have seen the longing for recognition written all over my hungry psyche. So he played on it, puffing up my ego like a balloon, because with a name like that I naturally assumed – as I'm sure he intended – that I was about to be chosen as his chief disciple and subsequently rise to global fame.

But the lesson wasn't over. Next, he asked me if I'd read his book of Zen stories, titled *And the Flowers Showered*. I shook my head.

"It starts with a story about Subhuti. You read it, hmm?" His eyes twinkled with a secret joke. Then he stood up, blessed us all with a Namaste – the traditional Indian greeting, with hands pressed together in front of the chest – and disappeared back into his house. I hopped in a rickshaw and went back to the hotel close to the train station where I'd checked in during the afternoon.

Next morning, impatient to understand the significance of my name, I was the ashram bookshop's first customer. It was nothing more than a small trolley, rolled into position outside Laxmi's office, with books containing Bhagwan's discourses for sale at modest prices in both Hindi and English. It opened for business after the mystic's morning discourse.

I bought the book, read the story, and got the point. Subhuti had indeed been a disciple of Gautam Buddha and was the first to become enlightened. But he did so in a way that was exactly opposite to my expectations.

Subhuti was a complete nobody. Nobody knew his name. Nobody knew he was there. He was just one among thousands of *bhikkhus*, or monks, who formed the Buddha's *sangha*, his commune. There were many disciples who were well known . . . Sariputta, Mahakashyapa, Manjusri, Ananda . . . but Subhuti's name was not among them.

Sitting anonymously in Buddha's presence, Subhuti came to understand "the potency of emptiness". He realised that the ego, or sense of self, is nothing but a mishmash of opinions we have gathered, over the years, from other people's ideas about us. By becoming nobody, Subhuti dissolved all those opinions and disappeared, leaving only a silent inner space, a blissful inner emptiness.

Bhagwan's way of giving me my first lesson in ego-awareness was intriguing, because it was existential, not intellectual. By appearing to feed my ambition, Bhagwan had given me the opportunity to feel my ego puffing up, like a balloon being pumped with air. Then, when I understood Subhuti's experience of being a nobody, I could feel my ego deflate, again like a balloon, only this time with the air squeaking noisily out . . . I'm sure you know the sound, rather like a well-delivered raspberry.

So, I figured I'd better stick around and learn some more. I was already familiar with the world of wanting to be somebody, so it was a challenge to experience the opposite.

But it wasn't that simple. Diving deeper into the paradox, I soon came to understand that you can't desire to be nobody. If you do, then you create a new ambition, a new goal, and your "nobody" becomes another form of "somebody".

The ego reappears, standing on its head: "Hey, dude, look at me! I'm a bigger nobody than you are!"

What, then, can be done? The answer I would soon learn, as one of Bhagwan's sannyasins, can be summarised thus: meditate, watch the ego, don't take yourself too seriously and, above all, have a good time.

What Was He Like?

As we speed through the second decade of the twenty-first century, people still ask me: "What was it like to be with Bhagwan? What was he like as a person? How did it feel to meet him face to face?"

Let me put it this way: on those occasions when I sat in front of him in darshan, for those moments, it felt like I was the most important person in the world, or the only person in the world, or both. This wasn't just my experience. It was everybody's experience. It was the result of sitting in front of a human being who is giving you his total attention, a man who is one hundred percent present, here and now.

When he looked at you, smiled and gently asked, "How about you?", everything else disappeared. It was just you and him. The entire population of the world and, indeed, the universe itself, had just become completely irrelevant and probably non-existent. Not only that, I had the feeling — and again, this was something many people commented on — that he had the capacity, the love and compassion, to look past the superficial layers of my personality and see my essential nature.

Bhagwan often made the point that we human beings are, in our essence, made of the stuff called "consciousness". We may not be aware of it, we may behave in all kinds of stupid and unconscious ways, but this doesn't alter our inner reality. When we sat in front of Bhagwan in darshan, many of us had the feeling that he was addressing this essential core, which he sometimes also referred to as our "buddha nature".

In those days, anyone could come to Bhagwan and ask him anything. It didn't matter what it was. People came to complain that they couldn't sleep, or tearfully report they'd just lost their boyfriend, or were becoming heroin addicts, or contemplating prostitution as a way to make fast money . . . oh yes, and also to ask questions about spirituality and meditation. Bhagwan's door was wide, wide open and his darshans were spontaneous affairs with no fixed agenda. As I said, you could ask him anything. Sometimes this became a matter of regret later, when people looked back and recalled the trivia they'd brought before him.

"When I think I used to talk to him about my dog I could shoot myself," bemoaned one American lady who'd been with him since the beginning.

He would offer initiation into sannyas to anyone, including very young children. Asked why he gave sannyas to sleeping babies, held in their mothers' arms, he replied: "In the first place, I have never given sannyas to anyone who is awake."

Whoever sat before him got the same treatment: one hundred percent attention and one hundred percent respect as a buddha-in-becoming. Small wonder, then, that we floated out of such meetings on a white puffy cloud of bliss, gliding along the footpaths of the ashram, our feet barely touching the ground. It usually took a couple of hours to come down.

As you can imagine, these kinds of experiences caused problems at the office. Dreamy-eyed women would wander into Krishna House, sit down in front of Laxmi and announce that "Bhagwan wants me to move into the ashram". Then Laxmi would have to patiently explain that the ashram's accommodation programme wasn't run via messages received through divine communion, mystical dreams or on the astral plane. Any changes Bhagwan wanted to make would be transmitted verbally to her during their daily meeting.

It wasn't only the women. On one occasion after darshan, I became convinced that if I could slip a note to Bhagwan's personal caretaker, a young Englishwoman called Vivek, instead of going through the bureaucratic channels of the office, he would be sure to offer me a room in the ashram. I was living outside at the time.

Of course, Vivek gave the note to Laxmi and I was told to grow up and act my age.

Poor Laxmi! The things she had to deal with.

As an aside, it is a curious fact that almost all of Bhagwan's personal staff were English, including his caretaker, his doctor, his dentist and his laundry woman. To me, it was an amusing depiction of the British

Raj in reverse – karmic payback for the way Englishmen had ruled over India for more than 200 years.

But, really, it was amazing the ashram functioned at all, because all kinds of esoteric experiences were happening to many people, including me.

One time, during darshan, I was lying on the marble floor at the back of the little auditorium, not really participating, while Bhagwan was doing some kind of energy event at the front with another sannyasin. Suddenly, without warning and without any effort or intention on my part, I popped up, out of my body, and was floating about a metre above it. It was like escaping from a high-security prison. I had the sensation that I'd been contained not only by my physical body but by several layers of subtle energy bodies, all of which had now opened.

Bhagwan had in one of his daily discourses described these subtle bodies, listing a total of seven, with the inclusion of the gross physical body. The second, or etheric body, extended just beyond the skin and was emotional in nature, while the astral body lay further out and included mental energies as well as the possibility of astral travel. There were four more, each one being more subtle and further away from the physical form.

I'd heard about these bodies, too, in the work I'd done with Arica back in London, and could sometimes seem to sense the energy field of my second body, but this was the first time I'd actually passed through all seven – on my way out of town, so to speak. It was a short excursion. I barely had time to realise what was happening when "whump!" I was back inside, with all doors closed. It was then that I realised how powerfully we are bound to the body.

On another occasion, later on when I was living inside the ashram, I'd skipped the early morning Dynamic Meditation and was lying sleepily in my bed when a massive roar erupted in the distance – from Buddha Hall – as the meditation entered its cathartic stage and everyone started screaming and shouting. Somehow, the energy of that sound rolled like a wave through the ashram, into my room, into my feet and up through my body, pushing me gently out of the top of my head.

"Ooh, I'm out!" I exclaimed myself, in a kind of nowhere land. But then I panicked. What if I couldn't return to my body?

"My legs!" I shouted and kicked them hard. In a second, I was back inside and immediately regretting my cowardice.

"You fool! Couldn't you have stayed out a bit longer, so we could've had time to look around?" I scolded myself. It might have been fun, walking through walls, poking my nose into other people's rooms. Now it was too late. The opportunity had passed. Time to get up, take my physical body for a shower and then to breakfast. This was the real challenge of being in Pune in those days: to accept all these strange goings on and still lead a relatively normal life.

But what was "normal" now? Well, there were parallels with my earlier drug experiences. In both cases, I was being propelled outside my mind's ideas about the limits of human perception. There were differences, too. These new happenings weren't chemically created. They seemed to be a by-product of living and meditating within the energy field of an enlightened mystic and, as such, might well be part of a new "normal".

It reminded me of a line from *Alice in Wonderland*, after Alice had fallen down the rabbit hole:

"Curiouser and curiouser!" cried Alice.

Honey, I'm with you.

Welcome to the Tardis

In the weeks that followed, I became familiar with the ashram and its surroundings, so let me take a moment to set the scene. In the mid-1970s, Koregaon Park was, as I said, a sleepy suburb, descending slowly into a kind of refined poverty. It consisted of four parallel lanes, named, somewhat unimaginatively – presumably by some bureaucrat in the long-departed British Army – as Lane One, Lane Two, Lane Three and . . . yes, you got it . . . Lane Four.

On either side of each lane there were ten houses some were classical-style bungalows with wide verandas, while others were large, rambling, two-storey mansions. Nearly all of them were in varying degrees of neglect and disrepair. The suburb was rendered elegant and beautiful by large banyan trees that lined the lanes and by the absence of traffic, apart from the occasional bullock cart and, rarely, a made-in-India Ambassador car.

The Rajneesh Ashram had begun with the purchase of a single, averaged-sized house on Lane Two, which Bhagwan had christened "Lao Tzu House", naming it after the Chinese mystic and author of the *Tao Te Ching*. The deal was financed by a donation from a Greek woman, who was divorced from a wealthy businessman, and who became the ashram's chief gardener.

It was into this house that Bhagwan moved in March 1974, in the hope that his fragile health would improve away from the heat, humidity and pollution of Mumbai. People close to him told me he suffered from asthma, diabetes, was allergic to strong smells – especially perfume – and preferred to live in air-conditioned rooms to avoid the heat.

Once settled in Lao Tzu House, Bhagwan didn't waste time. He immediately began to give morning discourses, held on a large balcony upstairs, while his meetings with individual disciples – evening darshan – were held in a room downstairs. His bedroom, dining room and kitchen were also located on the ground floor. Upstairs rooms were given to close disciples, while the rest of his visitors had to find accommodation in local hotels, or by renting servants' quarters in nearby bungalows.

Very soon, a second house was purchased, which Bhagwan called "Krishna House". This building was on Lane One, in exact alignment with Lao Tzu House on Lane Two, so the gardens of the two houses joined back-to-back. Once the dividing fence was torn down, the two houses became, effectively, one ashram.

The secretary's office, where I'd met Laxmi, was in Krishna House, as was the main office, where correspondence with sannyasins around the world was conducted and where book-keeping and other administrative essentials took place.

What about the meditations? Well, at the rear of Krishna House there was a large car porch, located under the house itself, which was quickly given a marble floor. This became "Radha Hall", the first venue for regular daily meditations. A maximum of about 50 people could meditate there. Meditations began at 6:00am with Dynamic and continued throughout the day, at regular intervals, concluding with a technique called "Kundalini Meditation" at 4:15pm. (I would explore all of these so-called "active meditations", and describe the basic principle on page 47.)

Both Lao Tzu and Krishna House had a number of smaller rooms attached to them and these, of course, were quickly filled with sannyasins planning to stay with Bhagwan as long as possible.

Just before I arrived, a lovely, semicircular auditorium, paved with marble and open to the garden, had been added to Lao Tzu House. The upstairs balcony had become too small for the growing number of visitors and so this new venue was created for Bhagwan's morning discourses.

I loved that auditorium. It was a magical place, with morning light filtering through the trees and birdsong mixing eloquently with the sound of Bhagwan speaking. It was named "Chuang Tzu Auditorium", after another famous Chinese mystic whom Bhagwan loved. Chuang Tzu used riddles and paradoxes to teach his disciples and was famous for the saying: "Easy is right."

In the early days, there were probably no more than 40 to 50 people in the auditorium for discourse, but this number was growing fast and within a few months of my arrival, two or three hundred people were trying to squeeze into Chuang Tzu.

Most of the arrivals from abroad were young, white, middle-class Europeans, Americans and Australians. But, naturally enough, there was also a significant percentage of Indian sannyasins, plus a scattering of other nationalities, including Japanese, Brazilians, Iranians and Indo-Chinese.

Meanwhile, evening darshan had been shifted from inside Lao Tzu out onto the bungalow's car porch, which had been paved with white marble. It was split level, raised at the rear, in the form of a small plat-form, and here Bhagwan met and spoke with newcomers, visitors and sannyasins. This was where I and many others took sannyas.

This, then, was the basic set-up when I arrived. But it was an ever-changing scene, because soon another house, standing side by side with Lao Tzu House on Lane Two, was purchased, giving the ashram an L-shaped look. The ashram now comprised three plots, covering about one and a half acres in all.

Bhagwan named this newly-acquired building "Jesus House" and immediately it was filled with disciples, including some who created makeshift sleeping quarters on the roof, in the form of flimsy bamboo huts.

A publishing office was established in Krishna House, where the audiotapes used for recording Bhagwan's discourses were transcribed by a couple of sannyasins. All day long, they sat listening to tapes with their headphones, while banging out the written word on old-fash-ioned typewriters; there were no word processors in those days. The typed transcripts of Bhagwan's discourses were then edited to create books. One discourse filled one chapter. A series of 10, 15 or 20 discourses filled a book. Some series were longer and were divided into volumes.

One of the most memorable series, for me, was *The Search*, describing the ten bulls of Zen, about which Bhagwan was speaking when I arrived. I loved the image of a bull symbolising the life force and the quest of the spiritual seeker who searches for it, finds it, tames it and rides it to enlightenment.

I also enjoyed reading *Hsin Hsin Ming: The Book of Nothing*, Bhagwan's commentaries on a famous Japanese Zen poem, which he gave two years prior to my arrival in Pune and which had been published as a book. This poem began with a line so simple, and yet so profoundly important for spiritual seekers, that I have never forgotten it:

The Great Way is not difficult for those who have no preferences . . .

Bhagwan was giving two or three discourse series in a month – either in English or in Hindi – so as you can imagine, the publishing office was kept pretty busy. The actual printing was done commercially in Pune city, under close supervision by sannyasin editors and production managers.

A small kitchen and canteen were established at the back of Krishna House, just behind the meditation hall, serving basic Indian food for breakfast, lunch and dinner. Sannyasins chopping vegetables often sat outside Radha Hall, where the meditations were happening, so it was an intimate, casual and cosy scene.

After my arrival, one of the first new developments as I recall was the creation of a proper fence along the road in front of Krishna House and the erection of a very grand, teak gate with brass studs. This instantly became known as "the gateless gate", reflecting Bhagwan's offering of unlimited access to thirsty souls seeking spiritual refreshment.

Somewhere in front of Krishna House, tucked away to the side, amid low-roofed buildings that once housed servants, was "the mala shop". Here, sannyasins with woodworking skills were fashioning the beads and lockets needed for the malas that Bhagwan would hang around the necks of new initiates. Naturally, the mystic's portrait was also needed for each mala, so a makeshift darkroom and photography lab were created inside Krishna House, behind the offices.

Meanwhile, underneath the building, accessed through a steeply descending staircase and strung together along a very narrow corridor, were three soundproof chambers with padded walls. Here, the noisy groups were held, like Encounter – a shocking and extremely challenging form of self-help therapy that I describe in detail later in the book. There was a claustrophobic, dimly lit, oppressive atmosphere down there – the perfect setting for provoking long-repressed emotions.

Up in the daylight, the whole ashram was a hive of industry and activity, with sannyasins working at a huge variety of jobs, including basic tasks like cleaning, cooking, gardening, carpentry and general handyman-style maintenance. We tried to do everything ourselves.

Physically, the ashram was small, but in some strange way it didn't seem crowded. To me, it was rather like the Tardis in *Doctor Who*: on the outside, the Tardis looked small, since it looked like an old-fashioned British police box, but, when you opened the door and went inside, it was vast, almost a world unto itself. To me, the Pune ashram was like that. The experience of being there had so many dimensions and provoked so many different moods and emotions that it seemed boundless. Moreover, during the meditations, discourses and darshan, the inner space we tasted seemed vaster than the universe itself.

I don't know if Bhagwan had ever heard of Doctor Who, but I rather fancy these two magicians had much in common. They both wanted to help people and they both fashioned ingenious ways of doing so. Doctor Who had his sonic screwdriver. We will see what Bhagwan had up his sleeve in the chapters that follow. The main difference between the two, of course, was that Doctor Who's enemies were externalised forces, such as the notorious Daleks, whereas Bhagwan could see that the forces of darkness were all inside our own heads.

The favourite battle cry of the Daleks was *"Ex-ter-min-ate!"*

No no, dear Daleks. At least, in this ashram, try something new: *"Med-it-ate!"*

This shift in emphasis may seem comical, but it neatly symbolises the switch required in the human condition: from outer conquest to conquest of oneself.

Bhagwan's Back Story

If you go to Google Images and enter "Maharishi Mahesh Yogi" and "Acharya Rajneesh" there is a good chance you will find an old photograph, taken in 1969, showing the two mystics sitting together on an outdoor sofa, discussing meditation, before a gathering of Western and Indian seekers in Pahalgam, Kashmir.

It was the first, last and only time the two gurus met. It was also the first time that Bhagwan addressed a Western audience and the first time he spoke publicly and at length in English. "Acharya" is a respectful Hindi term indicating a spiritual teacher, and this was how Bhagwan was known in the sixties.

By this time, the Maharishi was almost a household name, thanks to his endorsement by the Beatles. Acharya Rajneesh, on the other hand, was unknown outside India. His controversial book, *From Sex to Superconsciousness*, published in 1968, compiled from a series of discourses about sex and delivered in Mumbai the same year, had made him notorious in India, but it wasn't yet known in the West. Even in those early days, Bhagwan was admired by India's intellectual elite, who recognised the scope of his knowledge and the depth of his insights into the human condition. But, more often than not, they took care to keep a careful distance, especially if they had a social reputation to protect.

In September 1969, the Maharishi had been conducting a meditation camp in Pahalgam for Transcendental Meditation enthusiasts. When some of them learned that Acharya Rajneesh was also in town, they invited him to a joint discussion with the Maharishi – after obtaining the Maharishi's permission, naturally.

I have listened to an audio recording of their debate and could feel how the Westerners became frustrated and irritated with the Acharya, because all Bhagwan would say, in a dozen different ways, was that no technique could help people attain to enlightenment. This was the opposite of the Maharishi's teaching, and although the two mystics sat side by side in an apparently friendly manner, they were poles apart.

The Maharishi described TM as a technique that takes the mind from the surface to subtler levels and eventually into the state of pure, transcendental consciousness.

Acharya Rajneesh disagreed. "There is no validity to this whatsoever. How can you have a technique to go somewhere that is everywhere? If it's already everywhere, where is there to go? Why would you need a technique to go there?"

When asked to state his own position, Bhagwan told the crowd: "There is nothing like my position, because to have a position is to be untrue. I have no position, I am totally negative. There is no possibility of there being any path."

This didn't go over too well with the Western audience and Bhagwan must have realised he couldn't reach people this way. Soon afterwards, a remarkable shift happened. Within a year, he was developing his own meditation techniques, including the Dynamic Meditation I'd encountered in London. Two years after that, he was offering initiation into "neo-sannyas" – his own version of discipleship – and also started giving discourses in English as well as Hindi, speaking on a wide variety of spiritual paths.

The transformation worked. An iconoclastic rebel had morphed himself into a helpful spiritual mystic and seekers started coming – from abroad as well as India. The Rajneesh movement was under way.

In 1972, just as the first Westerners were being attracted to Bhagwan, an interesting event took place in the Himalayas that throws a fascinating light on the mystic and his mission to spread meditation.

One of Bhagwan's early disciples, an Indian sannyasin called Govind Siddharth, had become intrigued with stories about Tibetan lamas and their occult powers, which Bhagwan had occasionally mentioned in his discourses. Since he was visiting Sikkim, where many Tibetan monks had relocated after the Chinese invasion of Tibet, Siddharth decided to investigate these stories for himself.

Arriving in Gangtok, Sikkim's capital, he was advised by the local tourist office to go to Rumtek Monastery, about 25 miles distant. He arrived without an appointment and was at first told the monastery was closed to visitors, but then, in an unexpected twist, he was invited for an interview with the 16th Karmapa, Rangjung Rigpe Dorje.

The Tibetan teacher was 48 years old and preparing for his first world tour, which would include many of the "Black Crown Ceremonies" that made him known to thousands of Westerners. (By this time, too, the Karmapa had gained a formidable reputation within his Karma Kagyu sect for recognising reincarnated monks and lamas, and reminding them of their previous lives.)

Siddharth takes up the tale, upon meeting the Karmapa:

One interesting point is that His Holiness looks exactly like Bhagwan – exactly: so jolly, so light-hearted, so warm! He is about the same age too – about forty – between forty and fifty.

When I first entered, he immediately told me, "I know from where you are coming." It was a great surprise for me. And then he said, "I am seeing that you have somewhere some photograph, or something which is printed on two sides, of your Guru." I answered, "I have nothing like that which is printed on two sides." (I had completely forgotten the locket hanging on my mala with Bhagwan's photograph on both sides.)

There was an English lady who acted as an interpreter, since Lama Karmapa does not know English and speaks only in the Tibetan language.

She immediately saw my mala and said, "What is this?" I then remembered that the locket was printed on two sides and said, "This is the photograph of my Guru." She was curious to see it, so I took it off and showed it to her. Immediately His Holiness said, "That is it."

He took the locket of Bhagwan in his hand, and he touched it to his forehead, then he said about him, "He is the greatest incarnation since Buddha in India and is a living Buddha."

The Karmapa then explained to Siddharth that mystics who have become spiritually awakened need special training if they want to help others attain similar states of consciousness and Bhagwan had already passed through this training in previous lives as a Tibetan lama.

"Now in this life, Bhagwan has taken birth specially in order to help people spiritually – only for this purpose," he declared.

Intriguingly, the Karmapa added that although Bhagwan's disciples might feel he was speaking just for them, the mystic was really speaking for future humanity via the Akashic Records, which, according to legend, is a record of events and words stored on some non-material, astral plane of existence.

Apparently, the Karmapa was unaware that all of Bhagwan's discourses were also being recorded on audiotape (and later videotape) and transcribed into books. Or maybe to the Karmapa it was the same process, happening simultaneously on two different planes.

Siddharth continued:

Then he asked me about what methods of meditation Bhagwan teaches. I described to him our four-stage method. When I told him about the third stage, the shouting of "hoo-hoo-hoo," he said that this "hoo" comes from the "hum" in the Tibetan mantra "Om mani padme hum".

He was so much excited about this that he just grabbed my two hands, saying he was "very much delighted" and that "this method is absolutely right; this is similar to some of the Tibetan ways of these practices, and whatever work we are doing, you are doing the same thing." Many differences are only in language. For example, when we use the term "kundalini", they use "the burning fire" to mean the same thing. But about Bhagwan's method, he just said, "Perfect!"

Their interview continued, but we must leave it there. It was subsequently published in a book titled *The Silent Explosion* containing some of Bhagwan's early discourses. The mystic's approach to "kundalini", by the way, is explained in the next chapter.

Clearly, the description of Bhagwan as "the greatest incarnation since Buddha" is a remarkable statement, coming from one of the most important figures in Tibetan Buddhism, carrying with it the implication that Bhagwan was, and is, one of history's greatest and most powerful spiritual teachers. Personally, though, I'm not so comfortable with this way of looking at Bhagwan, which, I feel, can be easily misunderstood. My own perspective on the mystic is more complex and will unfold as my story continues.

I sometimes wonder if the Karmapa could have foreseen the trouble and turmoil Bhagwan would eventually cause, and whether this would have shaken his conviction in Bhagwan's greatness, or, paradoxically, perhaps even strengthened it. Alas, we will never know, because the 16th Karmapa died in 1981, just as the most turbulent period of Bhagwan's life was taking off.

Now, let's take a brief look at the rest of Bhagwan's life story:

He was born Chandra Mohan Jain in a small town in Madhya Pradesh, central India, in December 1931. His father was a cloth merchant and the family followed the Jain religion, which like Buddhism emphasises non-violence and believing that all life is sacred, including animals and insects, but reveres its own prophet, Mahavira, who was a contemporary of Gautam Buddha.

For the first seven years of his life, Bhagwan was raised by his maternal grandparents. They called him "Raj" and he later changed this to "Rajneesh", which, according to some interpretations, means "Lord of the Full Moon". Later he decided to go to university, where his parents hoped he would study engineering or medicine. When he announced he was going to study philosophy, they were shocked.

"They all asked me, 'But what is the reason that you want to study philosophy?'" Bhagwan recalled later. "I said, 'The reason is that my whole life I am going to fight against philosophers. I have to know everything about them.'"

While a student, at the age of 21, he attained to spiritual enlightenment – for sure, it wasn't on the university curriculum, but it seems to have happened anyway. Perhaps here I should mention that there are many weird and wonderful tales about Bhagwan's childhood, youth, student days and his spiritual awakening – not to mention his past lives.

For example, in Bhagwan's home town there was a strange, silent sage called "Mugga Baba", whose only possession was a mug – hence his name – into which people put food, water, sweets and money. He recognised that Bhagwan had attained enlightenment, and one night when there was nobody else around, Mugga Baba spoke to him, urging him make the effort to share, through words, the spiritual transformation that had happened to him.

"My silence has not been understood," he told the young man.

Bhagwan decided to spend a few more years at university, becoming Professor of Philosophy at Jabalpur. At the same time, he was being invited as a guest speaker at religious gatherings and conferences all over India.

He may have changed his approach to spirituality and meditation, but he was as adversarial as he would be in his later meeting with the Maharishi, criticising Gandhi and his philosophy, condemning orthodox religious attitudes, attacking the Indian government's socialist economic policies and daring to openly discuss India's archaic attitudes towards sex.

The Mumbai lectures, compiled in *From Sex to Superconsciousness*, were both shocking and ground-breaking. As one woman who attended them commented afterwards: "I knew the word 'sambogh' meant 'sex', but I had never heard it uttered in public before."

Towards the end of 1972, Bhagwan reduced his travelling and settled in an apartment in Mumbai. As an indication of his growing popularity, crowds of up to 50,000 people would come to listen when he gave public discourses, usually at open air locations like Cross Maidan, a park in the centre of the city.

Two years later, in 1974, he shifted to Pune. That's where I caught up with him, in 1976. At the time, he was giving a 90-minute discourse every morning, and although on the surface he was apparently embracing a wide range of spiritual paths – Sufism, Zen, Yoga, Tantra, Hasidism – Bhagwan's basic message was always essentially the same: there is no need for any god, nor any kind of religious belief. The spiritual fulfilment you are looking for is to be found in your own innermost core of consciousness. Just go in and find it.

Which might explain why, within a short time of arriving at the Pune ashram, I found myself in an underground sound-proof chamber with padded walls, with about 20 naked young men and women, facing my worst fears. Before descending into this sannyasin version of Dante's *Inferno*, however, let's take a longer look at Bhagwan's philosophy.

Non-Philosophy for Meditators

Bhagwan's philosophy was simple: he didn't have one. Or, if he did, it could be described in two words: "Wake up!"

In this, he was similar to radical Zen Masters in Japan, who focused on creating devices and situations that might provoke in their disciples a sudden awakening of consciousness. It was Bhagwan's viewpoint that, essentially, we don't need to understand the nature of spirituality intellectually. We just need a bucket of cold water thrown in our faces. Describing our existential condition as "buddhas pretending not to be", he said he secretly giggled at our so-called problems and we didn't need his compassion. We just needed "to be hit hard on the head".

One of his favourite sayings was taken from Hakuin Ekaku, regarded as one of the most influential Japanese Zen mystics. In his "Song of Meditation", Hakuin declares in his first line:

All beings are, from the very beginning, buddhas.

In other words, all beings have, as their innermost core, cosmic consciousness, or buddha-consciousness, or whatever you wish to call it. In this way, we are already enlightened. We have never been anything else. But we are distracted from this core in a million different ways: our attachment to the world, to wealth, to social status, to love, ambition, greed, conquest . . . All of this blinds us to our true nature.

The function of a mystic is therefore to provoke in us a remembrance of our nature. That's why Gautam Buddha called his approach to meditation "*sammasati*", or "self-remembering".

So, even though commentators have done their best to label Bhagwan, calling him a Tantric Master, a Zen Master, a Hindu saint or sage, or even, as the Karmapa declared, "the greatest incarnation since Gautam Buddha", none of it adequately and definitively describes him.

If I am to describe Bhagwan's connection to the cosmos, then perhaps I can begin by relating a strange experience I had one evening in the meditation hall during one of the ashram's celebration days, two or three years after my arrival.

The mystic was sitting on the podium, in his usual chair, while I was sitting in the crowd, about one third of the way back. There were more than 1,000 people present and those who were sitting were singing, while those standing at the back were dancing. At a certain point, the singing ended and everyone closed their eyes and went into silence. For some reason, I kept my eyes open and watched as Bhagwan's eyes slowly scanned the hall, looking at everyone, seemingly showering love on all those present.

As he scanned the middle of the hall, his eyes met mine, passed me by, then stopped, returned and looked at me again. In that moment, it seemed as if he was showing me something, because, as I looked into his eyes, I could see a bright, white pinpoint of light, like a star, shining out at me and everyone else, but from far away, as if from behind the head of the mystic – perhaps in some other dimension that, for this precious moment, was made visible to me.

I watched for a couple of seconds and then Bhagwan's eyes moved on, finishing their sweep of the hall. It was a mystifying experience, defying explanation. But, even if it was inexplicable, it gave me a vivid sense of how mystics operate in connection with cosmic energy.

As I explained with the story about Gautam Buddha's disciple, Subhuti, when the meditator arrives at the door of the beyond and relinquishes the ego, he disappears as a separate self into cosmic consciousness. There is no longer any duality. The mystic and the ultimate source have become one.

Then, if the mystic is willing to be a channel, divine energy will flow through him, out into the material world. In particular, it will flow into the hearts of an enlightened being's disciples and other people who are open to him. This is what happened to me in Laxmi's office, when I first arrived at the ashram. Laxmi was surrendered to Bhagwan, his energy was flowing through her, and because I was open and vulnerable, it also jumped into me. Many sannyasins had similar happenings.

In Bhagwan's view, all mystics who become enlightened have the same experience of the beyond. It doesn't vary. It's the same divine source into which they have all merged.

"You can taste the ocean from anywhere and it is salty," commented Gautam Buddha, talking about this state of cosmic consciousness. From this perspective, there is no difference between Buddha, Jesus, Ramakrishna, Rumi, Gurdjieff and other mystics. They all had access to the same source of power.

In Bhagwan's case, as with many of these mystics, he was involved in the process of creating and expanding an energy field, in the form of an ashram, so that, just by being near him, people entering this field would feel the vibe and receive a taste of cosmic energy, in a much more tangible way than if, for example, they had been meditating at home by themselves.

Bhagwan often stated that for the spiritual seeker knowledge was a barrier to real knowing, but he was himself extremely well read. He talked about all religious scriptures – all those, at least, in which he could see some merit – and on all the different spiritual paths, like Zen, Tao, Tantra, Advaita, Sufi, Hasid. He included them all, but he was not confined by them. He embraced modern psychology and psychotherapy. He borrowed from the human potential movement.

Bhagwan was, based on my experience of him, a spiritual surgeon. In other words, he was a pragmatic, hands-on, try-anything guru. He used anything and everything that might help people awaken to their intrinsic Buddhahood.

Bhagwan also spoke about chakras, subtle bodies and auras, while at the same time making it clear that we were not to get too distracted by these esoteric phenomena. He wanted us to stay grounded in day-to-day life, not floating away into spiritual la-la-land.

For the same reason, perhaps, he was cautious about talking to us on the subject of reincarnation. He acknowledged that the cycle of birth, death and rebirth was a reality, but warned us against embracing this as a principle of faith. "It needs to be your experience, not a belief," he told us.

He was against seriousness, which he regarded as a disease. To keep things light, he told jokes in his discourses. A daily celebration called "Sufi Dance" was held mid-morning in the meditation hall. Truth to tell, it had little to do with traditional Sufism. It was more like an adults' playtime, with singing, dancing and heartfelt interaction. In the evening, there was "Music Group", where singing and dancing continued.

It is going to sound strange, but Bhagwan was against kindness. I'm reminded of this now, because although Sufi Dance and similar events gave people a taste of joy and bliss, it was not unusual for newcomers to complain that sannyasins in the ashram looked self-absorbed and were unfriendly to strangers. There was a certain truth in it. We weren't smiling, polite and welcoming – not unless we really felt like it. Here, Bhagwan took a very different approach than the Dalai Lama, who is well known for his saying, "Be kind whenever possible. It is always possible."

To Bhagwan, spiritual growth had nothing to do with being kind, and everything to do with being authentic. No growth was possible, he told us, unless we were ready to drop all our social games and masks, and accept ourselves as we really were, with all our faults and imperfections. So, naturally, if we didn't feel like smiling and being polite, we didn't do it. Kindness is such a central concept in mainstream morality that it's worth understanding Bhagwan's dismissal of it: "Kindness is an ego-attitude, it strengthens your ego," he explained. "When you are kind to somebody, you feel the upper hand. When you are kind to somebody there is a deep insult – you are humiliating the other, you are feeling happy in his humiliation. That's why kindness can never be forgiven."

Bhagwan gave great importance to the creation of an energy field, designed specifically for spiritual transformation, which he sometimes referred to as "the Buddhafield". This consisted of a physical space – in our case, the ashram – in which all those inside would focus on being as meditative and conscious as possible. The presence of an enlightened mystic, together with the pooling of so many people's energies, created the Buddhafield, which, in turn, would amplify the impact of meditation and make it easier for sannyasins and visitors to look within themselves.

Bhagwan adapted some methods from George Gurdjieff, too, especially the use of "friction" between people who were working intensely together in a confined space, which the increasingly crowded Pune ashram certainly provided. When personalities clashed – as they inevitably did and as we shall soon see – it was an opportunity for those involved to reflect on their habitual behaviour patterns and to become more alert and aware.

At the heart of the process of gaining awareness is meditation, but, in this ashram, it was meditation with a difference. According to

Bhagwan, modern man has become too tense and stressed to be able to simply sit down, close his eyes and go deeply inside. So, prior to sitting in silence, Bhagwan's methods required us to be very active, releasing tension through such stages as vigorous breathing, emotional release, jumping, shaking, dancing, humming, running on the spot . . .

The mystic had devised many methods along these lines, all lasting one hour, all with active stages and all followed by the more conventional meditative practice of sitting or lying down in silence. During the inactive stages, we were asked to notice our thoughts, moods and feelings. He encouraged us to see ourselves as "the watcher on the hill", who could witness all these inner processes as they arose in us, from a place of detached observation.

This practice of witnessing, he said, would slowly rob the mind of its energy and power, allowing more and more inner silence. According to him, a silent mind was the doorway to the beyond, where all duality would disappear, allowing us to melt and merge into the oneness of existence.

In the ashram, Bhagwan gave priority to two of his meditation methods: Dynamic Meditation, which I had already experienced in London, and Kundalini Meditation. Dynamic was offered at dawn, as night gave way to day, and Kundalini was his evening meditation, which we did at sunset. Bhagwan explained that these two times of day, dawn and sunset, were good times to meditate.

Since I have already given an account of my experience of Dynamic, I will also give the instructions for Kundalini, which, like those for almost all of Bhagwan's methods, were simple and straightforward. This meditation had four stages, each lasting 15 minutes:

Be loose and let your whole body shake. Become the shaking.

Dance freely to music. Let your body move as it wishes.

Sit or stand silently, listening to music, observing whatever is happening, inside or outside.

Lie down and be still, eyes closed.

Kundalini was my favourite meditation. Just to be able to walk into the meditation hall at the end of the ashram's working day and shake off any accumulated mental and emotional dust, in the company of several hundred sannyasins, was a real joy. Kundalini had great music for its first three stages – shaking, dancing and sitting silently – and this gave an extra boost to our daily sunset experience.

Bhagwan's ideas about "kundalini energy" were markedly different from the traditional view, held by some schools of yoga, that it is like a coiled serpent, sleeping at the base of the spine. According to this tradition, the kundalini serpent can be awakened through discipline and yogic practices, and made to rise through the chakras, or energy centres, up to seventh, where the thousand-petalled lotus of enlightenment can flower.

But Bhagwan didn't give any importance to such esoteric maps of how human energy flows and how enlightenment manifests.

"Be concerned with meditation and not with kundalini," he told us. "When you are aware, things will begin to happen in you. For the first time, you will become aware of an inner world that is greater, vaster than you have imagined."

When Bhagwan was giving his discourses, he was addressing not just the intellect but also helping to induce a meditative state in his listeners. Underneath the flow of words, an alchemical transmission of meditation was slowly occurring. When he suddenly paused, halting the stream of verbal sounds, we would find ourselves dropping effortlessly into the silent space between them. Listening to Bhagwan in this way became a form of meditation.

With all of this in mind, I can summarise by telling you a short story. When people ask me to describe Bhagwan's philosophy, I show them one of his books containing his commentaries on Zen.

The very first Zen sutra says it all:

A monk asked his master: "What is the first principle of Zen?"

The Master replied: "If I could tell you, it would be the second principle."

This is why I have called this chapter "non-philosophy for meditators" because Bhagwan's approach needs to be lived, not learned. However, if pressed to condense the mystic's teaching into a single sentence, I would choose this one:

"I want you to know a state of utter nothingness – that is your reality."

Bhagwan was fond of the well-known saying that philosophy is like looking on a dark night, in a dark house, in a dark cellar for a black cat that isn't there. To him, it is the darkness, or the nothingness, that holds the key, not the elusive cat:

"That darkness is not a hindrance – that is my experience," he explained. "That darkness is immensely helpful, because it is peaceful, it is silence. What appears as darkness in the beginning, slowly, slowly, becomes luminous. And the day it becomes totally luminous – that's what is called enlightenment, you have come to the true light."

Close Encounters

The situation didn't look too promising. I was sitting in a circle with about a dozen other people when this big German guy got up, slung a pillow over his shoulder, and started walking around the circle, looking for someone to hit.

This was the notorious ashram Encounter Group, where anything could happen . . . and usually did. It was part of the ashram's programme of therapy groups, which Bhagwan saw as a quick way of helping people to unload their emotional baggage, in preparation for meditation.

Often, in darshan, Bhagwan would suggest groups for people, but I hadn't waited for his invitation. I signed up a couple of weeks after arriving. I was scared of groups, but knew I needed them and also realised I couldn't hold up my head in the ashram without participating in them – everybody went into these groups and afterwards wore them proudly on their chests, like invisible campaign medals. So, I figured the best thing to do was to get them over with, as soon as possible.

What was my fear? Well, I was worried about the possibility of physical violence, which, so I'd heard, happened frequently in the no-limits Encounter Group. But my biggest fear lay somewhere else: I was secretly harbouring doubts about my capacity and courage to walk the path to spiritual awakening.

The key issue, for me, was energy. I just didn't think I had enough of this elusive quality, while in Bhagwan's ashram I seemed to be surrounded by vibrantly alive young people, all of whom were bursting with the stuff. Good-looking guys in their twenties, with long hair and beards, were walking around semi-naked, clothed only in a *lunghi* – the Indian term for a sarong – wrapped around the waist. Beautiful women were showing off their bodies, bronzed with a deep tan from living on Goa's beaches, while dancing wildly in the meditation hall.

Bhagwan was on his way to acquiring an international reputation for attracting good-looking men and women to his ashram, and I think it was mainly their youth and vigour that created this impression. A whole generation was in a restless mood, looking for something beyond conventional values, and the mystic's dual offering of meditation and sexual freedom drew some of the brightest and most beautiful to Pune.

It was hard not to compare. I saw myself as a balding, thirty-something English intellectual with a skinny body and little muscular strength, who'd spent most of his adult life sitting in front of a typewriter. In terms of energy, I judged myself as being dead from the neck down.

Dynamic Meditation, which I'd grown to like – "love' would be an exaggeration – was helping to open up my internal energy circuits through the breathing, screaming and jumping, but the challenge of the groups had to be faced.

The essential difference between an ashram meditation technique and group therapy was that in meditation your journey of self-discovery happened privately, within yourself, usually with closed eyes – many meditators in Pune wore blindfolds – whereas in many of the ashram's groups you used interaction with other people to gain insights into your own psychological and emotional make-up.

I decided to begin with the group with the worst reputation: Encounter. It was conducted down in a custom-built, padded, sound-proofed chamber beneath the ashram's office building.

Inevitably, my very first time, the moment I'd feared duly arrived, in the form of the angry German, armed with a pillow, prowling around the room, looking for someone to hit. I was nervous, sitting cross-legged in the classic yogic lotus posture, doing my best to remain calm, detached and buddha-like.

The German stopped in front of me and looked down. I closed my eyes, hoping to take refuge in the non-duality of meditation. Bang! I was knocked sideways by a forceful swipe from the German-held pillow. A little dazed, I righted myself and reassembled my legs in the lotus posture, hoping to regain my serenity. Then I saw the German was winding up for another crack at me. A little voice in my head said, "Fuck this!" and I forgot all about serenity and raised both fore-arms in time to block the blow. The German moved on.

At the end of the session, when we shared what we'd been experiencing, I confessed that I'd failed to meet the challenge of the situation, losing my composure and resorting to self-defence instead. The workshop leader smiled and shook his head. "No, Subhuti, it was good what you did, because you got in touch with your fear."

That was the first time in my life it had ever occurred to me that it was okay to feel fear. For the first time, I was able to appreciate that fear is a useful, protective mechanism. I could see how I'd been in denial of fear, because that was the message I'd been fed during my upbringing: cool guys don't feel fear.

One might think that insights such as these can be acquired in less dramatic ways, not necessarily delivered through a bang on the head. Well, maybe . . . and maybe not. In my experience, we seldom learn anything from reading books or listening to other people's advice. We learn best from living intensely, taking risks, making mistakes.

Not all lessons in the Encounter group were transmitted through fast-moving pillows. For example, we were all naked – that was the norm in Pune groups in those days – and were invited to comment on each other's bodies. When it was my turn to come under scrutiny, one guy told me honestly, "I envy your prick." I couldn't believe my ears. I thought he'd made a mistake, or was talking to someone else, But no, he was talking to me – and he wasn't gay and trying to come on to me. That was when I realised what a low opinion I had of my own body, especially my private parts. That was the beginning of a new way of looking at myself and my sexuality.

There were all kinds of groups happening in the ashram, mostly to do with unlocking repressed emotions and giving them expression, so there was a lot of shouting and screaming. There were also Tantra groups, which focused on releasing sexual energy, Primal groups looking at childhood issues and classical meditation groups like Vipassana.

I decided that a Vipassana retreat was next, because several sannya-sins informed me it was even harder than Encounter. So, of course, I had to face the challenge. But, for me, surprisingly, it turned out to be a cruise.

Vipassana is a Buddhist meditation method, handed down by the Gautama himself. You sit silently, eyes closed, spine straight, focusing your attention on the sensation of your breathing, noticing the cool air coming in through your nostrils, on your in-breath, and the warm air flowing out, on the out-breath. You can also focus on the rise and fall of your stomach, again, in time to the rhythm of your breathing.

Inevitably, thoughts generated by your restless mind constantly interrupt this process, seducing you away with memories from your past, plans for your future, or into imagination and fantasy. But, when you remember you're supposed to be watching the breath, you return to the method, until the next thought drags you away. Gradually, as you sit silently, session after session, your awareness sharpens, the mind slows down, gaps appear between your thoughts . . . the silence of meditation descends.

In Bhagwan's version of this meditation, one sitting session lasted about 40 minutes, followed by a slow walk of 20 minutes, around the meditation hall, making an hour in total. The first session was held at 5:00am and the last at 9:00pm, with breaks for food, Dynamic Meditation, Bhagwan's discourse and Kundalini Meditation in the afternoon. We followed this routine for seven days.

I must have been a Buddhist monk in a past life, because it seemed easy, like second nature to me. The next real challenge was Primal: a totally different kettle of fish.

Sex on the Brain

I was lying naked on the mattress-covered floor, exhausted from killing my parents, when this very attractive young American woman, also naked, crawled over to me from another part of the room and lay beside me. I was lying on my back, incapable of moving. I don't think I even had the strength to put my arm around her.

But it wasn't necessary. Softly, she began to play with my body, caressing my belly, hips and thighs. Then she gently took hold of my dick and, after stroking it long enough to create an erection, slowly began to suck on it.

There were plenty of other people in the room: about 15 or more group participants and three leaders of the Primal group. Most participants were busy with their own inner process, either smashing pillows on the floor, cursing and yelling at Mom and Dad, or punching the padded walls with their fists. The group leaders, I learned later, were watching me and the American.

"Thanks for the show," said one of them afterwards, with a broad smile and a friendly wink.

Even though my partner was beautiful to behold, I found myself closing my eyes in order to focus on the sensations in my sex centre. I thought she might stop, but she continued until I reached the point of no return. At the moment of climax, a strong pulse of energy began in my genitals, then rippled up my spine and exploded softly in my brain. This was my first direct, personal experience of something that Bhagwan had spoken about in discourse and which is now generally accepted: the sex centre isn't located only in the genitals, but also in the brain.

I didn't have too much time to think about it, because, as I opened my eyes, I saw my American companion grab a tissue and spit into it. Then she turned to look at me and, with a slightly shocked expression, said reproachfully, "You came in my mouth!"

Actually, to be accurate, I didn't do anything. Not a thing. It all happened by itself, while I was lying on my back, unmoving, tired from parent-bashing. But, when she said that, it was my turn to be surprised, because, after all, what was she expecting? Clearly, we had different ideas about the protocol of love-making in Primal therapy groups.

When I write about this kind of sexual encounter, it might seem to the reader that most of us were drawn to Pune because of the lure of exploring our sexuality, with many different partners, under the guidance of the "free sex guru". It conjures up visions of hundreds of horny young people rushing off to some exotic Club Med, ready to strip off, partner up and get going. The idea is partly true, but it wasn't that simple. In 1976, Bhagwan wasn't yet big enough to register as a major blip on the West's radar screens. I hadn't yet heard of his controversial book *From Sex to Superconsciousness*, I didn't know he was referred to as a "sex guru" and I don't think I'd even heard the word "Tantra" before arriving in Pune.

The ashram's reputation for "free sex" came a little later. Even then, I doubt if many people's arrival in Pune was motivated solely by its sex appeal. After all, to a Western way of thinking, there were easier ways to find sex partners than risking your health in a poor country like India, joining a bizarre cult and getting personal with a bunch of crazy meditators who were just as likely to scream at you as seduce you.

I was drawn to Pune because, since taking LSD – and probably even before that – I'd developed a thirst for personal exploration, driven by a nagging need to find out more about myself. The sixties counterculture movement had enshrined a vision of people being more loving towards each other, but drugs offered only a glimpse of this, and as the initial "good vibes" of the movement wore off, it was apparent that love was still in short supply. Bhagwan's revolution, as I saw it, was to encourage us to forget about Jesus' admonition to love our neighbours and focus on loving ourselves.

"I don't say love thy neighbour as thyself," he told us. "My teaching is simple: Love thyself. And my experience is this, that if you become capable of loving yourself, love for the neighbour will come of its own accord; it does not have to be practised. All practised love creates hypocrisy."

I was pulled by an intuitive feeling that Bhagwan was right to priori-
tise self-love and that he could help me do this more effectively than
anyone else. True, I was scared by his methods, but impressed by their
power – intrigued by the aura of overflowing energy that infected everyone who came in contact with the mystic. If there was one overriding
reason for Bhagwan's appeal in those early days, it was this phenomenon
of amped-up energy – life with the volume turned way, way up.

Sex was one vehicle through which this magnified energy could be
experienced, and many people in the West – like myself, with my
friend from Berlin – got a taste of this mysterious quality through
making love with a sannyasin who was returning from Pune. It wasn't
so much the sex itself, nor the character of the sannyasins involved,
but the energy that came with it.

"There was definitely a connection to the energy in my attraction
to male sannyasins in those days, which, on a physical plane, often
didn't match," reflected one female friend of mine, looking back on
the mid-seventies. In other words, the guy might not be her type, but
the energy pulled her to make love with him anyway.

Now, in the Primal group, this unexpected blow job had shown
me a new energy pathway, rippling up my spine from the sex centre
and creating an orgasm in my brain. Apart from being enjoyable, it
was also helpful, since it showed me how meditation, which seemingly focuses on the mind and its thinking process, influences other
areas of human experience, including sex.

It also showed me the futility of traditional acts of self-mutilation,
intended to achieve celibacy, such as self-castration by the Skoptsy
sect of Christians, in nineteenth-century Russia, who thought they
could attain perfection by removing sinful parts of their bodies. After
all, there's really no point in cutting off your balls – or tearing out
your eyes to avoid seeing beautiful women, as one Indian saint did –
when the real hook of sexual attachment lies deep inside your cere-
bral cortex.

The discovery also gives added significance to the common expression, "You've got sex on the brain", and also to the rather crude
remark, usually shared man-to-man, that "last night I fucked my
brains out". Judging by these remarks, even the mainstream has some
understanding of how the sex centre and the brain are linked, and, of
course, sex magazines and internet porn sites depend on it.

The experience gave me a deeper appreciation of Bhagwan's insight, which he expressed many times, that way back in time, meditation was discovered while making love. Why? Because in the moment of orgasm the mind stops and, with it, time also stops, opening a doorway into an inner space that is beyond mind and sexuality both.

"The experience of orgasm itself is always nonsexual," Bhagwan told us. "Even though you have achieved it through sex, it itself has no sexuality in it."

Sensing the nonsexual nature of this orgasmic state, the next step would have been to see if the same effects, such as awareness, thoughtlessness and timelessness, might be reached in other ways, without a partner, bypassing the sexual act.

"This is how man must have first discovered meditation," asserted Bhagwan.

Repressing sex in order to meditate was counter-productive, Bhagwan added, and he criticised Gautam Buddha for telling his *bhikkhus*, or monks, not to look at women, explaining that such a prohibition was sure to create more interest, making a woman seem even more beautiful and attractive in a monk's mind. It is familiarity that creates indifference, not prohibition. "If I were in the place of Gautam Buddha, I would give everybody a magnifying glass!" he joked.

On another occasion in Pune around the same time, I'd invited an attractive German woman to my room for the afternoon. After making love, the initial tension had dissolved and we were both in a relaxed mood. We began to make love for a second time and – probably for the first time in my life – I wasn't busy with the usual male preoccupation of either creating an orgasm for my partner or preventing my own from happening too soon.

In fact, I wasn't even thinking about climaxing when slowly, from somewhere deep inside, a glow of orgasmic pleasure started spreading outwards through my entire pelvic area. It was an involuntary happening, unlike any sexual experience I'd had before. Fool that I was, I thought I could enhance it by doing something, so I started to thrust more strongly with my hips. To my dismay, the sensation immediately disappeared and, try though I did, I couldn't make it come back.

This was the beginning of a new understanding about sex energy and, indeed, about life in general. There are things you can do to create pleasure, to satisfy your desires. But there are also things that you cannot do, which happen by themselves – usually in a state of relaxation, or non-doing.

This second category of experiences is elusive and mysterious. You try to grab them . . . they're gone. It's true of meditation. It's true of love.

I should say something more about the Primal group, because my sexual encounter, though remarkable, was incidental to the main focus. We were there to dig deeply into our past, into our early years, into our childhood, to re-experience and understand how our parents had damaged us. They may have done it with the best intentions. But they damaged us, nevertheless. They wanted us to be good, to be polite, to learn manners and, perhaps above all, to fit into the society in which they lived. This was the process that cut our energy, crushed our spontaneity and freedom, tamed the wild animal in us.

It wasn't their fault. They were just doing whatever they thought was right. But we were determined to undo the damage and, as part of this healing process, spent a good deal of time in our sound-proof chamber screaming at them and – in our imagination – killing them. The group lasted 15 days, the longest one I ever did.

I'm not sure Arthur Janov, the American psychologist who founded Primal therapy, would have approved of our activities – especially the blow job. But, what the hell. We took Janov's ideas and pushed them to the limit . . . and then some.

It was just one more wild ride on Bhagwan's rollercoaster of self-discovery.

Showering the Message

Six months, I'm sure you'll agree, isn't exactly the "forever" I'd promised Bhagwan. In fact, it's considerably shorter and that's how it proved to be, in terms of my stay in India. In spite of my new-found spiritual life and my declaration that I would be staying with Bhagwan indefinitely, I wasn't finished with the material world.

Why? Because when, after six months in Pune, my editor on the *Birmingham Post* offered me my old job, I was eager to go. It was a surprise to feel hunger for big-city life welling up inside me, brushing aside my assumption that I was done with my career.

It was strange: during those six months since my arrival in India, in March 1976, I hadn't felt any desire to leave. But as soon as I got the offer and this unexpected window of opportunity opened, my eagerness to go back to my old lifestyle rocketed up inside me. To be honest, I knew the reason perfectly well: some part of me was glad to be escaping from the ashram pressure cooker and from the challenging work of dissolving my social identity. Indeed, I felt guilty about it, as if I was getting away with something, because my ego was relieved and happy about leaving Pune. In this ashram, it had been given a spiritual death sentence and here was a reprieve.

I even made up a little song about it, borrowing from John Denver's classic ballad. My lyrics were:

Leaving, with my ego, don't know when I'll be back again . . .

The situation exposed my laziness and my hope for a short-cut in my quest for spiritual awakening. Up to this moment, I'd been hoping that enlightenment might be something easily attained, adorning my personality with another crown of accomplishment. To be totally honest, I'd fantasised that I would become enlightened within three months of being with Bhagwan, then go off and start my own ashram, surrounded by devotees and adoring, beautiful women.

Well, it didn't take long before I realised this was just naked ambition, which had been transferred from the material world to the spiritual world. Instead of wanting to be the Political Editor of *The Times*, I now wanted to be Jesus Christ Superstar. It was a new take on the old, old story of wanting to be king of the castle, the alpha male in the pack.

But Bhagwan had made it clear: for the inner explosion to happen, the ego had to disappear entirely. I could feel the truth of it, but still, I didn't like it. Going back to London took the pressure off, giving me a chance to once again display my skills as a political journalist, commenting wittily and sagely on important social issues.

Perhaps I should explain that in those days the *Birmingham Post* was a prestigious daily morning newspaper serving the West Midlands business community. Later on, hard times hit the paper and it shrank to a weekly with an online business website. But in the 1970s it aspired to rival the national dailies and for a while kept two reporters at Westminster, including myself.

However, before deciding to leave India, there was an issue to face: I was now in a "master–disciple" relationship with Bhagwan, so I felt the need to seek his blessing. I wrote a letter to him and nervously awaited his reply. What would he say? To my relief, the mystic gave me the green light, saying: "You can go, and let the message shower on the House of Commons, with orange clothes and mala on."

But when I went to darshan to say goodbye, I got a different take on the situation. Bhagwan looked at me, quite seriously, so it seemed, and asked, "When will you be back?"

His question floored me. I'd been so focused on taking up my career again, I hadn't really thought about coming back – just assumed it would happen one day, sooner or later. Now, in this moment, it seemed that Bhagwan really cared about me, which was in itself surprising. I'd always assumed it wasn't a personal relationship, in the sense that he might miss me, or be concerned for my welfare.

I shrugged and said, "When I feel the urge."

He did his best with my indifferent response, saying emphatically, "You will feel it. Listen to it, hmm?"

And that was that. I flew to London the very next day.

God knows what would have happened if I'd showed up at Westminster in a flowing orange robe, with my shaggy beard and the bright light of religious zeal in my eyes, trying to shower the message of meditation on Britain's politicians. Most probably, I'd have been fired, there and then. But I compromised. I trimmed my beard and bought myself a trendy, double-breasted, rust-coloured suit in the King's Road. I wore my mala inside my suit. I didn't talk to my fellow hacks about meditation.

Still, when I went back to work in the autumn of 1976, I did make them call me by my sannyasin name, and that was embarrassing enough. In those days, the Press Gallery in Westminster had a loudspeaker system, manned by the duty officer on the gallery's telephone exchange, which was used to inform correspondents they had calls waiting. In the beginning, I heard myself being publicly addressed with a jumble of names, including "Mr Peter Subhuti" or "Mr Subhuti Waight", as they struggled to combine my new name with my old one.

Eventually, I got them trained to just say "Subhuti," but still I cringed every time I heard it, because it seemed so out of place. I forced myself to do it, though. Having compromised on everything else, I clung to my new name as a lifeline to the rapidly fading memory of a reality beyond normality. My editor refused at first to use my new name and, as an uneasy compromise, we settled for the generic by-line "By *Birmingham Post* Political Staff". Steady persistence paid off, however, and when he realised it wasn't just a fad, I had the satisfaction of seeing front-page stories with the by-line "By Anand Subhuti". The editor still didn't like it, but he swallowed his objections, probably hoping I'd return to sanity soon.

The other journalists in the Lobby were curious about my name-change and semi-concealed mala for a few days, then forgot about it. I understood why: at Westminster, if you can speak the language of politics, you can be a green Martian and nobody cares. I did contemplate trying to offer an introduction to Dynamic Meditation, using the rifle range located down in the basement under the House of Lords, where the screams from Dynamic's second stage would remain unheard above us. But I chickened out. Lethargy took over. Compromise and convenience replaced any desire to spread the word. Someone loaned me a red Porsche and a mews cottage in Belgravia and I was set up for comfortable London living.

I stayed on the job for a year, then decided to fly to India to spend my two-week summer vacation at the ashram. Really, a fortnight was way too short for making such a long trip, but that was all I was given and I was expected to return to the UK in time to cover the annual party conferences.

In the late summer of 1977, when I arrived in the ashram, my friends took one look at me and commented, "You look terrible, where have you been?"

That was enough. I knew they were right, because I could see, in comparison, how much more relaxed and natural these sannyasins were; how loving they were to each other and how centred in themselves – all the qualities I'd started discovering in Pune and then abruptly given up.

And for what? Journalism requires a sharp mind, a sarcastic intellect, an aptitude for stringing words together and not much else. Journalists are, to use a phrase coined by Laxmi, "head people". Almost without knowing it, I'd shrunk from a multi-dimensional human being back into a walking brain again.

I wrote to my editor saying, "I'm not coming back."

I think he was as relieved as I was.

For me, the decision to quit represented a significant milestone in my journey towards spiritual maturity. When I'd first sat in front of Bhagwan in March 1976 and told him I would be staying "forever", I meant it, I was sincere, but I had not understood the implications. Now, returning to Pune and giving up my job in London, my earlier good intention was being turned into a commitment – not to Bhagwan, but to myself. The extra year in Westminster had given me, beyond a shadow of doubt, the understanding that whatever I was looking for in terms of personal fulfilment wasn't available in the UK. It was here, in the Pune ashram.

With that decision out of the way, it was time to focus on my new life. Working in the ashram seemed to be the next step. Among sannyasins, it was considered to be a kind of graduation from groups. Also, it would help my finances if I worked there, since entrance to the ashram became free and there was a possibility of being invited to join the commune, with free food and free accommodation as part of the package.

"Work Meditation", as it was called, was about bringing meditative awareness into daily activity. We were using interaction with each other, especially personality conflicts and differences of opinion, to notice what thoughts and feelings were being triggered. At the same time, on a practical level, it was our job to keep the ashram functioning. Cooking, cleaning, gardening, office work, making malas for the initiation ceremony, taking care of plumbing and electricity . . . it was a world in itself, crammed into an area of less than a couple of acres.

The real aim of Work Meditation was to experience the silent witness within, who could watch our thoughts, our experiences, our esoteric happenings, and know itself to be beyond all of it. Try doing that while arguing about whose turn it is to wash the dishes, and you'll soon see how the ashram functioned.

Here, we touch on Bhagwan's basic modus operandi in working with people. He didn't want us to sit in isolation in monasteries, or in caves in the Himalayas. He didn't want us to "renounce the world" like traditional Hindu sannyasins. He wanted us to test our meditative awareness through the challenges and conflicts of daily life. Trouble was not to be avoided, but welcomed, not just among ourselves, but in our interaction with the world outside the gate, even – as we would later come to know – on a national and international scale with politicians and governments.

"The politicians will create all kinds of troubles for you, but I know that only through those troubles will you grow," he once told us. "So, whenever I hear that people are going to create trouble for you, secretly I giggle! I say, 'Hee-hee!'"

Bhagwan's word proved prophetic. Trouble was coming our way, big time, and we had no idea what we were getting into.

Disappearing Disciples

I was sitting on the banks of the Ganges, in the ancient city of Varanasi, watching the river gliding past, enjoying a sunset that filled the western sky with an orange glow, as if the sky itself was on fire. A fine white ash was drifting down through the air, settling on my clothes. Along the river bank were the flames and smoke of a dozen funeral pyres. Close to me, a head and an arm, both attached to the same body, slowly rose through the flames of a burning pyre, but this wasn't a horror movie and the dead weren't coming back to life. As the flames scorched the flesh, the muscles tightened before being consumed, and there wasn't enough wood on the pyre to keep the body down, so it slowly rose, nearly to a sitting position, a flaming corpse that refused to lie down until everything was burned.

This was Shiva Town, holiest city of the Hindus, where the faithful came to die, so that they might free themselves from *samsara*, the wheel of birth and death. Such is the power of Varanasi and the holy River Ganges.

How did I get here? Well, my first venture into ashram work didn't last long. I started in the kitchen as a "chai wallah", boiling up huge cauldrons of spicy Indian tea for breakfast, lunch and dinner. It was enjoyable, but the day's work went on too long. I particularly resented having to scrub out big dirty cooking pots in the evening after creating my last brew of chai.

In addition, I realised I hadn't explored India. If I was going to dive permanently into ashram work, surely I should see something of this vast country first? So in November 1977, without consulting Bhagwan – I was afraid he'd say no – I travelled to Goa by bus, hung out with the hippies, smoked too much dope and made love on the beach with someone else's girlfriend.

When Goa became boring, I took a long train ride up to Delhi and from there caught a bus to the Himalayas. I stayed in Manali, exploring the mountains and enjoying nearby hot springs, but by this time winter was approaching and it was getting cold, so I took a bus back to Delhi, then caught a train to Varanasi.

There were parts of this ancient city that felt really, really old.

"So, this is what it was like to live a thousand years ago," I said to myself, walking through tiny, dark streets, passing temples, beggars and shopkeepers on my way to the Ganges. Every evening I sat by the river, watching the funeral pyres burn, gazing upon this extraordinary spectacle of death and rebirth along the river bank.

"What a metaphor for my own spiritual journey with Bhagwan," I thought.

It is said that the relationship between a master and disciple is a death and a resurrection. Bhagwan said this many times, and in my experience it's true. But in order to understand it, you need to be familiar with the phenomenon of black holes – the inner ones, not those lurking in outer space.

"How can I surrender to a black hole?"

The question had been asked by a Dutch friend of mine, as she sat in front of Bhagwan in darshan. She'd been telling him about an experience in meditation where she'd been on the verge of disappearing into a deep, dark nothingness.

He laughed. "To call it a black hole is not very polite," he chuckled, obviously familiar with the experience himself.

My friend couldn't accept it and left. But for me, the opposite was true. As far as I was concerned, I couldn't surrender to anything *except* a black hole. Because, as we all know, surrendering to another human being is a humiliation. That's why I was able to hook up with Bhagwan. Because I understood, from the very beginning, that he wasn't there. On a spiritual level, he'd already disappeared; he'd become a doorway to the beyond.

I had been back at the ashram from Varanasi for about a month when it happened to me – or nearly did. Through accident, ignorance, or pure dumb luck, I stumbled upon the very same black hole within myself and came within a fraction of a second of disappearing into it. I was lying in bed, in a rented room near the ashram, still asleep as morning was approaching. I was dreaming of being a vast expanded being, almost like a god, and found myself gazing down at the tiny forms of human beings, running around on Planet Earth, and wondering, "How could such an expanded being as myself possibly fit into one of those creatures?"

Then I heard Bhagwan's voice say "You have to disappear."

I understood his message: rather than this god-like being trying to fit into a human form, the opposite needed to happen. The god needed to be released from the form. Disappearing was the way out and, to my astonishment, disappearing began to happen to me. Somewhere between sleep and waking, I began to realise it wasn't just a dream. It was coming true.

It happened just like the Zen stories say: the dewdrop disappearing into the ocean. There was I, metaphorically speaking, a little droplet of water, sitting on the vast ocean of existence. And the bottom of the bubble opened ... the moment came ... the moment that all disciples, all seekers, hope and wait and pray for ...

Suddenly, I was gripped by fear, almost panic. I could not allow myself to disappear. It felt like death, with no guarantee of any kind of resurrection. Urgently rousing myself to full wakefulness, I cried out "No!" and immediately the door to the beyond closed and the opportunity vanished.

Then I understood the words of Ikkyu, a Japanese Zen mystic, when approached by a group of monks who asked why enlightenment is so rare, why more people don't attain it.

"What is the main obstacle?" they enquired. Ikkyu simply replied, "The taking of the self as real."

There you have it.

Which poses another, apparently sensible question: who, in their right mind, would want to disappear anyway? Which takes me back to the banks of the River Ganges and to the white ash that, every evening, had been softly, slowly, falling through the air, covering my orange clothes. That white ash is all that is left of me and you, when the body – as it must – ceases to harbour life and is consumed by flames on the funeral pyre. All our hopes and dreams, our passions, our loves, our ambitions, our desires ... they all come down to this ... this white ash. It was with this in mind that Gautam Buddha admonished his *bhikkhus*:

You are as a yellow leaf,
The messengers of death are at hand,
What will you take with you?

Bhagwan had the same insight, but put a different spin on it: knowing that death takes everything away doesn't mean you need to
renounce the world and become a monk, or *bhikkhu*. There is no
escape. Even if you run away and hide inside a cave, deep in the
Himalayas, you will dream of women and have sexual desires. Indra,
the King of Heaven, will send his divine *apsaras* – beautiful young
women – to dance around you in your lonely cave and tempt you
into lust. In modern terminology: your own imagination will create
sexual desire, even if no woman is actually present.

The real thing is to drop psychological attachment to what the
world offers, to enjoy it without clinging to it. Which brings me back
to the story of Buddha's disciple, Subhuti, because if you succeed in
dropping all your attachments, you drop the mind itself, and then . . .
yes . . . you disappear.

Consciousness remains, death is transcended and life continues on
its endless pilgrimage, but with no "I" attached.

Tricky business, isn't it?

That morning, after my scary experience, Bhagwan was talking in
discourse about jumping off a cliff, using it as a metaphor for the act
of surrendering the ego and disappearing into the divine. I'm paraphrasing, from memory, but he said something like: "You just have to
learn a little courage. One jump and you are gone forever into the
mysterious. You yourself become a mystery." Then he chuckled and
said: "You can jump from the top of the cliff, or, if that is too scary,
you can walk down the cliff a little more. But sooner or later you have
to jump . . . because the cliff has no bottom."

By now it was January 1978. A new year was beginning and I
decided it was time to start work again. To me, working in the ashram
seemed a bit like walking down the cliff Bhagwan was talking about.
If I couldn't jump from where I was now, maybe it would happen
later, through living and working inside Bhagwan's energy field, gaining more trust and courage.

But about one thing I was clear: no more kitchen work. Instead, I
asked to join the ashram's press office and got a nod of approval from
Laxmi. After all, where else would an ex-journalist want to be?

One more thing: it was the experience of "nearly disappearing" that showed me, beyond any doubt, that Bhagwan was an authentic enlightened being. It would never have happened without his presence as a doorway to existence, to the whole, to universal consciousness . . . whatever you want to call "IT".

The title of one of his early books neatly summed it up: *I Am the Gate.*

Indeed, he was. Many times, during my years with Bhagwan, I had glimpses of the beyond, especially while sitting in his discourses. Many times in his presence I'd slip into a a profound state of inner silence and bliss. Many times, all the problems and preoccupations crowding my mind would suddenly vanish, leaving me with a deeply relaxed feeling of being completely at home in myself, not needing anyone or anything.

The understanding gained from these experiences later became a thread that kept me with him through all the controversies, allegations, scandals and disappointments that came crashing down on our heads. No matter what happened, I could never deny the reality of his enlightenment – although sometimes I wished I could.

From Tardis to Starship

If the Pune ashram was like the Tardis when I first arrived, it had quickly evolved into the *Starship Enterprise* by the time I got back from my year in Westminster and trip to Varanasi. The whole place had expanded, becoming more organised and more streamlined to cope with the ever-increasing numbers of people wishing to "boldly go" – in the words of Captain Kirk – on this cosmic adventure with Bhagwan.

The main difference to the ashram – the difference that made all the difference – was the addition of Buddha Hall, a big, new meditation hall that now stood on a fourth plot of land recently added to the ashram's original three. There had been no house on this plot. It was lying vacant, covered with weeds and wild shrubs, but similar in size to the other properties. Our new hall took up nearly the whole space. It was oval in shape, raised above ground level by a couple of feet, and surfaced with polished stone slabs. You could get about 2,000 people inside, and although on my return there were around 500 people in the ashram, within a year the hall would be full.

The roof was crude but effective, being made of corrugated steel sheets all inter-laced together and supported by vertical wooden poles. It would have looked awful, but the entire ceiling and all the poles were covered with white cloth, and this gave the hall a surprisingly harmonious and aesthetic feeling.

Buddha Hall – named, of course, after the Gautama himself – was open to the surrounding garden on all sides and we were fortunate that Koregaon Park was, in those days, a very quiet neighbourhood. Rarely did any noise intrude into the hall, other than birdsong, although our neighbours certainly heard our noise – all day long. Fortunately, many of the nearby bungalows stood empty a lot of the time, being used only occasionally by owners living in Mumbai.

A small marble podium was erected on one side of Buddha Hall and here Bhagwan would sit, in a simple, bucket-shaped executive-style chair, while giving discourse. At eight o'clock every morning, he was driven in a Mercedes from Lao Tzu House to Buddha Hall and an hour and a half later returned the same way. A small, circular driveway had been fashioned around the hall to make the trip possible.

As for the rest of the ashram, it was also subjected to modification. Evening darshan was now too big for the Lao Tzu car porch, so this was shifted to Chuang Tzu Auditorium. I missed the intimacy of the porch, but more and more people wanted to meet Bhagwan and the shift became inevitable.

There was now a much larger kitchen behind Krishna House, named "Vrindavan" by Bhagwan after the holy town in northern India where Krishna is supposed to have spent his childhood. It served three meals a day to an outdoor canteen, packed with benches and chairs for visitors. This eating space wasn't enough, however, and a second canteen – supplied by the same kitchen – was opened for ashram workers on an upstairs balcony in Jesus House. Workers got free meals. Visitors had to pay.

Expansion cost money, I understood, but I didn't give much thought to how our growing ashram was being financed. The gate price was low, no more than five or ten rupees per day, and meals were cheap, but a great deal of money came through the fees charged for courses, workshops and trainings. There were also private donations from wealthy disciples, usually in exchange for a nice room in the ashram, but I didn't have a clue how much.

An open patch of ground to the side of Jesus House soon developed into a massive rectangular pit and I was curious as to what it might become. The pit was given a concrete floor, concrete walls and another massive slab of concrete was added as a roof. This, it turned out, was to be an illegally constructed "go-down", where stacks of Bhagwan's books were stored in a huge basement-like facility. On top of the go-down's thick roof was a busy despatch area, sending his books all over the world, plus a row of about ten tiny rooms standing at the back, with three people crammed in each one. Behind the go-down, hidden from view, were ten more little rooms.

Another row of rooms was hastily constructed on a plot of ground that had previously been used to grow vegetables for Bhagwan's meals.

Upon completion, it was instantly dubbed "Veggie Villas". These were also illegal. We never sought planning permission from Pune City Corporation, assuming, rightly as it turned out, that they would refuse it because we were so controversial. So we just went ahead without it.

Even this was not enough space and the ashram's activities spilled out into other properties nearby, including a large mansion on Lane Three, known, somewhat prosaically, as "Number Seventy". Curiously, I don't think Bhagwan ever gave it a name. Here, among other things, was the ashram's medical centre, a café and, of course, lots more accommodation for sannyasins.

What made this crowded ashram so beautiful was Bhagwan's instruction to plant fast-growing trees, shrubs and plants. With lots of daily watering, plus India's warm climate, this mixed vegetation grew swiftly into a lush jungle, which seemed to shield us from the outside world, enveloping us in a lovely, protective aura of greenery. One day, not so far away, this newly expanded ashram would also become too small. But for the moment it was Bhagwan's beehive, buzzing all day long with energy, enthusiasm and excitement.

For me, it was both a relief and a support to be part of a spiritual community. It was good not to be alone in my quest for self-knowing and comforting to feel that I was now part of a movement.

As Bhagwan said, in a 1977 discourse, shortly after I'd returned from London: "If you are alone it is difficult to keep awake. But if you are with a few people – laughing, talking, joking – you can keep awake the whole night very easily."

In the same discourse, he made a statement about the ashram that to me and many others was new and exciting, raising our ballgame to the next level:

"This whole experiment is to bring a kind of Buddhahood into the world. This commune is not an ordinary commune. This is an experiment to provoke God."

With a chuckle, he added: "You may have come to me only to solve your problems. That is secondary. I am cooking something else!"

The Orgasmic Hug

Journalists have special talents. They can write about events without actually being there – this would happen many times when reporting about Bhagwan and his sannyasins. One reporter made up most of his stories in his Pune hotel room. But journalists can, occasionally, be there and also write accurately about what happens. When they did this at our ashram, almost all of them mentioned the orgasmic hug. I don't blame them. It was a remarkable phenomenon.

For example, I might be walking through the ashram from the press office to the front gate, in order to meet and talk with a visiting journalist. On the way, I'd very likely pass a couple standing in the middle of the path, wrapped in each other's arms. No passionate kissing, no making out, but with full body contact . . . usually, they were completely motionless, eyes closed. Most probably, the couple wouldn't actually be a couple, in terms of being in a relationship. Most probably, they just happened to meet, by chance, at this spot on the path and decided to have a hug.

So, then I'd meet the journalist, sit down, have a cup of chai with him or her, and arrange interviews with Laxmi and other ashram residents. About half an hour later, I'd walk back towards the press office and yes, the couple would still be there . . . motionless, full body contact, eyes closed.

This happened a lot. I also enjoyed these hugs myself. Why? Because they were orgasmic. They were like low-grade nuclear fission: two pieces of radioactive material coming close enough to each other to start a chain-reaction.

This may give you an indication of how strong the energy field was around Bhagwan. It was like an electric grid: you walked in the gate and you got plugged in. The more you participated in the "active" meditations and therapy groups, getting rid of inhibitions, opening up your body's energy channels, the stronger these sensations became. Sometimes the hugs were sexual, with both partners getting turned on, in which case it was probably time to skip work and make love, or make a date for later. But mostly they were orgasmic in a non-sexual way, focusing on the heart and whole-body sensations, a general melting and merging in which energy could be felt streaming up and down your body, or, more likely, between your two bodies.

To allow an ashram in which this kind of thing went on was a revolution in India. Really, it's a wonder we weren't shut down, because it went against centuries of cultural and spiritual tradition. But it was an essential part of Bhagwan's approach to spirituality – and to life itself. The greatest crime ever committed by religion, according to Bhagwan, was that it divided the world in two. It separated the spiritual from the material, the body from the soul. It created a deep split, making us schizophrenic, incapable of living whole, healthy and happy lives.

It wasn't always like this. Back in the days of the Upanishads, thousands of years ago, the mystics of India used to live with their wives and families. Then along came Gautam Buddha and Mahavira, who both taught renunciation: turn your back on the world and its fleeting pleasures if you wish to attain eternal truth.

The impact of Buddha on India was enormous, dealing a huge blow to the Brahmins and their caste-oriented approach to religion. Then Hinduism went a stage further: Adi Shankara preached an even more extreme view than Buddha, declaring the world is not even real; it is *maya* . . . illusion.

Shankara is regarded in India as the man who consolidated the doctrine of Advaita Vedanta, one of the main traditions of Hindu philosophy. On the face of it, Bhagwan fitted nicely into this tradition: Advaita teaches that the true self, or Atman, is the same as the ultimate reality, or Brahman, which was no different, in essence, from Bhagwan's vision of dissolving the ego-self into the absolute.

But there the similarity ended. Bhagwan attacked Shankara's idea of the world being illusion, saying this had created deeply life-negative attitudes in India and turned millions of people into hypocrites: they pretended to give little value to human desires, but nevertheless continued to be ruled by them. This was especially true in regard to sex, which in conventional Hindu philosophy has been regarded as one of the biggest obstacles to renouncing "the world" and all its temptations.

In Hindu ashrams, men and women lived, prayed and worshipped separately. Many saints could not permit themselves even to look at women, and required a wait of ten minutes before sitting where a woman had sat – lest the warmth left by her thighs created a disturbance in their celibacy. This is how it was for centuries and centuries. Until Bhagwan arrived on the scene with his orange horde of hugging sannyasins.

Perhaps the most provocative aspect of Bhagwan's new version of sannyas was that he asked us to continue to use the traditional orange colour worn by Hindu saints and sadhus who'd given up all their worldly possessions, while encouraging us to enjoy everything life had to offer. Bhagwan was against renouncing anything. He found it cowardly. The real challenge was to relish what ordinary life had to offer while using meditation to remain free of attachment.

Sometime in early 1978 I was arrested for hugging in the street, outside a cinema in downtown Pune. I'd just emerged with a girlfriend after the movie ended, and we were holding hands while trying to flag down a rickshaw to take us back to Koregaon Park.

For some reason, I gave her a hug and immediately a policeman, whom I hadn't noticed, came over and ordered us to stop.

"Please behave properly," he cautioned us.

Being in a carefree and arrogant mood, I hugged my girlfriend again, right in front of him. Of course we were both wearing orange clothes so, to him, it must have been like watching a monk and a nun making out on the street.

"Not like this?" I asked, jokingly.

At that moment a police jeep was passing and he hailed it.

"Get in," he ordered, so we did.

"Where are you from?" he asked me.

"England," I replied, loftily.

"Get ready to go back there," he snapped.

I realised it was time to sober up. My girlfriend was still giggling, thinking the situation was hilarious, but I whispered to her to get serious, or we'd find ourselves in all kinds of trouble.

At the police *chowki*, or station, I did some smooth talking, apologised for my ignorance about local customs, wrote and signed some bullshit statement – I don't think they could even read it – and hurried my girlfriend out of the door. There were limits to how much we could provoke the locals with our carefree antics.

This incident serves to underscore Bhagwan's biggest and most controversial innovation in the long history of Indian spirituality: meditation should be fun. Life should be a carnival. Inner and outer worlds needed to meet. Metaphorically speaking, Gautam Buddha needed to get up from his meditative lotus position and join Zorba the Greek in an ecstatic dance . . . then spend the night with Marilyn Monroe.

Local Living

The ashram was tight for space, and as everyone wanted to live inside, being accepted as a worker didn't automatically come with a bed. At first, I lived outside, renting a small, funky room in a run-down two-storey house nearby, for the modest sum of 100 rupees a month – about ten quid by 1978 currency values.

For possessions, I had a mattress on the floor, a mosquito net, a change of clothes and that was about it. My landlord was also a tenant, squeezing himself, his wife and his four kids into one other room, so he could sublet mine.

They were a low-caste family, so his wife had to clean the toilet for a higher-caste family living on the same floor. At first, I didn't understand, and when the smell from the other toilet got too bad, I bought a large bottle of disinfectant and pointedly left it outside our neighbour's door. Instantly, it was whisked away by my landlord's wife. Then the caste penny dropped. She was one of those whose destiny, by birth, required her to clean up other people's shit.

Occasionally, I had uninvited guests. One night, for example, there was an almost-silent thump as something landed on the top of my mosquito net. I slid out from underneath, stood up, switched on the light and saw a rather pretty-looking rat, sitting frozenly on the net, having fallen off one of the rafters supporting the roof. I opened the door and waited quietly, looking expectantly at my guest. He, or she, got the point, jumped off the net and ran daintily out of my room. Nice, wordless communication.

But my landlord had a large, nasty dog who, sensing my fear, made a point of barking loudly at me whenever I returned home. One evening, he bit me on the leg as I tried to get past him in the corridor. Actually, to be accurate, he bit me twice, because he was blocking the corridor and I was stepping gingerly over him, so he nipped me high on my inner thighs, on either side of my private parts. My landlord apologised for his pet's behaviour, saying the dog was upset because they hadn't given him his usual chapati that evening.

My thin cotton trousers were no protection and the skin was broken, which posed a dilemma. Rabies was common among dogs in India – it still is – and to be safe I should have gone to a local hospital and endured the horrendous procedure of seven periodic injections of anti-rabies serum into my stomach, which was the only available cure in those days.

I eyed the dog speculatively. Did he have rabies?

Since he wasn't frothing at the mouth – the dog, not the landlord – and had good reason for his irritation, I decided to take the risk. Instead, I went to a nearby medical centre and asked for a tetanus shot. The doctor thought I was crazy not to have the rabies injections, but the gamble paid off. I didn't die.

One day, my landlord brought home a green parakeet and stuffed it into a tiny cage on his balcony, where a much smaller bird was already in residence. The parakeet had a bloody head, so somebody had whacked it in order to catch it, but otherwise it seemed healthy – although it was, of course, completely freaked out and squawking desperately.

I couldn't stand it, so the next day when my landlord was out I opened the cage. With a loud shriek, the parrot shot out and disappeared into a clump of nearby trees. I waited for the smaller bird to fly out, too, but it had been in the cage so long it wouldn't leave – a metaphor, perhaps, for the state of many of us humans. We love our cages.

The landlord came home, saw the parakeet had flown and looked at me angrily. I looked back at him with cool defiance. He hesitated, decided to say nothing and let it pass. Nice, wordless communication.

My routine as an ashram worker was pretty simple. If I wanted to do Dynamic, I'd be up by 5:30am and in the hall by six, when this meditation started each morning. As Dynamic began in darkness and ended an hour later in daylight, the metaphorical transition from darkness to light appealed to me.

But unless I was feeling angry or upset about something, and needing urgently to blow off steam, I'd usually skip Dynamic, get up around

seven, take a bucket shower and walk to the ashram for an early morning mug of chai and a breakfast of porridge and bananas. Chai was
available almost all day long and was free for workers. Then I'd line up
for Bhagwan's morning discourse, which started at eight and lasted
about 90 minutes. We all sat on cushions on the floor of the hall and I
could see that our numbers were growing, almost week by week.

Seating in Buddha Hall had a structure: the first two or three rows
were reserved for Bhagwan's personal staff and the ashram's group
leaders, who kept increasing in number as the range of therapies
offered continued to grow. In these rows, Bhagwan himself chose
exactly where each person would sit, which – so I was told later by
an insider – could be an agonising experience. If, for example, you'd
become accustomed to sitting in the first row and were one day given
the message that, from now on, you'd be sitting in row three, it could
easily feel like "spiritual demotion".

"Bhagwan definitely used that as a way of showing us our attachment to being high on the spiritual pecking order," commented one
insider. "Of course, the pecking order was in our minds, but . . .
ouch! It felt real enough, if you lost your front-row seat."

Ashram workers were given the next few rows, with the general
crowd of visitors behind them. Even though I was a worker, I sat
mostly at the back of the hall, which gave me the option of lying
down when sitting became tiring. Watching old videos from those
days, I can't see myself anywhere, so I must have been horizontal most
of the time. Bhagwan was easy about people lying down and even
sleeping through his discourses, but coughing and making any kind
of noise was taboo. This made sense, because, paradoxically, the basic
aim of his discourses was to talk us into a state of inner silence.

After discourse, there was a short break and work usually started
around 10.00am. I'd walk down the leafy, gravel pathway alongside
Lao Tzu House, climb over the balcony, sit down in front of my typewriter and start work. This tiny space was the press office and four of
us were packed into it, plus, of course, our desks, chairs and
typewriters.

My daily work consisted of three things:

Writing a press release about something newsworthy that Bhagwan
had said in discourse that morning – "the pill is the greatest invention
since the bullock cart" is one classic that comes to mind.

Writing a letter to the editor, in response to some negative news-paper article that had been recently published about Bhagwan.

Writing an article about the mystic and his ashram, in the hope that it would be published in some Indian or Western magazine.

Bhagwan's house was regarded by many of us as the "holy-of-holies" and everyone dreamed of living there. This might have generated fierce competition, but there was really no point, since Bhagwan himself chose the residents and he, so it seemed, was above any kind of manipulation by ambitious, unenlightened disciples.

For us workers, there was a mid-morning chai break, and in addition I sometimes went to Buddha Hall for the Sufi Dance celebration of singing and dancing. Nobody in the press office seemed to mind my absence. Lunch break was around one o'clock and lasted an hour. It was vegetarian food and, to be honest, not very nutritious. I don't know why, but locally farmed veggies lacked the vitamin-powered punch of their Western cousins. Maybe the soil was tired from over-use.

Amoebic dysentery was always a problem, but not because of ashram hygiene. It was when we tempted fate by going outside for fresh-squeezed orange juice, or a roadside-pressed sugar cane juice, or – god forbid – drank a glass of water in a restaurant, that the trouble usually began. Cures were tedious but eventually effective. Nevertheless, due to chronic stomach issues, many of us acquired that thin, pale, nearly-gaunt look that, when combined with long hair and beards, could easily be mistaken for spiritual asceticism.

Hepatitis A was a lesser danger, but not uncommon. We called it "the spiritual disease" because, in addition to turning our skin and eyes a deep yellow colour, it completely robbed us of our energy. All one could do was lie in bed for about six weeks – a kind of involun-tary Vipassana group – until the illness passed and our energy came back. Some people were convinced they'd become enlightened while suffering from hepatitis, simply because they lacked the strength to be upset about anything, or even to think. In such cases, the return to health proved very disappointing.

Work in the press office continued in the afternoons, made pleas-ant by the sound of bells and chimes from Bhagwan's "Nadabhrama" humming meditation that was held every day, like Dynamic and

Kundalini, in the nearby Buddha Hall. We stopped work at five, with more chai, followed by supper. Then people either got ready for evening darshan with Bhagwan, or went for dancing in Buddha Hall, with live music supplied by sannyasin musicians.

After that, well, either you went home alone, or with a date. Since my room was so close and accommodation in high demand, I occasionally found myself being solicited for inappropriate reasons. I remember making love with a South African woman, who, soon afterwards, held my hand, looked at me softly with her deep, sparkling blue eyes, and started talking about developing an intimate relationship with me . . . and, oh yes, moving into my space. This was puzzling, since it was our first date and neither of us seemed the type to be struck by love at first sight. Then I understood the true object of her affection. It wasn't me. It was the location. I laughed, gave her a hug and said, "Nice try, but I'm staying single."

She laughed, too, and fessed up to her real intention. In any case, not long afterwards we were both invited to move into the ashram. Just in time, really, because the owner of my bungalow showed up and sent a message to me, via a young girl also living in the house, that if I didn't leave immediately I would be badly beaten by a gang of thugs.

This was a shock, but, recovering quickly, I surprised myself by saying calmly to the girl: "Tell the owner that if he doesn't leave me alone, I will bring 50 sannyasins from the ashram and burn his bungalow to the ground." Shortly afterwards, the owner invited me to tea. He explained that he needed me to move out, gave me a month's notice, and I agreed, having already received my ashram invitation. Neither of us mentioned our exchange of macho-style ultimatums.

It left me wondering: was this how the locals did business? Well, not too many years later, a male member of the family who owned the bungalow was murdered for his part in a mafia-controlled business of selling low-grade petrol as high-octane fuel. I guess that answered my question. All in all, it was a relief to move into a large, newly erected bamboo hut squeezed between two ashram buildings that could house about half a dozen of us.

It was pretty basic: there were square holes for windows, cut into the bamboo matting walls, but no window panes or shutters. There was a spacious doorway, but no door. I didn't mind. We were *inside* and that was all that mattered.

As Noah no doubt said to the animals when they walked two-by-two into his hastily constructed Ark, ready for their voyage into uncharted waters: "It's not much, but it's home."

Looking Out, Looking In

"Self-indulgence to the point of madness."

That was how one indignant British journalist described our lifestyle with Bhagwan, in a magazine article published in the spring of 1978.

I could see his point. Journalists are heavily invested in trying to make sure the public maintains a high level of interest in the world surrounding us. This includes the "serious issues" of our time – economic problems, political crises, unemployment, poverty, famine, conflict, war – and also trivial stuff like fashion, sport, gossip, scandal and entertainment.

How can one simply turn one's back on it all and look within?

Well, actually, for me it was easy.

By the time I went to India, I'd already studied the sayings of several spiritual mystics and one of Gautam Buddha's statements stuck with me:

We are what we think. With our thoughts we make the world.

In other words, the state of the world is our own creation. Not the natural world of rivers, mountains and deserts, but the social world of human beings. We are continuously thinking it into existence, because this is the way we want it. For example, there is no such thing as "the United Kingdom". It's just an idea. It's nothing more than a thought, sustained by several million people. A piece of coloured cloth becomes a "national flag" and an ordinary old woman is transformed into a "queen" just because we agree to think so.

The media's job is to support the kind of reality we want to see, by continuously reflecting our thoughts back to us. Gossip about the Royal Family, votes in the House of Commons, football games, TV talent contests, celebrity interviews . . . it all feeds and sustains our social paradigm.

As the Canadian philosopher Marshall McLuhan once famously

said, "the medium is the message". And the media's message is: "Believe in this world we create together."

So, having understood my role in sustaining the collective illusion, I had decided to explore my personal reality instead. That's why I had quit Westminster in 1974. When I arrived in Pune, two years later, and Bhagwan began one of his discourses with the words: "Only individuals exist – society is an illusion," I knew I'd found a mystic who was speaking my language.

However, your inner world as an individual is no less complex than external society. When you begin to look inside your own mind, you open a Pandora's Box of issues and emotions that need sorting out on the way to self-realisation.

For example, as a young man and as a political journalist, I had been ... well ... something of an arrogant asshole and had developed an attitude of feeling superior to others. This changed radically when I joined the ashram press office, which placed me under the wing of one of the most arrogant people I've ever met in my life. His name was Krishna Prem, a tall, gay and supremely self-confident Canadian with a splendid Van Dyck beard and a way of walking around the ashram like he owned it. He could be bitchy, disdainful, with a waspish sense of humour – "I don't drink water, dear, fish fuck in it" – but, all in all, he wasn't a bad guy.

No, the problem was me. Somehow, through meditation and groups, I'd begun to peel away the outer layers of my personality, revealing that my sense of my own superiority had, all along, been masking deeper feelings of inferiority and low self-esteem. And now, in "the perfection of introspection", I found myself working with someone who, simply by being himself, exacerbated my new-found sense of inferiority. We would be working together day in, day out, for four long years, sitting together on that narrow little balcony.

Right from the start, I'd begun to compare myself negatively with other sannyasins and this was now magnified: I had doubts not only about my energy resources, but also my physical appearance, my level of consciousness, my writing abilities, my sexual potency ... all these doubts and fears came bubbling up.

Eventually, though, I was cured. The alchemy of exposing this psychological wound, for four long years, in the light of meditative awareness, gradually healed me. I began to see Krishna Prem's human side, his weaknesses and his vulnerability, and to feel that we were equal partners in the press office, doing valuable work for Bhagwan, rather than me being a kind of unwilling servant or subservient word-smith. I can't say I was grateful. I never managed to bow down to Krishna Prem and say thank you. But at least I didn't kick him in the butt or push him under a passing rickshaw.

One more example, from my inner closet of hidden skeletons: I had carried with me, from childhood, a habit of seeking negative attention. So, having been in Pune for a while, and having not received what I considered to be sufficient attention from Bhagwan, I decided to provoke him. I wrote a negative article about him using my best journalistic cynicism, and sent it to him to read.

It was titled "The Rip-Off Artist" and alleged that all the material in his daily discourses was lifted from other spiritual teachers. I had no grounds for saying this and I didn't send the article to any newspaper for publication. I just wanted to see how Bhagwan would respond to it. I was expecting him to turn the other cheek, as recommended by Jesus, saying something like, "It is good that you can express your negativity, just bring more awareness to it . . ." Some kind of detached spiritual guidance.

His response was delivered to me the next morning by a woman who lived in his house. Her face looked pale and tense as she said, "Tell Subhuti you will be doing everyone a favour if you drop sannyas."

Bam! I'd slapped his face and, far from offering me the other cheek, he slapped me right back.

Later on, I heard Bhagwan saying in discourse that he agreed with Friedrich Nietzsche, the German philosopher, who accused Jesus of insulting people. Nietzsche pointed out that, by offering the other cheek, JC was trying to prove he was spiritually superior to the people who attacked him. Well, there was nothing "holier-than-thou" about Bhagwan's message to me. It was more like a punch on the jaw by Muhammad Ali.

But I had no intention of dropping sannyas. I went to my room, stayed there for three days meditating as best I could, watching my mind go around and around, and, when I finally managed to slip out of its grip and into my heart, I wrote to Bhagwan, apologising for my behaviour.

"I won't do it again," I promised, and felt relieved that he hadn't kicked me out of the press office. But old habits die hard. It wasn't the last time he had to deal with my mind. Such is the destiny of mystics who try to awaken others.

However, lest you begin to feel sorry for Bhagwan, I have to say that he seemed to thoroughly enjoy hitting people. He didn't do it with a stick, as in the Zen Buddhist tradition of masters whacking their disciples on the head. He did it through his words and his responses to situations like mine. On a couple of occasions, Bhagwan spoke about verbally hitting his disciples "just for the joy of it", explaining that in Zen it is a loving and playful gesture, as well as a useful method for creating alertness in sleepy disciples.

He was, by his own admission, a lazy man. When someone presented him with an authentic Zen stick from Japan, he gave it to one of his disciples to hit people publicly, in discourse, on his personal instruction. He couldn't be bothered to do it himself.

"God Sir" in Esalen East

"What does 'Bhagwan' mean?"
  "It means God."
  "He calls himself God?"
  "Yes."
  "And Shree?"
  "Hmm, it kinda means 'sir'."
  "So his name is 'God Sir?'"
  "Right."

That was how *Time* magazine came up with the headline "God Sir in Esalen East" when it published a one-page feature on the ashram. The year was 1978 and Bhagwan was getting noticed in the States, categorised as a self-help guru, with an ashram comparable to Esalen, a popular personal growth centre in Big Sur, California.

For me, it was always an embarrassment, having to explain the meaning of "Bhagwan" to journalists. Every time, I could see the reporter's built-in scepticism meter shoot skywards, from doubt to incredulous disbelief. Later on, we found an easier way to explain the name after hearing Bhagwan remark in discourse that it could also mean "the blessed one". That let us off the theological hook, so to speak, and gave us an easier time with the media.

So, let's take a brief look at Bhagwan's approach to God, the universe and metaphysics. The mystic was against theology and philosophy both, but a little detour into these realms may shed light on his approach to life, with a little help from the world's most famous schoolboy, Harry Potter.

In her seven-book saga about Harry's adventures, author J.K. Rowling combined two exotic worlds: magicians at war with each other and children growing up together in a boarding school. It was a truly magical mix, but the basic concept on which she built her make-believe world, called "conflict dualism", is as old as human history.

Conflict dualism is the struggle between opposites. The tension that is created between two opposing polarities forms the basis of almost all novels and movies: the good guy fights the bad guy and, after a long struggle, the good guy usually wins. It is this tension that grips the audience, keeping us on the edge of our seats, compelling our attention until the conflict is finally resolved. In a novel or a movie, conflict dualism works well. But, unfortunately, it is also fundamental to the way we have traditionally looked at universal forces, dividing them in two: good and evil, light and darkness, God and the devil.

Our concept of a massive cosmic conflict between good and evil arose from religious traditions, including Zoroastrianism and Judaism, together with Judaism's two main offshoots: Christianity and Islam. In other words, for thousands of years we have been hooked on a cowboy philosophy of white hats and black hats, good guys and bad guys. Hence, George Bush Junior could justify his attack on Iraq by making that nation part of his "Axis of Evil". Never mind that hundreds of thousands of people have died in Iraq as a result of the American invasion in 2003. The important thing is: evil has to be defeated.

In Bhagwan's vision, the only conflict lies within the human mind, which projects its warped view onto the natural world around us. In reality, the universe is a harmonious dance of complementary opposites, like the Taoist polarities of *yin* and *yang*, summer and winter, male and female, day and night, birth and death . . .

"The whole existence is in continuous celebration," he explained. "Just we have to drop our constant traffic of the mind, which goes on keeping us away from existence."

The human mind, in his understanding, consists of a thick wall of thoughts, including our dreams, imagination, feelings, emotions, sentiments. It is this thought-wall that separates us from existence.

Bhagwan had a poor opinion of the Christian doctrine of the Trinity because it lacked the female element, referring to it as a "gay trio". He also said it was ugly of God to create Adam and Eve as lesser beings than himself. "Any father worth the name would want his children to eat from the Tree of Knowledge and the Tree of Life," he explained.

He chastised Jesus for claiming to be the Only Begotten Son of God, when in reality we all possess the same divine essence within ourselves. As for Christ's teachings, Bhagwan stated that Jesus learned most of it from Buddhist and Hindu mystics during a long stay in India between the age of 12 and 30 – the gaping hole left in the Bible's account of Christ's life. He claimed that records of Jesus' visit to India still exist in the library at Hemis Gompa, the Buddhist monastery in Ladakh.

He mocked not only the idea of Creation but also the Big Bang theory, saying that our idea of *the* beginning was untenable. The so-called "bang" event may have been *a* beginning, but only as a continuation of other cosmic events preceding it. The universe is an eternal phenomenon, with no beginning and no end. According to him, God is not something separate and above humanity, but something hidden within humanity, as our potential – the cosmic consciousness.

As for heaven and hell, Bhagwan referred to them as psychological states, not physical locations. "Hell is optional," he informed us, which still today remains one of my favourite quotes, because it makes us entirely responsible for both our joy and our misery.

"This is the most perfect world possible, it cannot be improved upon," he said. "Enjoy its beauty. Relish the celebration that goes on around you."

Live totally, explore everything. These were the key elements of Bhagwan's philosophy of life and he summed it all up in the synthesis of Zorba the Greek and Gautam Buddha, producing a new vision for human potential: "Zorba the Buddha."

To Bhagwan, Zorba represented the celebration of a sensual life, with wine, women, song and dance, while Buddha represented the richness of the inner world of consciousness. In both cases, celebration was the key, because in the mystic's view, everything in nature from the birds to the stars exists in a state of celebration.

"Existence is so incredibly beautiful, that all that you need is just to relax, rest, *be*. Let the separation between you and the Whole disappear," he declared.

Just relax and let the separation disappear. Sounds simple, doesn't it? But here's the problem: for the separation between us and existence to disappear, our egos also have to disappear. And this, apparently, is the last thing any of us want. Our consciousness is glued to the ego. The ego is all we know. So except in moments of deep meditation, the death of ego looks like the death of us – hence my panic at the prospect of dissolution that I described earlier.

Gautam Buddha was well aware of this problem and in what, to me, ranks as the greatest understatement of all time, described it thus:

"The tendency of the ego is to want to persist."

When seekers come to mystics like Buddha and Bhagwan, they somehow already know they are more than the ego. They want to wake up, in the spiritual sense, but they don't want to experience how scary and painful it can be to let go of their dreams. When it gets too painful – as it usually does – they get angry and usually tell the mystic to fuck off.

So, the question facing any enlightened mystic is surely this: why bother? When you have awakened from the collective dream and are living in a state of ultimate bliss, why go through the unrewarding hassle of trying to wake up other people? For this very reason, India has a long tradition of *silent* sages. Down through the centuries, scores of sadhus, yogis, ascetics, sannyasins and *bhikkhus* . . . those who succeeded in lifting the veil of illusion . . . chose to keep their mouths firmly shut. Having attained to universal oneness, they gazed upon those still trapped in duality and decided not to share their wisdom.

After all, if the world is *maya*, illusion, and the destiny of human beings already determined by their karmic burden, accumulated during numerous past lives, what would be the point? "Jai Ram! All is God!" they murmured to themselves, shrugging their spiritual shoulders, then closed their enlightened eyes and disappeared into eternal silence.

Nevertheless, some seers did decide to speak, doing their best to convey what they'd experienced. Buddha did it because his heart was filled with compassion for the suffering and sorrow of humanity. Jesus did it for similar reasons, taking all the suffering of humanity upon himself in order to wash away our unoriginal sins.

Bhagwan, however, did it for an entirely different reason, which, in the long tradition of enlightened saints, is almost heretical:

He enjoyed it.

Please Touch

"I do my thing and you do your thing."

This was the first line in the so-called "Gestalt Prayer", composed by Fritz Perls, the noted German-born psychiatrist and psychotherapist. After an extraordinary life, which included escaping from Hitler and pioneering Gestalt Therapy, Perls ended up living at the Esalen Institute in California. There he collaborated with Dick Price, one of the founders of Esalen, which in the late 1960s rapidly grew into a Mecca for anyone interested in experiencing new techniques for personal growth. The institute, with its fabulous location in Big Sur, on high cliffs overlooking the Pacific Ocean, soon acquired an international following.

After Perls died in 1970, Price started looking around for more teachers. Eight years later, in 1978, at the time I was working in the press office, he made the trip to India to see Bhagwan, asked for initiation into sannyas and was given the name "Geet Govind".

But his stay at the ashram was a short one. After Bhagwan had suggested that he should do two groups, Encounter and Tantra, Price ran into trouble. He couldn't handle the "no limits" paradigm and threat of physical violence in the Encounter Group. He soon freaked out and left. From then on, as far as his relationship with Bhagwan was concerned, Price definitely adhered to the opening line of the Gestalt Prayer: "I do my thing and you do your thing" – at a distance of several thousand miles.

As for Bhagwan, when he heard of Price's hasty departure, he commented in discourse: "Although he had been a disciple and a colleague of Fritz Perls, he had not learned anything. Although he is the founder of Esalen, he must have been avoiding his own deep problems. I had given him these two groups. If he had passed through these two groups he would have attained to a great insight – a satori was possible – but he escaped, he ran away."

I'd already heard the news and, in a way, I sympathised with Dick Price, because some of the things we did in those groups were completely off-the-wall. I remember a face-slapping exercise, where we sat in pairs, and took turns to slap each other's faces, as hard as we liked. It was brutal and bizarre, but I have to say, for me personally, it was also brilliant, because it took so much courage for me to stay in that structure, all the way until the end, that it helped to blow away my negative self-image of being a weak and cowardly person. I'm not saying I'd recommend it to anyone else. I'm not saying I'd ever do it again. But when it was over, I felt like a warrior, having bravely survived a battle, and it was a fantastic feeling. For the first time in my life, I was able to acknowledge my male strength.

However, Dick Price left early and this was a newsworthy event, because by this time his Esalen Institute was well known in America. That's why *Time* magazine used it as a parallel reference point for introducing the public to Bhagwan – hence their headline "God Sir in Esalen East", mentioned earlier.

Bhagwan gained notoriety in Germany that same year, again because of the Encounter Group. Eva Renzi, a well-known German film actress and director, who once starred with Michael Caine in the 1966 British spy film, *Funeral in Berlin*, came to the Pune ashram.

Initially, Renzi signed up to participate in a gentle introductory group, but after a short time asked to be transferred to the Encounter Group, a request that probably should have been denied, since Renzi did not seem to understand the main purpose of this intense process: to dare to go beyond one's normal attitudes, preferences and limits.

One of the first challenges in this particular group was that people were invited to spend the night with another participant who was a stranger. Paired off with a 50-year-old Dutchman, Renzi had dinner with the man, but then decided to return to her hotel room alone.

The next day in the Encounter Group she found herself being slapped by the Dutchman, who was calling her a "phony bitch". According to Renzi, the whole group then turned on her, ripping off her clothes, slapping her and leaving her naked with a bleeding nose. Deeply distressed, she ran out of the ashram and contacted the consulate, the police and DPA, the German international press agency. Her dramatic story soon appeared on the front page of *Bild Zeitung* and all over the German media.

Commenting in discourse, Bhagwan said he felt sorry for Eva Renzi, because she'd missed a great opportunity. He dismissed her allegations as wildly exaggerated and also saw the advantages in even this negative publicity: "Now it is all over Germany. Everybody knows my name – this is something great – and everybody is asking about me, 'Who is this man?'"

In the press office, we came to understand Bhagwan's approach to negative news very well. "Just create the negative and the positive starts coming. Create the positive and the negative starts coming. They always balance, so never be worried about negative things; it is always like that," he told us.

Pretty soon the Netherlands press heard about the incident and wanted to know the identity of the Dutchman. To their surprise, it was a well-known psychologist and author, Jan Foudraine, who had written a best-selling book about alternative psychiatry called *Not Made of Wood*. He spent days on the telephone, giving long-distance interviews, giving his version of what had happened.

So Bhagwan and his controversial ashram were making news in Germany, Holland and the US. One particular phrase from the *Time* magazine article stuck in my brain. I still remember it today, more than 30 years later. Describing the workshops offered by our ashram, the magazine's Asia correspondent sarcastically referred to them as "please touch" therapies. *Please touch*? To me, this was an odd phrase, conveying some kind of prurient interest in the sexual content of our groups, yet couched in terms of moral disapproval. This was something we would come to know well after shifting to the US, this strange cocktail of sexual curiosity combined with distaste, which I assume must be a legacy from the Mayflower and its cargo of UK-exported Puritans. It was a pathetic understatement of what was really going on. Maybe "please make love" would have come closer to the truth. But, in any case, no one ever used the word "please". Either you felt the buzz or you didn't.

My own sex life at this time seemed to swing between several unsatisfactory alternatives: if women were attracted to me, I didn't usually find them attractive. If I was attracted to a woman, she seemed unavailable. Or if an undeniably beautiful woman, such as Bhagwan's English caretaker, Vivek, let me know she was attracted to me – which happened a couple of times – I'd freeze like a rabbit caught in the headlights. Fortunately, the energy field was so strong that sex happened anyway, and occasionally all my issues faded away. I remember one elegant young Frenchwoman who had a small bamboo hut just at the back of the ashram on a piece of waste ground. I'd often pop round there and while away an enjoyable hour or two on her bed.

As for the journalists, they stuck with the tried-and-true label of "sex guru" for Bhagwan, and we sannyasins were seen as enthusiastic recipients of his instructions, trying out his "sexual prescriptions" – to borrow a sarcastic term from a British reporter. I don't think any of them grasped the basic concept of using daily life as "meditation in the marketplace", which is the art of watching your own mind.

Please touch? Well, sure, touch as much as you want, but more significantly, please *watch*.

Mum and Dad

My parents must have wondered what hit them. First, my brother decided to be "born again" with Jesus. Then I gave up my reporting job at the Houses of Parliament, went off to India, changed my name to Subhuti and started wearing orange clothes.

Mum and Dad were not religious people. They paid lip service to the Church of England, but were actually members of what I call the NGB – the *Non-God-Botherers*. In others words, they didn't bother God with prayers and hymns and he, in return, didn't demand their presence in church on Sunday mornings.

At first, after taking sannyas, I tried to share my new spiritual perspective with them: "I'm not really your son, I just took birth in this life through you . . ."

Many parents got letters like this, arriving through doors around the world from Pune. It must have caused a lot of angst. But when you begin to understand how you've been programmed as a child and start to rebel against it, you inevitably blame your parents. With the very best of intentions, they were the ones who indoctrinated you. Who taught me to sing "God Save the Queen?" Who told me "life is a competition and you must try to win it"? Who explained proudly that "British is best" and that England is the greatest nation on Earth? Yep. You got it.

A little background may help create the context: Born in 1945, I was part of the post-war baby boom. My father, who'd served as a lieutenant in the Royal Navy during the war, returned to his old job as a bank clerk, in a small town on the Sussex coast, while Mum kept house and fed three meals a day to me, my dad and my brother, who was 18 months older than myself.

We were neither poor nor wealthy. I vaguely remember ration cards, drinking National Health orange juice, using an outside lavatory, taking a bath once a week and playing on lineoleum floors because we couldn't afford carpets.

As I grew into adolescence, I sailed effortlessly into the A Stream of my local grammar school, listened to Radio Luxembourg until my father could afford to buy us a television set and, as my hormones kicked in, started awkwardly fondling girls' breasts in the bushes behind our local golf course.

Having gathered my A Levels, I went to Bristol University to study Politics and Philosophy and finally lost my virginity at the end of my first year at the age of 20 – about five years late, in my estimation. Two years later, in 1968, I graduated with a BA degree, discovered that journalism was the right career for me because it didn't feel like work and, two and a half years after that, thanks to a combination of modest writing skills and the blessings of Lady Luck, landed a plum job in the Houses of Parliament.

On one level, it was a story filled with safety, security and good fortune. On another level, it had crippled me. Now, I was trying to explain this to my parents.

But I soon saw that my efforts to convey my new ideas were only hurting them, so in January 1979 I tried a more practical approach: I persuaded them to come to Pune. I rented a sweet little bungalow at the rear of Koregaon Park and tried to make them feel at home. They sat in Bhagwan's morning discourses. They went to evening darshan. They liked Bhagwan's style and sense of humour, but they never became sannyasins.

"Well, half of what he says makes sense, but the other half is pure Indian," pronounced my mother in her best English manner, defiantly waving the Union Jack. My father, impressed by all the hugging and loving in the ashram, commented: "Any man who creates a religion that mixes spirituality with sex has struck gold, as it were."

As for me, I found myself being stretched and stressed by their visit. On the one hand, I felt I owed it to my parents to bring them to Bhagwan and show them the spiritual path I'd discovered. After all, how many kids have the opportunity to introduce their parents to the contemporary equivalent of Gautam Buddha?

On the other hand, I was acutely aware of the fact that they had been the cause of the childhood issues I'd discovered in Primal, although they didn't have a clue they might conceivably have done anything wrong. On the contrary, if asked, they'd have said they made great efforts to give me the best possible upbringing, which from their perspective was true enough. Nor did they really understand what sannyas was and how it could help transform people's lives.

But something did get through eventually. Walking out of darshan with Bhagwan, my father commented, admiringly: "What an amazing personality he has!" So, I had to be content with that. Really, I was giving them an excuse for a colourful holiday in an exotic country, and meeting Bhagwan was just part of the overall package.

Speaking of exotic experiences, both my parents had a taste of what India can offer, by way of unfriendly natives. One morning, just before discourse, an insect flew into my mother's ear and was unable to find its way out again. The buzzing sensation, generated by this panicky little insect so close to her ear drum, was driving my mother crazy. "I'm not the hysterical type, but that brought me as close as I could be," she told me afterwards, "It was awful, as if that insect was crawling all over my brain."

This was not the time to tell her: "This is a wonderful metaphor for the noise created by your own mind," although, as a way of introducing my mother to meditation, I was sorely tempted to do so. Fortunately, Frederika, my friend from Berlin who back in London had helped introduce me to sannyas, was a doctor and happened to be passing by. Using a pen torch and a long, sharp instrument, she managed to extricate bits of the flying insect, piece by piece. My mother almost wept with relief when it was gone.

Then my father got bitten on his leg by another insect and it started to swell and become infected. My doctor friend put him on antibiotics and sent him to bed. When I visited him later that day, bringing chai and biscuits, he asked me if there were any ghosts in the old bungalow.

"I keep hearing a deep sighing sound," he told me. He wasn't scared, just puzzled. I shrugged and said I didn't know, but then the sound started once more.

"There it is again," exclaimed my father. "Listen!"

I did so, and, after a couple of minutes, realised what we were hearing.

"That is the young sannyasin couple next door making love," I told him. We both laughed.

Since I was busy during the day, working in the ashram, it fell to my mother to fill various prescriptions for my father and she became quite expert at jumping into rickshaws and moving around the neighbourhood. The local shopkeepers loved her: she was so very, very English.

The ashram management used the opportunity of my parents' visit to test public reaction to a new film called *Ashram in Poona*, which had just been completed by a German film-maker called Wolfgang Dobrowolny. He'd been given access to the Encounter Group, albeit a staged form of it – all the participants in the film had done the group before and were brought together for a few hours to recreate the atmosphere.

So Mum and Dad sat in Laxmi's office, watching scenes of naked men and women screaming at each other, rolling around on the floor, fighting each other . . . it looked and sounded like a madhouse. Afterwards, they didn't say much. "A bit of a shock," I think my father said. But thereafter, whenever we sat in the ashram's main dining area, where we could hear muffled screams coming from beneath Krishna House, my father would smile and refer to the underground location as "the chambers of correction".

After about three weeks, Mum and Dad returned to the UK, apparently pleased with their visit, but also relieved to leave behind the hazards of Indian life. I was glad they'd come. Even though I was busy removing their influence from my psyche, I still loved them and wanted to stay connected.

In Bhagwan's vision, it's not that you need to stay mad at your parents forever. But a little distance and an angry "Fuck off!" delivered to Ma and Pa with heartfelt conviction – preferably in therapy rather than face to face – are a tonic for the soul and a necessary part of growing up.

What was it Jesus said, when his mother came to one of his public meetings, asking for him?

"Tell that woman I have no mother."

JC knew what he was talking about.

An Empty Chair

I didn't ask many questions in discourse. Some of those I did ask, he didn't answer. But, once in a while, something clicked. A question that came spontaneously, out of nowhere, was met with a response that transformed it into a sublime experience.

This was one of those occasions. In the spring of 1979, Bhagwan was due to begin a series of commentaries on *The Dhammapada*, a central text of Buddhist literature containing 432 sutras, or sayings, by Gautam Siddhartha. By this time, Bhagwan had already given talks on two other collections of Buddha's sayings: *The Heart Sutra* and *The Diamond Sutra*.

I loved listening to Buddha's sutras, especially when they were read aloud in the silence of our early morning assembly of sannyasins – I'm guessing there were about a thousand of us by now – sitting with the master, in an open-sided hall surrounded by trees and bushes, with only birdsong and the occasional, distant, mournful train whistle as accompaniment. In that precious atmosphere, I understood the meaning of the word "sacred".

I've never had much of a feeling for past lives, but if I had them, one must have been as a Buddhist *bhikkhu*, because Buddha's utterances went straight to soul-depth. It didn't happen that way with Lao Tzu, Jesus, Bodhidharma, Patanjali, Zarathustra, the Sufi mystics, the Hasidic masters, or the Zen masters, although Bhagwan spoke on them all.

I was enthralled by *The Diamond Sutra*, not least because it takes the form of a dialogue between Buddha and Subhuti – the original Subhuti – who, having attained enlightenment, was being further guided by his master in the ways of *bodhisattvas*. This was Buddha's term for those who are able to reach nirvana, but who delay doing so out of compassion for all sentient beings who are suffering unnecessarily, in ignorance of the Dharma teaching.

Bhagwan liked the idea of *bodhisattvas*, saying that anyone who becomes enlightened needs to share it, and for a while he addressed us collectively as such. He made it clear, however, that we were as yet only seekers, not finders, of the awakened state. His talks on *The Dhammapada* were planned as a huge project, eventually filling 12 volumes of books. But on the morning he was due to begin, he fell sick and couldn't come to the meditation hall. In his absence, we sat together in silence, facing an empty chair on the podium, where he usually sat.

Afterwards, on my way to the press office, it struck me as the perfect introduction to Buddha, a man who preached *shunyata*, inner emptiness and silence. A little poem flowed into my mind and I immediately typed it out and sent it to Bhagwan in the form of a discourse question:

> *Beloved Bhagwan,*
> *An empty chair, a silent hall,*
> *An introduction to Buddha.*
> *How eloquent! How rare!*

He answered it as the first question of the new discourse series:

"Yes, Subhuti, that's the only way to introduce Buddha to you. Silence is the only language he can be expressed in. Words are too profane, too inadequate, too limited. Only an empty space, utterly silent, can represent the being of a buddha."

"You are right," he continued. "An empty chair . . . Yes, only an empty chair can represent him. This chair *is* empty, and this man talking to you is empty. It is an empty space pouring itself into you. There is nobody within, just a silence."

I loved the parallel we'd created with a dialogue that happened 2,500 years earlier: Buddha speaking to Subhuti, Bhagwan talking to me. My little verse seemed to carry the fragrance of the original Subhuti's questions, in which he'd used the word "rare" to describe his master.

There was, however, a significant difference, which Bhagwan pointed out:

"This chair, Subhuti, is certainly empty, and the day you are able to see this chair empty, this body empty, this being empty, you will have seen me, you will have contacted me. That is the real moment when the disciple meets the master. It is a dissolution, a disappearance: the dewdrop slipping into the ocean, or the ocean slipping into the dewdrop. It is the same! – the master disappearing into the disciple and the disciple disappearing into the master. And then there prevails a profound silence."

In other words, as I already knew inside my heart, it had not happened yet. That was the difference between me and the original. *Way to go, dude.*

Special Guests

"Are you taking sannyas tonight?"

Diana Ross didn't know what to say. I don't think she even knew what sannyas was. She looked for guidance to Werner Erhard, her boyfriend, but he was already through the gate and heading towards the auditorium. So, the famous American singer nervously shrugged and followed him.

A few minutes later, after darshan had begun, it was Erhard's turn to be called up. He was the creator of a hugely successful two-week-end seminar programme offering personal transformation – the Erhard Seminar Training, more popularly known as "est".

Since its inception in 1971, hundreds of thousands of people had passed through est, so, in terms of popularity, he was way ahead of the man in front of him. Yet now, eight years later, Erhard looked decidedly uncom-fortable as he sat on the floor in front of Bhagwan. He didn't ask a question, just said something like, "Well, Bhagwan, it's really good to be here."

Bhagwan welcomed him, asked if he had anything to say – he didn't – and that was pretty much it. A high-speed darshan with no real content. So why, I wondered, had Werner Erhard bothered to come all the way from the United States to Pune?

The only answer I could come up with was that perhaps he wanted to be acknowledged as a master himself. But, of course, he couldn't directly ask Bhagwan for an enlightenment certificate, in case his application might be rejected. He couldn't even ask a question, because that would imply that he himself didn't have all the answers. So he just sat there, said "hi" and left. Diana Ross, for her part, looked like she'd landed on Mars and couldn't wait to catch the next shuttle back to her home planet.

The year was 1979 and the "saffron superstar" – by then the Indian media's name for Bhagwan – was attracting a trickle of celebrities from the West. It never became a flood for two reasons:

Not many famous people cared to risk their health by visiting India.

Not many cared to risk their reputation by visiting a controversial mystic.

One of the first well-known people to come was 6th Marquess of Bath Henry Frederick Thynne, a British aristocrat and landowner. It was he who created the Lions of Longleat, the first safari park in the UK, to help pay his taxes and save his ancestral home. Thynne arrived as early as 1975 and, as I recall, asked Bhagwan to shed light on an altered state of consciousness he'd experienced, in which his breathing had completely stopped for several minutes.

British actor Terence Stamp was another early bird, arriving in 1977, who had several darshans with Bhagwan. In one of them, Bhagwan told him that actors have an advantage over other people when it comes to spiritual growth because they already know how to slip out of one personality and into another. Stamp was a sociable fellow, mixed freely with other sannyasins, and delighted me one night with a hilarious impression of British Prime Minister Ted Heath conducting an orchestra.

Around 1978–9, Alan Whicker, a British TV personality who globe-trotted with his travel programme *Whicker's World*, spent several days at the ashram. When Whicker commented on a general atmosphere of "suppressed hysteria" among the community, Krishna Prem, my colleague in the press office, immediately replied, "Oh no, Alan. It's called love."

Bernard Levin, elegant and erudite columnist for *The Times*, was allegedly introduced to Bhagwan's books by his young girlfriend Arianna Huffington, who later co-founded the *Huffington Post*, the news website. In 1980, Levin visited the Pune ashram, then wrote three feature articles about us in *The Times*. Levin compared the silence preceding Bhagwan's morning discourse to "the Bayreuth hush", which I found puzzling until someone explained that Levin was a devotee of composer Richard Wagner and a regular visitor to the annual opera festival in the town of Bayreuth, Bavaria. The "hush" happens just as the curtain goes up.

Jimmy Carter's sister Ruth passed through during a tour of India. A Christian evangelist and preacher back in the States, she asked us not to publicise her visit and we agreed – at least, until she was out of the gate. Then we notified the Indian press. No opportunity to make headlines was lost and, besides, Bhagwan didn't like people to visit him in secret. He found it cowardly.

Once in a while a celebrity did make his or her admiration for Bhagwan known in a very public manner. Vinod Khanna, who in the seventies competed with the legendary Amitabh Bachchan for the privilege of being India's No.1 male movie star, caused a sensation when he asked to be initiated by Bhagwan. Vinod wore his orange clothes and mala on the Mumbai movie sets, changing into his actor's clothes only at the last moment before shooting. He was a frequent visitor to the ashram and later shocked his Bollywood colleagues by dropping out at the height of his film career and following Bhagwan to the Oregon Ranch, working there as a humble gardener.

To borrow the title of a popular self-help book, Vinod Khanna literally became, for a while, *The Monk who Sold his Ferrari*.

From Freud to Tantra

The freelance Indian photographer was stressed out and I knew exactly why. There was a goldmine waiting for him here inside the ashram, hovering tantalisingly just out of reach, but he wasn't being allowed to get to it. We escorted him around our beautifully tended gardens, invited him to take photos of people meditating in Buddha Hall, of newcomers walking in through the gate, even of hugging sannyasins. But it wasn't enough. It wasn't what he wanted and we all knew it. The year was 1979 and the photographer had heard enough rumours about what was going on to know he was missing out on the real story.

Eventually, in sheer frustration, he sent a message to Bhagwan complaining that Laxmi wasn't allowing him to take "interesting" photos. Obligingly, Bhagwan overruled his secretary, saying any therapist who wished to do so could invite the photographer into their workshops and groups. Several did, and instantly the veil of social conformity was ripped away. Photos of naked sannyasins – screaming, shouting, hugging, massaging each other – soon appeared in a Delhi magazine, then in *Stern* magazine in Germany. They were indeed shocking and are still being republished, even today. As we have already seen, Bhagwan knew how to hit the headlines.

A reporter from *Stern*, called Jörg Andrees Elten, came to write an article on the ashram, took sannyas himself, then wrote a book, published in 1979, called – in German of course – *Totally Relaxed in the Here and Now*. It became a best-seller, motivating thousands of young Germans to come to Pune.

As for the good citizens of India, they nodded their heads and said to each other, "I told you so." The controversial author of *From Sex to Superconsciousness* and his disciples were living up to their expectations. From then on, whenever I took a group of Indians on

FROM FREUD TO TANTRA

a tour of the ashram, I could see men peering into the bushes and undergrowth, hoping to catch a glimpse of a naked couple making love.

They never did, but that did nothing to allay the rumours. In any case, the sight of scantily clad sannyasin couples standing motionless on the ashram pathways, entwined in intimate hugs, was more than enough evidence to confirm their suspicions.

So, what was going on, behind the sensationalism?

If you want to understand Bhagwan's approach to sex, you need to begin with Sigmund Freud. The good professor, as is well known, had a dismal view of human nature. Having peered into the depths of the Unconscious and discovered the instinctual urges of the Id and the driving passion of the Libido, he concluded that if civilisation is to exist we have no choice but to suppress our instincts – especially our sexual instincts. Suppression creates neurosis, Freud acknow-ledged, but this is the price we must pay for an orderly society. The best we can hope for, therefore, is to be normally neurotic.

Wilhelm Reich, one of Freud's disciples, came to a different conclusion. Experimenting with methods to release suppressed energy, both sexual and emotional, he declared it perfectly possible to be a happy and orgasmic being without bringing about the destruc-tion of civilisation.

Aneesha Dillon, an American therapist who'd studied Reich's methods and who was invited by Bhagwan to practise her craft at the Pune ashram, describes it thus in her book *Tantric Pulsation*: "Reich advocated sexual freedom for all human beings. He also pointed out the social cost of repression, including sexual perversion, pornog-raphy, prostitution, domestic violence, rape, depression and all kinds of psychological problems."

Bhagwan agreed with Reich, saying that methods developed by this psychotherapist to release energy had been known in India's Tantric traditions for hundreds of years.

But Bhagwan painted a bigger picture: "There is no such thing as sex energy," he said, answering a question about whether it was possible to spiritualise sex. "Life energy is one and the same, but there are many directions for it."

If sex remains the only focus, then it becomes a wastage, he contin-ued. "It is like laying a foundation and going on laying the foundation, without ever building the house for which the foundation is meant."

Sex energy, according to Bhagwan, is the unrefined crude oil out of which the high-octane gasoline of consciousness is refined. For this refining process, two things are needed: a free-flowing energy system and a growing meditative awareness that would, by its very nature, transform energy into higher manifestations, such as love, compassion, prayer and enlightenment.

One of the first of Bhagwan's books to attract attention in the West was titled *Tantra, the Supreme Understanding*, in which he commented on the life and teachings of a Tantric mystic, Tilopa, who lived in India about 1,000 years ago. Even though Tilopa's personal life included sexual exploration, such as working for a time as a bouncer and pimp in a Bengal brothel, the focus of Bhagwan's commentaries was not on sex, nor, as one might expect, on descriptions of Tantric rituals and ceremonies.

Around this time in the late seventies, Tantra was becoming known in the West as a form of sacred sexuality, with courses and books offering step-by-step progression of exercises designed to enhance sensuality, intimacy, sexual ecstasy and orgasm. This approach was loosely based on old Tantric scriptures, some of which declared that god-like powers could be acquired by channelling sexual energy upward through the body's seven chakras, or energy centres.

One might suppose that an ashram run by a "sex guru", or "Tantric mystic", would be filled with couples sitting in the classic *yabyum* Tantric embrace, sexually conjoined, busily channelling energy up their spines, in an attempt to illuminate the seventh chakra and experience ecstatic oneness with all things.

But it wasn't like that. Bhagwan wasn't interested in these kinds of techniques. His approach was to help people unblock their energy and then encourage them to follow it freely and uninhibitedly, enjoying sex as a dance or play of two energies meeting naturally and spontaneously. It was the function of the Tantra groups to help people experience sexual freedom, encouraging participants to explore nudity, masturbation, sensitivity to energy, body-to-body connection and sex with as many partners as occurred naturally within the five days that the group lasted.

Combined with Dynamic, Kundalini and morning discourse, this created the alchemical mix of sexual energy and meditation, aliveness and consciousness that gave Bhagwan's vision and his ashram their unique flavour.

He did talk about one technique, which he called "the valley orgasm":

"Once the man has entered, both lover and beloved can relax," Bhagwan explained. "No movement is needed. They can relax in a loving embrace. When the man feels or the woman feels that the erection is going to be lost, only then is a little movement and excitement required. But then again relax. You can prolong this deep embrace for hours with no ejaculation, and then both can fall into deep sleep together. This is a valley orgasm."

To Bhagwan, the path of Tantra wasn't only about sex, but about life as a whole. In a nutshell, Tantra meant saying "yes" to life, in all its aspects. His commentaries on Tilopa focused on the man's philosophy, including Tilopa's best-known insight into the task of freeing oneself from worldly desires:

The problem is not enjoyment. The problem is attachment.

In terms of sexual exploration in the ashram, we certainly got to experience the pleasures of enjoyment and the pain of attachment. It was energy that brought people together, both in daytime hugging and in nightly love-making. But energy knows nothing of commitment, or relationship, so when two people felt drawn to each other and spent the night together, they had no idea if this magnetism would last.

Inevitably, all of us had to face the sudden pang of jealousy that stabbed through our guts when, rounding an ashram corner the next day, we suddenly came upon our most recent lover in an intimate, melting embrace with someone new.

There were a few committed partnerships among sannyasins, but the majority of us were eager to be swept along in the ashram's maelstrom of sexual energy that pulled us together, wrenched us apart, spun us through a whirlpool of agony and ecstasy, then threw us into Bhagwan's morning discourse as welcome relief from our own emotions.

This, then, was the background to the so-called "sex guru". Some of us understood the philosophy; some of us did not. But all of us sensed the magic of going all-out to enjoy the body and its pleasures while at the same time plunging as deeply as possible into meditation.

It was a heady mix and if nobody on the outside could figure out what was going on . . . hey, who cared? We were having a blast. As a concession to the front office, we did try to keep sexual activity behind closed doors, or on the ashram's flat rooftops, so that visitors could be shown around without seeing couples in the bushes.

But there was another side to Bhagwan's approach, which the media completely missed: he also acknowledged that no society that hadn't repressed sex had managed to evolve beyond the tribal stage. Why? Because an energy surplus was needed to create the fabric of more advanced, sophisticated social structures and this surplus could be gained only by diverting sex energy.

So sexual repression had been a useful stepping stone in our social development. The problem was, however, that it created life-negative attitudes, especially life-negative religions that condemned the body. As Reich discovered, it is this self-condemnation that makes people miserable and neurotic.

So, where do we go from here?

According to Bhagwan, a new stage of social development has now been reached in which we can stop repressing our energy. Compared to primitive societies, we live in a state of abundance. We don't need to spend our time occupied with survival issues – hunting, fishing, food gathering, etc. We can just pop down to the local supermarket whenever we want. Therefore we can enjoy our sexual energy, take care of our survival and have surplus energy for other aspects of life, all at the same time.

Like I say, we didn't spend a whole lot of time thinking about such matters. It was far more interesting to live it.

All for Love

"I am all for love, because love fails."

OMG! This statement must rank as one of the most shocking things I ever heard Bhagwan say and I'm sure this was true for many other sannyasins. To our romantic psyches, this was serious heresy, for had we not been raised on Hollywood's deepest, most enduring, most powerful myth – that true love lasts forever? Had we not, deep in our hearts, nurtured the belief that, somewhere on this planet, our soul mate is waiting for us, and that if we follow the longing of our heart we will surely find that person and experience everlasting togetherness?

Bhagwan disagreed. In his view, the only human state that has any possibility of lasting forever is aloneness – let's face it, not a very romantic concept. But this didn't mean he was against love. On the contrary, he saw it as a wonderful opportunity for waking up. Why? Because it fails – *has* to fail, is *bound* to fail – by its very nature as an impermanent state. Love might last a day, a year, or a decade, but no matter how deep, passionate and intimate the experience may be, there comes an end to it – sooner or later. If you go through this experience enough times, Bhagwan explained, you come to understand the need for meditation, because only meditation brings you in touch with the timeless, the eternal. Love can't do it.

"I'm going to prove him wrong," declared one determined female friend of mine. Twenty years and several relationships later, she allowed the possibility that he might have a point.

Personally, I have the feeling that Bhagwan's approach is . . . well . . . shall we say . . . a little optimistic? It's a huge leap from love to meditation. The vast majority of us, devastated and broken-hearted at the end of a love affair, fail to view this as an opportunity to turn inwards and start contemplating our navels. Rather, we drag ourselves up off the floor and stagger onward, looking for the next big romance.

Love seems to hold tremendous significance for us. Sometimes I think it's the only religious experience that people can know without meditating – certainly, far more powerful and meaningful than anything offered by organised religion. The biologists and neurologists tell us it's just a flood of chemicals like dopamine and serotonin that stimulate the brain's pleasure centre and suppress our ability to think rationally. But that's not what it feels like. When it hits us, it carries a whiff of magic, a fragrance of the divine, a conviction that *"this is real . . . this is it!"* Which, of course, makes it so much more painful when it's over.

Allow me to make a time-shift, for a moment, in order to offer three very public illustrations:

When Paul McCartney married his second wife Heather Mills in 2002, he threw a lavish reception in the lovely, mystical setting of an old Irish castle, and when Mills asked the veteran Beatle if he wanted her to sign a prenup contract to safeguard his fortune, McCartney shook his head, saying, "It's not very romantic." Six years later, McCartney found himself in a highly unromantic, acrimonious, fight-for-every-penny divorce battle with Mills, who eventually walked away with £24 million.

When Monty Python's John Cleese married American psycho-therapist Alyce Faye Eichelberger in 1992, he too waived his right to a prenup, even though it was his third spin on the wedding merry-go-round. Their love disappeared in a 2008 divorce and, after a two-year bitterly contested struggle with a £12 million settlement, Cleese was so angry he created a one-man show called the "Alimony Tour", which included photos of his ex-wife taking "my money" out of an ATM.

Wealthy women are equally vulnerable, as Athina Onassis, heir to her grandfather's shipping fortune, discovered when divorcing her husband for 11 years, Brazilian Olympic showjumper Alvaro de Mirando Neto. The handsome-looking rider went after a sizeable chunk of Onassis' $270 million fortune and was only thwarted by timely revelations that he'd been in a parallel relationship with a Belgian model.

Do we ever learn? That's why I say Bhagwan was optimistic in thinking we'd eventually come to understand how meditation can deliver what love cannot. Looking at our track record as an evolving species, we just don't seem to have the IQ needed for such a paradigm shift. But then, even though he was talking to the whole world, maybe Bhagwan already knew that only a few people could hear him.

However, in case you think love is best avoided, I have news for you: that doesn't work either. I speak from personal experience. For a long time I stayed single, content to continue dating and enjoying short affairs, justifying my lifestyle by citing Bhagwan's negative views about marriage. Then I realised why I'd developed this habit: I was avoiding intimacy out of a deep fear of opening my heart and being hurt. This kind of cowardice wasn't part of Bhagwan's vision. On the contrary, he was encouraging us to open up to life and love as much as possible. Eventually, I got the message and allowed myself to go deeper in my love affairs.

My point is this: to avoid love is to deprive ourselves of one of life's most precious experiences and it's not what Bhagwan means by "love fails". In his vision of life, we need to have the courage to go headlong into it, while at the same time knowing it can never give us the lasting fulfilment that Hollywood myths suggest.

While on this theme, one more statement by Bhagwan that stunned me was a comment he made in one of his discourses, saying that "even to use the word 'couple' hurts me".

"The moment love becomes a relationship, it becomes a bondage," he explained. "There are expectations and there are demands and there are frustrations, and an effort from both sides to dominate. It becomes a struggle for power. I want the world to consist of individuals. A couple is not a thing of beauty."

On another occasion, Bhagwan said that, during his time in Mumbai, newly married Indian couples would come to seek his blessing. Jokingly, he recalled how Vivek used to try to warn them:

"She used to tell them, 'Don't ask for his blessing, because his blessing means divorce' – because she had seen, year by year, whoever had asked for my blessing was finished, asking for my blessing was the end of the relationship. But they could not understand it. They had come to ask the blessing that for their lives they remain devoted to each other, that their love goes on growing, their love should not know any end, it should be endless."

Where does this leave the romantic myths of Bollywood and Hollywood? Alas, *Gone With the Wind*, sunk with the *Titanic*.

Courtesy of Her Majesty

While on the subject of romance, I need to pay tribute to the services of Her Majesty the Queen as one of the most popular and effective match-makers in our ashram. This sounds outlandish, I know, but allow me to explain the background.

In India, in the late seventies, the cosy, red after-glow of the British Raj still shimmered in the air. The sun had set on the Empire, that's for sure, but many Indians, especially the older ones, looked nostalgically backward and sighed.

Never mind that the British had methodically sucked India dry of its great wealth, including the fabulous Koh-i-Noor diamond now decorating our monarch's coronation crown in the Tower of London.

Never mind that two million Bengalis starved to death in the 1943 famine that could have been alleviated by the redistribution of grain by British officials who had other priorities.

Never mind that the country was cut in pieces and a million people died during the 1947 Partition between India and Pakistan.

No, somehow none of that mattered. Still in the 1970s, the British were admired and welcomed. Which is why a certain young Englishman, desiring to stay indefinitely in Pune, had no trouble with his visa. Why? Because, as a British citizen, he didn't need one. He could come and go as he pleased. His big, blue, imperial-looking passport was all he needed.

Other sannyasins were not so fortunate:

"Three hundred rupees or a fuck."

The short, bald, fat Indian man didn't mince his words. His message was simple: pay the price or have sex with me. In response, the slender, frail and attractive young European woman sitting across the table from him in a downtown Pune café wilted visibly. It was clear from her body language that she didn't have the money and regarded the alternative as horrendous.

But this was how it went. The man sitting opposite her could, and did, deliver six-month visa extensions from the Pune Police Foreigners Registration Office – at a price. Three hundred rupees, in those days, would be worth 6,000 rupees today (about £67 or $85) so it was quite a sum and many of us were penniless hippies. I didn't stay in the café to see what happened, but I'm told some women did choose the alternative method of payment, which, given the physical character-istics of the middle man, must have been a real challenge.

There was, however, a third alternative: marry a Brit . . . like me, for example. Get a big blue passport and stay as long as you like, cour-tesy of Her Majesty the Queen and the former glories of world domination.

Needless to say, British sannyasins were in demand.

I was solicited by a beautiful Latin American woman and, after making love with her, it was impossible to say no. Not that I even tried. It was in the spirit of the times that we all helped each other in our collective, overriding desire to stay with Bhagwan. A few years later, for the same reason, we had to divorce and marry Americans.

The first wedding, conducted in 1979, seemed to go smoothly enough, although I couldn't help reflecting on the unique nature of our contract. Mostly, when foreigners married UK citizens, they did so in order to enjoy the blessings of moving to Britain, and living and working in a first-world country. We sannyasins were the only people, I'm sure, who were marrying UK citizens in order to remain in India.

Obtaining a British passport through marriage in those days was easy – nothing like the hassle it is today. However, my visit to the Pune registry office with my bride-to-be proved to be shockingly insightful. When my companion signed the registry and entered her birth date, I saw that she'd been born on the same day as my mother. Not the same year, of course, but the same day and month.

I had married my mother! Sigmund Freud would have clapped his hands in delight, his monocle popping out of his eye socket. Oedipus complex proven!

Fortunately, or unfortunately, our relationship didn't last long. On our wedding night, my wife left me for a French lover.

Thank God we enjoyed the honeymoon before the wedding.

The Cosmic Orgasm

"Subhuti . . ."

My name was called. I got up from among a group of about 30 seated sannyasins and walked forward to where Bhagwan was sitting in his chair.

"Amano . . ."

Another male sannyasin was also called and we both sat on the marble floor, just in front of Bhagwan. We weren't facing the mystic. We were sitting sideways to his chair, facing each other.

Then he called two women, who were in regular darshan attendance:

"Radha . . . Shunyo . . ."

Bhagwan started arranging his female "energy mediums", with one sitting closely behind me and another behind Amano. More mediums sat behind these two women, then the rest were arranged in a loose semicircle surrounding us.

"Everyone, raise your hands in the air, close your eyes and start humming and swaying," instructed Bhagwan.

The music began. The lights went off, operated by a push-button switch, lying on the floor close to Bhagwan's right foot. He personally controlled the lighting during each energy darshan, with his foot. The humming was loud. The music became wild, chaotic and fast. Some of the mediums were soon squealing and moaning in ecstasy. I felt the medium's hands on my shoulders and her breasts pressing against my back as we began to surrender ourselves to the experience. Within seconds, I found myself engulfed by a cosmic blackout that was somehow both inside and outside me.

To say that I was lost in a vast, empty space is one way to describe it. But it was more than that. This darkness was tangible and silky soft. This emptiness was luminous and filled with energy. This space was vibrating with wild music and yet, paradoxically, was seemingly drowning us all in an ocean of silence. At a certain point I felt Bhagwan's finger rest firmly yet delicately on my third eye, just between my eyebrows. He vibrated his finger vigorously, ramping up the voltage that was pulsing through my body.

To me, it was like meditating without having to make any effort. I had no choice. I was simply overwhelmed by the energy and could relax into it, thanks to the warm feminine presence that was embracing me from behind. The feeling of the medium's body against mine was sensual and delightful. She was so open, so available, so intimate. In some other context, I might have assumed we were making love and she was having an orgasm. But this was different. This was a willingness to abandon oneself and be lost within an energy phenomenon that was so big it filled the entire ashram.

It wasn't sexual, in the sense of being physically turned on, but it was orgasmic, which is probably why Bhagwan once described meditation as "orgasm without sex". The mystic arranged matters so that, while these "energy darshans" were happening in the auditorium adjoining his house, the rest of the ashram would be plunged into darkness. This meant that, while lying on my bed in my room, or dancing in Buddha Hall, I could still feel the power of this extraordinary event. It wasn't quite as strong outside the auditorium, but strong enough to transport me effortlessly into a meditative space.

Meanwhile, in my personal "energy darshan", the lights flashed on and off, the music became even more frantic, the mediums gasped and sighed, and I was leaning back in ecstasy against this soft female body, feeling like I'd probably died and gone to heaven. I had a sudden vision of a secret, orgiastic ritual in a witches' coven, back in medieval Europe, and knew for certain that every single one of these women would have been burned at the stake, hanged from a tree, ducked in a pond, or tortured to confess their evil deeds as a witch. Bhagwan, of course, would have been condemned as the devil incarnate.

Suddenly, the lights came on, stayed on, and the crazy music stopped.

"Okay, come back now," instructed Bhagwan, with a satisfied chuckle.

It was only when I tried to stand up that I realised how powerful the experience had been. I felt completely stoned and it was difficult to move; one of the nearby male "lifters" stepped forward and gently helped me to stand up, so I could return to my seat.

Bhagwan gave several more energy darshans, to both men and women, and then the event was over. He rose from his chair, gave a beaming smile to us all, accompanied by his usual Namaste, and returned to his room. Slowly, we filed out of the auditorium. It usually took a couple of hours to come down off the high that we'd experienced.

Bhagwan had selected about a dozen women to be his regular mediums, with a few more invited as occasional guests. Most of these women were voluptuous, with shapely bodies, but aside from any personal preferences Bhagwan might have had, my feeling was that femininity and receptivity were key qualities for these women, allowing surges of energy to rush easily through the body. As far as Bhagwan's mediums were concerned, the sexual element in their role in the energy darshans was clear from the beginning:

"While you are absorbing my energy, feel utterly sexual, sensuous," he told his mediums, while instructing them. "In the beginning it will look very sexual. Soon there comes a point of intensity when it starts changing, when it starts becoming something that you have not known before at all, something that can only be called spiritual."

I was reminded of the image of an electrical grid, in which the mediums acted like booster stations for the main charge that flooded out, seemingly from a source inside Bhagwan himself. He requested confidentiality from his mediums about what happened to them during the energy darshans. "This has to be remembered, that whatsoever transpires between me and you is an absolute secret," he told them.

Years later, there was controversy over whether Bhagwan sexually stimulated his mediums during the blackouts. In particular, it was rumoured that he would sometimes slide his foot under a medium's robe to connect with her sex centre. Some women hotly denied it, while others quietly agreed that it happened.

My opinion? From what I gather, it did happen with some of the women. And since the Indian spiritual tradition of Tantra has known about the powerful connection between sexual energy and the state of meditation for hundreds of years, in a way Bhagwan's experiment was nothing new. To an outsider reading about it now, it might seem sleazy – turning out the lights in order to have a quick grope – but at the time there seemed to be nothing tawdry about these energy darshans. As I understand it, Bhagwan was interested in voltage, not vice.

These energy darshans, beginning in 1979, continued on a nightly basis for over a year, but at a certain point Bhagwan abruptly discontinued them. Some years later, in discourse, the mystic gave us the reason: he told us we were becoming too reliant on his energy, whereas the real work of spiritual development happened only through our own ability to meditate, with or without him.

This basic message came back to me again and again during my time with Bhagwan, and became especially important after he died. In a nutshell, when you hook up with an enlightened being, there is good news and bad news: The good news is, his energy field can give you glimpses of states of consciousness way beyond what you can achieve alone. The bad news is, when he's gone, all you can take with you is what you've done yourself.

The Fuck Tape

Bhagwan didn't just call a spade a spade.

"I am against all the repressive traditions, all the so-called moral, puritan stupidities. I simply call them stupid," he explained. "I am not a polite person. If a spade is there, I call it a spade – in fact, a fucking spade! I want to be clear and straightforward."

Just to prove his point, during one of his discourses in 1979, Bhagwan delivered a brief educational sermon on the word "fuck". Even though it occupied just a couple of minutes in a 90-minute talk, history was made and this discourse thereafter came to be known among his sannyasins, and by the media, as "the fuck tape".

The catalyst was a question from a female sannyasin who confessed: "I am still shocked when I hear you say the word 'fuck'."

Bhagwan replied: "It is one of the most beautiful words. The English language should be proud of it. I don't think any other language has such a beautiful word."

Referring to his notes, Bhagwan continued: "One 'Tom' from California has done some great research on it. I think he must be the famous 'Tom' of 'Tom, Dick and Harry' fame, and he says that one of the most interesting words in the English language today is the word 'fuck'. It is one magical word: just by its sound it can describe pain, pleasure, hate and love. In language it falls into many grammatical categories. It can be used as a verb, both transitive (John fucked Mary) and intransitive (Mary was fucked by John) and as a noun (Mary is a fine fuck). It can be used as an adjective (Mary is fucking beautiful). As you can see there are not many words with the versatility of 'fuck'."

Besides the sexual meaning, he came up with the following uses:

Fraud: I got fucked at the used car lot.

Ignorance: Fucked if I know.

Trouble: I guess I am fucked now!

Aggression: Fuck you!

Displeasure: What the fuck is going on here?

Difficulty: I can't understand this fucking job.

Incompetence: He is a fuck-off.

Suspicion: What the fuck are you doing?

Enjoyment: I had a fucking good time.

Request: Get the fuck out of here!

Greeting: How the fuck are you?

Apathy: Who gives a fuck?

Innovation: Get a bigger fucking hammer.

Surprise: Fuck! You scared the shit out of me!

Anxiety: Today is really fucked.

Concluding his soon-to-be-notorious sermon, Bhagwan added: "And it is very healthy too. If every morning you do it as a Transcendental Meditation – just when you get up, the first thing, repeat the mantra 'Fuck you!' five times – it clears the throat. That's how I keep my throat clear!"

Now, tell me, dear reader, it's not the first thing you expect when you wander into an ashram in the middle of India and listen to a discourse from the local guru, is it?

Quest for Peace

People with all kinds of national identities and ethnic roots were arriving at the Pune ashram in the late seventies, including significant numbers of Germans and Jews. The Germans were the biggest group coming from outside India. The Jews were mainly from America and Europe, although some Israelis did manage to come, slipping through the embargo that was imposed against their country in those days by the Indian government. Bhagwan joked that it was easy for Germans to come to him, because whenever they looked back over their shoulders at their own past, they saw Hitler standing there.

"The whole credit goes to Adolf Hitler," he explained. "Hitler led the German youth into such a hell, into such suffering and misery, into such utter failure, that the German mind since then has been searching for somebody who is just the opposite of Hitler. They have found the anti-Adolf Hitler in me."

As for the Jewish seekers who came to him, Bhagwan seemed to have personal experience of their ethnic roots. "I myself am an old Jew," he said once, in an offhand way, although whether he was talking about a past life, or about some stereotypical Jewish qualities he'd acquired, was left unclear. I noticed that, among the Americans who came to Bhagwan, a high percentage were Jewish, which could perhaps be attributed to their long cultural tradition of prophets, giving them an approximate understanding of the function of a spiritual master. Either that or they were just more adventurous and inquisitive than other Americans.

In 1979, one Jewish-American artist wandered into the ashram with a long backstory. Born in eastern Europe, Samudaya was barely in his teens when the Nazis invaded his country, rounded up his family and sent them to Auschwitz. He later told me about the long rail journey into Poland in the cattle wagons, the sense of foreboding in his family and the innocent honesty of his younger brother, who said, as they neared the camp: "Mother, I think we're all going to die."

He told me about the Angel of Death, Josef Mengele, who stood at the railhead while the band played music, saying "To the right . . . to the left . . .", sending people either to immediate execution or to work camps.

He told me how the prisoners became so immune to death and suffering that, one freezing winter morning, as the dead lay naked in front of their huts, they laughingly turned all the men's penises to one side, in a kind of macabre salute.

He told me about the English attitude to Hitler's "Final Solution". In a perfect Oxford accent, he exclaimed, "I say, old boy, you can't do that!" Then, lowering his voice to a murmur, he added, "Do it quickly."

God knows how Samudaya survived, but he did. After the war, he went to Israel and did a spell in the army. But living in Israel brought no peace to his tortured soul and some years later he emigrated to the US, where he became an artist, seeking to purge the horrors of his past through his paintings. One of them portrayed a tall Auschwitz smokestack, its chimney belching smoke filled with tiny, glittering, six-pointed Stars of David, while the shadow from the chimney made a Christian cross on the ground. The name of the painting was simply: *Why?*

Eventually, Samudaya became interested in meditation and that's why he ended up in Pune in the late seventies. I wouldn't meet him until we were in Oregon, when I recorded his story for our community newspaper, but something he told me about those earlier ashram days with Bhagwan is worth remembering.

He was participating in one of the ashram's therapy groups, which as I've already indicated had an international reputation for no-holds-barred experiencing of everything that is normally taboo. As an evening assignment, he was sent home with a young German woman; they were told to spend the night together and pretty soon they were making love.

Afterwards, as they drank tea together in Samudaya's room, he told her his life story and she became very quiet. When he finished, there was a long pause.

"Do you know what my name is?" she asked, finally.

He shook his head.

"It's Goering."

The girl was the great-niece of Field Marshal Hermann Goering, commander-in-chief of the Luftwaffe.

They looked at each other. They laughed. They embraced. As for Samudaya, that moment must truly have been a revelation in his personal quest for peace.

Pune Stinks

J. Krishnamurti had a long career as a spiritual teacher. At the age of 34, he split with the Theosophical Movement, which tried to proclaim him as the World Teacher, the Lord Maitreya. In August 1929, in Holland before an assembly of 3,000 people, mostly members of the Theosophical Society, he repudiated the title, turned his back on the organisation and walked away.

Thereafter, he developed his own style of teaching – ironically, he became a sort of world teacher anyway – and continued until his death at the age of 90. Krishnamurti's message was similar, in some ways, to that of Bhagwan: drop the ego, discover the inner flame of consciousness that lies at the core of every human being, become one with the "isness" of all things.

But Krishnamurti never became a controversial figure. He never irritated priests and politicians to the point of them wanting to wipe him out. The same goes for Eckhart Tolle, the German-born spiritual teacher living in Canada, who has sold 10 million books of his teachings worldwide, including his breakthrough work *The Power of Now*.

Tolle's spiritual vision has similarities to that of Bhagwan. For example, he talks about the "mind-made self", which needs to collapse in order to experience a state of "no self", which he describes as "a sense of presence or beingness, just observing and watching".

I can almost hear Bhagwan saying the same thing. But Tolle isn't a controversial figure. Why, then, did Bhagwan choose to become so notorious? Why did he provoke people?

My answer: because otherwise, the transforming power of the mystic does not go deep or far enough. We listen to people like Krishnamurti and Tolle, but we are not shocked by their words. We are not startled and provoked into experiencing how identified we are with our deeply held attitudes and beliefs – the glue that keeps the mind-made self together.

In attacking Jesus, for example, Bhagwan was attacking all those Christian beliefs and moral attitudes that constitute the building blocks of our Western egos. I particularly liked Bhagwan's dismissal of JC's resurrection of Lazarus:

"Even if it is a miracle, even if Lazarus comes back to life, he is not transformed. We don't hear anything else again of Lazarus," he commented.

I enjoyed the point Bhagwan was making: the masses might be impressed by Christ's superhuman powers, raising a man from the dead, but these feats didn't change anything in the man's consciousness.

The New Testament never mentions Lazarus again, so we have to assume that sooner or later the man died once more – this time for real, just like the rest of us – as an unconscious, unaware human being. There was no transformation. He didn't even become the thirteenth apostle of the man who brought him back from the dead.

"A man who has died, a man who has gone through the process of death to the beyond, who comes back, cannot be the same. Lazarus would have become a great master, but he remained the same person – no change at all," Bhagwan asserted.

India was Bhagwan's home and also his refuge, but it was not spared. After all, he had Indian disciples to take care of, too. In one discourse, as I recall, Bhagwan devoted about half an hour to analysing the peculiar morality of a country that didn't allow kissing in public, but permitted people to piss anywhere.

"Pissing is allowed and kissing is not?" he mocked. "The whole country is a latrine!"

He hated poverty and blamed it on overpopulation, saying that India's political leaders were too cowardly to tackle the problem. In order to fulfil their personal ambitions to win elections, Bhagwan explained, they had to grovel before religious heads – Hindu, Muslim and Catholic – who, in competition with each other over numbers, encouraged large families and condemned birth control.

As a solution, Bhagwan advocated a 15-year-dictatorship with a nationwide programme of compulsory birth control, which sounds brutal until you fast-forward to recent times and read a headline in the *Times of India* announcing that 230 million people in this country go to bed hungry every night because they don't get enough to eat.

Neither was Pune neglected by Bhagwan. Noting how this academic city prided itself on being "the Oxford of the East", he reminded us that the assassins of Mahatma Gandhi were natives of Pune, and that the city itself was polluted and strewn with uncollected garbage.

"Pune stinks," he concluded.

Working in the ashram's press office, I was in the thick of it. Inevitably, some local newspapers started condemning Bhagwan as "anti-Indian", which was a dangerous turn of events, since we didn't want an angry crowd marching on the ashram. I did my best to point out – in press releases and letters to editors – that Bhagwan's comments were out of compassion, not hostility.

"This country has so many problems and no one except Bhagwan has the courage to expose them as they really are, which is absolutely necessary if these problems are to be solved," I explained. This was a constant theme of mine. Sometimes, giving in to my tendency toward purple prose, I admonished the readers thus:

"Oh generation of vipers! India lies bleeding of her mortal wounds, and you bury your yellow fangs in the undefended body of the doctor!"

To my surprise, this letter was actually published, under the headline "Doctor Bhagwan".

Being in the press office was hectic and fun. My main task was to attack people who wrote articles attacking us, which, given Bhagwan's notoriety, certainly kept me busy. But I don't know if it did any good. I rather think that our greatest protection was the natural fear and awe with which most Indians regard their mystics. They have a centuries-old habit of steering well clear of such people while they are alive, then praising and worshipping them when they're safely dead.

Don't mess with mystics – that was his real protection. After all, you really don't want to come back in your next life as a stray dog on the streets of Pune, just because you crossed the local guru.

Guru Voodoo

I'm not a great believer in voodoo or black magic. But still, sometimes my experiences around Bhagwan were so strange it almost felt like the mystic was practising a kind of witchcraft. It began within days of my arrival, on my first visit, and continued all the way through my time with him.

For example, I'd hardly walked in the door when I learned that a 27-year-old Dutch woman called Vipassana had "left her body" – as the sannyasin saying goes – in a nearby hospital, dying from some kind of breathing complication.

Bhagwan called his sannyasins together for a short talk, then invited us to give her a joyful send-off before carrying her body to the nearby burning ghats, the sacred spot near the river where her body would be burned on an open funeral pyre. The next thing I knew, Vipassana's body was lying in the meditation hall and scores of orange-robed sannyasins were dancing around her as if this was some kind of party.

I was also trying to dance, but in a state of shock. I'd never seen a dead body before and it was hard enough to accept the fact that I was in the presence of death, let alone celebrate the occasion, as Bhagwan had invited us to do.

"This is all phony," I thought, closing my eyes to avoid comparing myself with the ecstatic-looking people around me.

Bang! Next moment, my head had collided with another head. I abruptly opened my eyes to see another bald-headed intellectual, this one from Germany, looking at me with the same astonishment with which I was looking at him. I knew immediately that he was in the same space as me. We were both caught up in judging what was happening around us, going through the motions of dancing but really completely disconnected from the celebration. At the same moment on some higher plane of existence, I could distinctly hear, or rather, feel, that Bhagwan was laughing at the pair of us. I'm not sure if the other guy felt it, but I certainly did.

Had Bhagwan knocked our heads together? I tried to dismiss it as nonsense, but, looking back on those Pune years, I can't begin to count the number of times this kind of thing happened to me. The timing of these incidents was uncanny. I would be in some cynical, negative mental space, so very familiar to me as a political journalist, and then . . . thump! I'd suddenly hit my head on something. This was particularly frequent in Pune's rickshaws, while zipping around the streets of Koregaon Park or heading downtown for shopping or entertainment.

A rickshaw's plastic hood is held up by a frame of two steel bars and, time after time, I'd be in some negative space, mentally bitching away at Bhagwan, or some aspect of his ashram, and . . . bump! My head would knock against one of these bars, which were inches above my head in the passenger seat.

One day, during my time in the press office, I thought I'd foiled him. I was travelling in a rickshaw, realised I was in a cynical mood and deliberately slid down in the seat. "Ha ha!" I chuckled, looking up at the steel bars. "You don't get me this time!"

At that moment, a local mother and child who'd been walking hand-in-hand on our side of the road decided, for no apparent reason, to cross the road without looking behind them. My rickshaw driver swerved to the right in order go around them – the road was no more than a narrow track – but they also kept moving to the right, so he had to go off the road. The grass verge was soft and the wheels sank in. In slow motion, the rickshaw keeled over on its side and lay there.

I climbed out. The rickshaw driver was distraught. "Ayeee, I am unlucky!" he wailed.

I smiled, dug into my pocket and gave him whatever cash I had for repairs. "No, don't worry, you have good luck," I assured him. "It's my bad luck to have a spiritual master with a weird sense of humour."

Next morning, in discourse, Bhagwan was talking about Moses and the burning bush, which was covered in flames and yet not consumed. He chuckled, dismissing it as an old-fashioned magical trick. "God doesn't do that anymore," he added.

Right. But Indian gurus probably do.

By the way, maybe I should explain: the name of the game around Bhagwan wasn't to replace negative thinking with positive thinking. He had no time for such "cheap American philosophy". So it wouldn't have made any difference if I'd gone around thinking "Bhagwan is wonderful". Most probably, I'd have got my head knocked just the same. The real deal is to become free of the mind; to free oneself from the habit of thinking itself, "good" thoughts and "bad" thoughts included. And how do you do that? By obeying the three laws of spiritual growth:

Meditation.

Meditation.

Meditation.

Mystical Powers

Producing Swiss watches out of thin air was the spiritual trademark of a guru in South India called Satya Sai Baba. He was a contemporary of Bhagwan, attracting an enormous following. He would sometimes sit in his chair, producing gold bangles that seemed to come out of his mouth. He would then hold them up, as evidence of his miraculous powers, before an admiring crowd of thousands of people.

Secret filming of some of these "miracles" indicated that Sai Baba's magical powers might have had more to do with sleight-of-hand tricks normally associated with street magicians. A great deal of controversy arose in the Indian press about Sai Baba's "miracles", whether they were real or not, but Bhagwan, as usual, took a different approach:

"Even if you expose Satya Sai Baba, that doesn't matter – another Baba will arise because these people have a need," he explained. "They will say, 'Yes, that Baba was bogus, but this Baba is true.' You go on exposing, it makes no difference, because you don't understand that there is a basic need in people. Unless people are raised in their consciousness, Satya Sai Babas will continue."

Bhagwan was right about the Indian mentality. In that country, spirituality and magical powers go hand-in-hand. Almost every village has its tales of saints and sadhus, either dead or living, who flew through the air, walked through fire, cured the sick, or never ate a mouthful of food, or even drank water, for the whole of their lives.

And of course this isn't just an Indian phenomenon. Almost everyone is fascinated by magic and the possibility of miracles. It reflects our need for wonder and conjures up dreams of unlimited wealth and power – if only such tales might be real.

So where does the truth lie? Early on in this book I described my experiences of leaving the physical body as a result of living inside

Bhagwan's powerful energy field. Just now, I talked about those irritating moments when the mystic seemed to be banging my head. So, to me, there is no doubt that mysterious things do happen around enlightened beings.

One more example: during my Arica days in London, I'd discovered that when I looked at a photo of Oscar Ichazo, gazing into his eyes, he seemed to come out of the photo towards me. So when I got to Pune in March 1976 and bought a photo of Bhagwan, I tried to see if the same thing would happen with him. In a way, I was challenging Bhagwan, saying: "Okay, you think you're such a hot mystic, can you do what Oscar did and move towards me out of a photo?"

I was in for a shock! As I gazed at the photo, looking into Bhagwan's eyes, he seemed to practically leap out of the photo towards me, so much so that I had to pull back and stop looking. It was clear to me that he was a mystic with a lot of energy and power.

So, leaving aside fraudsters and charlatans, the question arises: what about manipulation? Can enlightened beings use their connection with the divine to actually influence and change the material world? For me, it is a grey area. Of course, just by their presence, mystics help to transform the world around them, without trying to "do" anything. Everyone they meet is likely to benefit in some way.

Moreover, if they choose to create the special energy field that Bhagwan did in his ashram, and as many mystics have done in the past – in India, Tibet, Japan and China – then this will increase the charge in the power-pack, so to speak, and boost the potential for transformation. As we saw with Bhagwan's energy darshans, when disciples are capable of acting as mediums, the power of the meditative field increases.

Apparently, nature also responds to the presence of mystics. It is said of Gautam Buddha that when he walked through the countryside, flowers would bloom out of season. It may not be just a myth. And in the West, we know the story of Saint Francis of Assisi, whose rapport with all kinds of animals was legendary.

But this is not manipulation of energy. It is, rather, the response of nature to the presence of enlightenment. And the bumping of my head on rickshaw roofs could be explained as coincidence, or maybe a better word is "synchronicity" – simultaneous events that appear to be related but have no apparent causal connection.

I know that Bhagwan was able to leave his body and "visit" his sannyasins. This happened to many of us. For example, I would be sitting in my bed, in the evening, perhaps reading a book, when suddenly a feeling like a soft breeze would enter the room and I would feel Bhagwan's presence, clearly and unmistakably. So many sannyasins related these kinds of experiences that it would be foolish to try to deny it.

I also got used to him appearing in my dreams. One time, I dreamed he was walking along a path and I wanted to meet him, but there were so many people on either side of the path it was impossible to get near him. I gave up, stayed at the back of the crowd, closed my eyes and as he walked by . . . whump! A gentle blast of energy hit my heart, just like in Laxmi's office. I woke up and found the sensation was really there, in my heart.

On another occasion, I was sick in bed with a bad cold. It was winter and the weather was unusually chilly for the normally mild Indian climate. I dreamed that Bhagwan came to see me, looked at my miserable condition, chuckled and said, "Wear a hat!" And promptly disappeared. I was surprised he'd bother with something so mundane, but it was a good idea and after that I did wear a hat, at least until the weather warmed up.

But this, again, is not manipulation. So, in my view, if Bhagwan had paranormal powers, they had limits – or at least they were limited in the ways he chose to exercise them. Clearly, he didn't have the power to create the ashram he ideally wanted, which, according to his own statements, would have been located somewhere in the Himalayas, with everyone living inside the ashram walls, rather than us all being scattered across a city suburb like Koregaon Park.

On the other hand, there are tales of other mystics wielding impressive magical powers, which to me have a ring of truth about them. For example,

The great Tibetan yogi Milarepa, who lived about 1,000 years ago, is said to have conjured up a thunderstorm that sent huge hailstones crashing down on a wedding party of his relatives in revenge for the way his mother had been abused by her brother-in-law. I think this story may be true, because I have had my own experience of guiding a thunderstorm, while meditating in the French Alps back in the early 1970s. I was chanting a Sufi Zikr, or devotional prayer, with about a dozen other people in a big tent at a Sufi camp high in the French Alps, under the guidance of a lovely old Sufi mystic called Pir Vilayat Inyat Khan. On this occasion, the mystic wasn't with us in the tent he used for teaching; he had left for the afternoon and was further down the mountain. I poured myself wholeheartedly into chanting the Zikr and my intensity seemed to bond in perfect synchronicity with an approaching thunderstorm. As I became more and more passionate in my devotion, so the storm grew steadily in magnitude, to the point where we seemed to become one and the same energy – it was almost like making love with nature itself.

Eventually, the storm was at full power, right overhead, with thunder crashing and a screeching wind threatening to blow away our refuge. I stopped chanting and looked around the tent. My fellow meditators had given up on the Zikr and were standing outside the madly flapping canvas walls, hanging onto tent ropes, trying to stop the whole thing from taking off.

I knew the tent wouldn't be destroyed, because, at the very moment I'd opened my eyes, the storm's peak had been reached and was now passing. As soon as I'd stopped chanting, it began to subside. It could have been coincidence, but it felt like a genuine rapport. If someone like me can influence a natural event like that, what to say of a powerful yogi like Milarepa, burning with the passion of revenge?

But, like I say, such powers are limited. In 1903, during the British invasion of Tibet, local lamas tried to use their spiritual powers to protect Tibetan soldiers, who were sent to block the advance of British troops. The lamas gave their soldiers sacred amulets to wear, promising they contained powers that would prevent the soldiers from being harmed. They didn't work. The Tibetan force, armed only with antiquated muzzle-loading rifles and swords, was shot to doll rags by the British, who were armed with Maxim machine guns. It quickly developed into a massacre.

In more recent times, Maharishi Mahesh Yogi attracted media attention in the early 1990s when he claimed he could teach people "yogic flying". At first, this was purported to be a method of actually levitating off the ground for significant periods of time. What it turned out to be, in reality, was a form of energetic hopping with crossed legs. Nobody stayed in the air for more than a split-second. Apart from this, yogic flying never took off.

As I recall, the Maharishi once told Indira Gandhi she could protect India from Pakistan's aggression by chanting sacred mantras. Dismissing this claim in discourse, Bhagwan told the story of Hindu priests in the tenth century who thought they could protect their wealthy temple from Mahmud of Ghazni, the so-called "Idol Breaker", with their sacred chanting. Mahmud arrived with his army at the temple, looted it, then smashed it to pieces.

As I said earlier, the 16th Karmapa's recognition of Bhagwan as "the greatest incarnation since Gautam Buddha" may have provoked expectations of powers similar to those claimed above, but in my experience Bhagwan manifested no powers beyond those I have already mentioned.

Bhagwan himself made it clear: "The person who goes to Satya Sai Baba because miracles are happening must be living somewhere two thousand years back, when these things were thought to be spiritual," he said. "These are just ordinary magical tricks. A buddha is not known to have done anything like that. It would have been foolish."

Just to emphasise the point, he added: "With me you will fail in the world. Of course, very few people are ready to fail in the world. With me you can succeed in the inner, but very few people are mature enough even to desire for that."

No superhuman powers? No magical short-cuts to enlightenment? With nobody waving a fairy wand over our heads, we had no choice but to take the long road to salvation, by sitting down, closing our eyes and meditating.

To quote an ancient Chinese proverb:

The journey of a thousand miles begins with a single step.

Quickies

Bhagwan loved to talk. It was his thing. Often his answers to questions in discourse would last 20–30 minutes, even an hour or more, because ultimately the words didn't matter.

He was, in a way, singing a lullaby to the mind, keeping it relaxed and occupied while creating a backdrop of silence. Sometimes when I closed my eyes and listened to him, the sound of his words was like musical notes, dancing across a vast inner emptiness. But Bhagwan also enjoyed interspersing his longer talks with quickies, so here is a selection:

A starry-eyed newcomer once asked him: "Bhagwan, I believe that nothing is impossible. What do you say?"

His answer: "Try sharpening a pencil with a bar of soap."

Another question: "Bhagwan, what is 'going in'?"

His answer: "Not going out."

On one occasion, the office sent out a message that they were running short of questions, so, in a playful mood, I sent him this one:

"Beloved Bhagwan, what is going on?"

I didn't expect him to answer it. But next day he read it out as the last question and replied, "Subhuti, I am surprised, because that's exactly what I was going to ask you all! I don't know."

He then quoted the famous Zen saying: "Not knowing is the most intimate," and left the hall.

Around the same time, I saw an article in a British newspaper reporting a survey by the London Polytechnic showing how candidates trying to become Labour MPs had a better chance of being selected by constituency committees if they were ugly. I clipped it, sent it in and a couple of days later Bhagwan read out a question in discourse that I'm sure he made up himself: "I am so terribly ugly and have suffered much because of it. What should I do?"

His answer: "Use it, this is a great opportunity: become a politician."

He then mentioned my report, adding: "Ugly, stupid-looking, unintelligent people have poll appeal. Why? Because they look so like the masses, the masses think they belong to them. The beautiful person, the intelligent-looking person, immediately is felt as belonging to the aristocracy. Naturally, he is not of the masses, he belongs to the leisured class. The masses feel him as the enemy."

A few more quickies come to mind:

A visiting journalist pointed out that Bhagwan seemed very inconsistent in his statements and asked, "Do you change your mind, make mistakes, or are you just inconsistent?"

"In the first place, I don't have a mind," answered Bhagwan.

Another journalist asked if he encouraged the media to think of him as a "sex guru".

"I am the most anti-sex person in existence, because my whole work is to transform sexual energy into spiritual consciousness," he replied.

A disgruntled visitor from England sent Bhagwan a question, saying he was disappointed to see so many "power trips" being played out among sannyasins in the ashram and this didn't make him want to stay.

He ended his question by asking, "Should I leave?"

Bhagwan's answer: "Please."

Another critic objected that being a disciple was unnecessary and declared: "I believe in the philosophy of 'do it yourself'. What do you say?"

Bhagwan: "Why are you asking this question? Do it yourself!"

The media constantly referred to Bhagwan as a guru, and although he himself, in his early talks, seemed to accept the role, he later denied it, probably because the term began to acquire a negative slant.

"A guru is one who gives you knowledge," declared Bhagwan. "I am an anti-guru! I take away your knowledge so that you can again become innocent."

This didn't change the media's attitude, though. When journalists think of a convenient tag, they won't let it go. To them, he was still a guru, and for those who bothered to heed his words it didn't change much.

Not a guru? No teaching? Then he must be an anti-guru guru who teaches that there's nothing to teach.

Problem solved.

Power to the People

As I mentioned right at the start of this book, Lady Gaga was attracted to Bhagwan's idea of being a rebel, and it's worth taking a closer look at this aspect of Bhagwan's work. As his sannyasins, we certainly didn't look like rebels, more like a bunch of singing and dancing hippies, so how did it become a central theme of the mystic's vision for humanity?

Growing up in the West, I was familiar with the idea of rebellion in a historical sense: the War of Independence in the late eighteenth century, when the American colonies broke away from the English Crown; the Russian Revolution of 1917, when the Bolsheviks toppled the Tsar; the Cuban Revolution of 1953, when Fidel Castro seized power . . . and so on.

Bhagwan's take on all of these social upheavals was as simple as it was radical: all revolutions fail. The overthrow of one social elite – capitalists, aristocrats, monarchs – creates a fleeting sense of liberation, but the power vacuum is swiftly filled by another elite: bureaucrats, communist party leaders, bankers, multinational corporations, etc.

"The revolutionary is created by the old society against which he is revolting," Bhagwan asserted. "His values, his ideals are not much different from the old. The only difference for him is that the right people are not in power."

Looking back on my own life, I could see the same tendency applied to the so-called "Flower Power" revolution of the sixties, which mutated from innocent wonder to political demonstrations to eventual compromise with the status quo. Finally, when Bob Dylan played for Pope John Paul II and Mick Jagger accepted a knighthood from the Queen, the very last gasp of sixties revolutionary romanticism sputtered, coughed and died.

But my most profound insight came in 1972 when I was a political journalist on a visit to communist China, so if you will forgive me for backtracking for a moment, I will relate this cautionary and hopefully instructive tale.

In that same year, President Richard Nixon had opened the door to communist China with his "ping pong diplomacy", following it up with a personal visit. Then, of course, his Western allies wanted to go too. It was really quite shameless and, to me, almost embarrassing: the way Western Europe's leaders lined up behind Nixon, like obedient little ducks, and waddled into the People's Republic of China, which had been a no-go area since the 1940s.

Ted Heath, the British Prime Minister, was too busy to go, but he sent his Foreign Secretary, Sir Alec Douglas-Home. A former Prime Minister himself, Sir Alec was the exact opposite of what the People's Republic of China was supposed to symbolise. The 14th Earl of Home was a blue-blood English aristocrat, educated at Eton and Oxford, whose idea of gainful employment could not have been more removed from a Chinese worker's experience. But off he went, with a large number of British journalists in tow, including myself. I celebrated my 26th birthday as we crossed the famous bridge that joined Hong Kong with the People's Republic. It was via this bridge that captive foreigners came staggering out of China, dazed and delighted to be alive, having sustained years of brainwashing by their Marxist-Leninist-Maoist captors.

Once on the Chinese side, we were greeted by members of the local Revolutionary Committee – these committees greeted us wherever we went, even at midnight, at airport refuelling stops – then we were whisked off on a tour that included Canton, Shanghai and Beijing.

We caught up with Sir Alec on the Great Wall, toured the Forbidden City – the last emperor was off being re-educated – and were taken to meet Premier Zhou Enlai, Mao's No.2 and a veteran of the fabled Long March. Mao himself was still alive, but rumoured to be sick and slowly dying. Later, we visited a People's Army barracks, where bands of soldiers would suddenly erupt from behind rows of huts, marching in perfect step while singing songs in praise of Chairman Mao and flourishing little red books.

The economic, political and social disruption caused by Mao's Cultural Revolution was all around us, but carefully hidden from view, although one or two bruised and battered Chinese academics in Shanghai dared tell us what a nightmare it had been for them.

On the last day of Sir Alec's tour, he was invited as Zhou Enlai's guest to an official banquet in the Great Hall of the People, an immense, square building in the very heart of Beijing. It was clearly modelled on Soviet neo-Stalinist architecture and completely lacking in any kind of aesthetics. We were all waiting with our Chinese hosts, when Sir Alec walked in. As he did so, the People's Army Band struck up a refrain that was familiar to me, although I could scarcely believe it was being played by a group of Maoist-Leninist-Marxist musicians.

It was the Eton Boating Song:

"*Jolly boating weather . . .*"

Outside, on tall buildings around the city of Beijing, banners proclaimed: "Death to the American Imperialists and their Running Dogs." Inside the Great Hall, this Eton-educated running dog was being feted by communist leaders.

Sir Alec smiled, went over and toasted the band master. Then we all sat down and tucked into roast duck – all comrades together. It reminded me of George Orwell's *Animal Farm*, in which the animals, having overthrown their human masters, make the revolutionary declaration that "all animals are equal". But they are outsmarted by the pigs, who gradually take control. In the final scene, the animals peer through the farm window, where the pigs are having dinner with local human farmers. Hanging near the window is a new sign:

"All animals are equal, but some are more equal than others."

When I came to understand Bhagwan's vision of being a rebel, I could see it was radically different, in the sense that it did not involve any attempt to change the structure of society, nor to replace one system of government with another. Rather, it encouraged the individual to look within and dissolve the psychological structures created by society inside the mind. In this way, meditation and rebellion went hand in hand, the mystic argued, because it was through meditation that the individual freed himself from identification with belief systems and social attitudes programmed into his, or her, personal bio-computer as part of the process called "education".

For myself, while I love Bhagwan's vision of individual rebellion, I also allow more shades of grey than his black-and-white view that social revolution doesn't work. As I see it, these upheavals do sometimes have positive effects, in the sense that they create better conditions for a majority of people: the end of feudalistic attitudes in Russia with the overthrow of the Tsar in 1917, for example, or, 73 years later, the democratisation of Russia by Mikhail Gorbachev. The hippie revolution of the sixties also had several lasting, beneficial effects on mainstream society: initiating a new sense of appreciation for nature and care for the environment; ushering in more relaxed attitudes about sexual freedom and living together outside of marriage.

But these are relative social gains, not profound personal transform-ation. For that, you need to be a spiritual rebel. You need to look in.

Sex and Celibacy

The young Indian yogi sat before Bhagwan in darshan and asked for initiation. It was rare for a man of his obvious spiritual discipline to come to Bhagwan. Traditional sannyasins and sadhus tended to avoid the controversial mystic. His ashram was off limits. Even to enter a place where men and women were openly affectionate and touching each other was unthinkable and would have destroyed their reputation with their followers.

This yogi was very good-looking: tall, well-built, with long, silky black hair and a beatific smile on his face. He sat in a classic yogic posture, spine erect, legs crossed, very much at ease, as if he'd been sitting this way all his life. When he closed his eyes to receive sannyas, his face looked so radiant that to me he seemed already enlightened. Bhagwan gave him a new name and welcomed him into the growing community of sannyasins that were crowding into the ashram in Koregaon Park. Then, as the yogi started to move away, Bhagwan added: "Remember, you are not to be celibate, hmm?"

Later, for good measure, he encouraged a voluptuous young Italian woman to keep the yogi company, just to make sure he didn't fall back into old habits.

Among India's traditional sadhus, saints and sannyasins, nothing is more impressive than a man who has renounced women and "conquered" his sex drive. It is viewed as proof of spiritual attainment. In the West, celibacy has also been held in high regard as a religious quality, especially in the Catholic Church. But after three successive popes – John Paul II, Pope Benedict XVI and Francis I – have felt obliged to apologise for a worldwide epidemic of sexual abuse of young children by Catholic priests, it would be instructive for the current pontiff to meditate over Bhagwan's approach to celibacy.

The mystic was dead against it. Why? Because it doesn't create spirituality. It creates sexual perversion. It doesn't make you holy, no matter how much it impresses others. It simply twists your sex drive. Sex energy, according to Bhagwan, cannot be stopped. If you deny its natural expression, it will find some other outlet, either in sexual perversion, pornography and prostitution, or in anger and pride, violence and aggression.

It wasn't an accident that Ancient Greek warriors developed the habit of staying away from their women as much as possible. They understood that love-making softened them, made them less tough. They knew it took the edge off the killer instinct. They were fashioning sex energy into a weapon of war.

"It is a strange phenomenon that for ten thousand years no thinker has been against celibacy, has not said the truth, that it is criminal to teach such an unnatural thing," stated Bhagwan, in one of many discourses on the subject. According to him, celibacy is possible, but only after a man or woman has fully lived and explored their sexuality. If this is allowed, the sex drive gradually lessens and fades away with the approach of old age.

"Sex has existence only from the fourteenth to the forty-second year, *if* things go naturally," he explained "But they don't go naturally – the priest jumps in. He starts talking about celibacy. When all that was needed was the art of love, he starts talking about celibacy. He creates guilt. Sex energy becomes repressed, goes underneath, into the unconscious. Real celibacy is the fragrance of sex lived truly. Celibacy is sexuality become mature. Otherwise hypocrisy continues."

Maybe it's because I was around Bhagwan so long that the solution to the Roman Catholic Church's problem with its perverted priests seems so blindingly obvious: just drop the rule of celibacy; stop equating celibacy with spirituality. It won't guarantee that perversion will cease, but it will be a huge step in that direction. It doesn't guarantee that child abuse won't happen, but it will lessen the pressure on the priesthood by allowing the natural release of their sexual drive.

Interestingly, celibacy wasn't widely enforced in the Catholic Church until the twelfth century, so historically it's never been a fundamental doctrine that cannot be changed. One notable milestone came in 1531, when Martin Luther accused Pope Leo X of vetoing a measure placed before the Lateran Council that would have limited the number of young boys to be kept by cardinals for their pleasure. "Otherwise, it would have been spread throughout the world how openly and shamelessly the pope and the cardinals in Rome practice sodomy," declared Luther.

Today, there's no sign that celibacy will be dropped. Responding to the epidemic of abuse, Pope Benedict talked about better screening of priests, more safeguards, a quicker response to complaints from bishops and cardinals. But he stubbornly continued to defend celibacy as "the sign of full devotion, the entire commitment to the Lord and to the Lord's business, an expression of giving oneself to God and to others."

His successor, Pope Francis, seemed at first to be open to making celibacy optional, but later closed the door, saying celibacy was "a gift to the church".

Fine words from both pontiffs. The harsh reality is that every young man who goes into the priesthood and takes a vow of celibacy is being condemned to a lifelong war with his own energy, with perversion as a likely outlet – thus guaranteeing a life of torment and anguish for victims and perpetrators alike.

Dethroning the Mahatma

The idea that Mahatma Gandhi was a violent man is one that is hard to credit. It seems not to make sense, because the Mahatma's name has over the years become synonymous with non-violence and the achievement of noble goals through peaceful means.

Bhagwan, as one might expect, presented this modern saint from an entirely different perspective. He wasn't about to let us cling to such an obvious icon. Repeatedly, in discourses during the Pune ashram years, and later during the Ranch, the mystic was pointing to Gandhi's hidden violence.

"Mahatma Gandhi was the uncrowned king of India for the simple reason that he was able to torture himself more than anybody else could," asserted Bhagwan. "For any small reason he would go on a fast-unto-death."

Gandhi preached non-violence, Bhagwan conceded, but he directed his violence against himself and used it as a means of forcing others to agree with him. Gandhi would go on a fast, claiming that if those around him did not support him, then it must be because he himself was not yet sufficiently pure. If he was really pure, in spiritual terms, then others would see the correctness of his viewpoint.

This put enormous pressure on those who disagreed with him, because they would feel responsible for the fact that Gandhi was starving himself to death. Moreover, they would be blamed by public opinion for endangering the Mahatma's precious life.

I would one day gain my own intimate insight into Gandhi's strategy, when I volunteered to play the role of an English politician in a film about the life of Dr Ambedkar, the man who wrote the Indian Constitution. The movie was made in the mid-1990s, but by then I already knew the story, because Bhagwan had spoken on several occasions about the conflict between Gandhi and Ambedkar.

Ambedkar was a rare man. Born into a caste of Untouchables, his natural intelligence was spotted by an Indian prince, who paid for his education and sent him to London and New York to study law. He became a barrister, then returned to India to try to better the plight of his oppressed caste.

Meanwhile, India's British rulers were slowly waking up to the fact that they needed to change the way they governed the country. In 1927, they dispatched a Commission under Lord Simon to examine constitutional reform. In the movie, I played the role of Clement Atlee, Labour MP and member of the Commission who later, as Britain's Prime Minister, would personally oversee the granting of independence to India and Pakistan in 1947.

Dr Ambedkar was requesting that the British give the oppressed castes a separate electorate – the right to elect their own MPs. The British were sympathetic, but Gandhi objected. The Mahatma feared that if the Untouchables had a separate vote they could ally themselves with the Muslims and thereby outnumber the Hindus.

Gandhi went on a fast-unto-death in order to try to force Ambedkar and the Untouchables to drop their demands. I watched the story unfold at close quarters, while the movie was being made, recalling Bhagwan's description of how Gandhi effectively destroyed the hopes of the oppressed castes:

"For twenty-one days Ambedkar remained reluctant, but every day the pressure of the whole country was increasing. And he started feeling that if this old man dies then there is going to be great bloodshed. It was clear – he would be killed immediately, and Untouchables would be killed everywhere, all over the country: 'It is because of you that Gandhi died.' When the whole arithmetic of how it would work out was explained to him – 'You figure it out soon, because there is not much time, he cannot survive more than three days,' – Ambedkar hesitated."

In the end, Ambedkar came personally to Gandhi with a glass of orange juice, agreeing to drop his demand for a separate electorate and requesting the Mahatma end his fast. Gandhi agreed and drank the juice.

Bhagwan observed that Ambedkar had been right to ask for a separate electorate and it was Gandhi who should have backed down, commenting, "This orange juice, this one glass of orange juice, contains millions of people's blood."

Politicians' Brains

The Prime Minister leaned back against the table and gave us her warmest smile. Indira Gandhi seemed genuinely pleased to see us and the feeling was mutual. This was our big moment. The year was 1980 and we'd come to Delhi as the Rajneesh Theatre Company, about to put on a performance of *A Midsummer Night's Dream* at a theatre in the capital.

By way of background, I should explain that a group of English sannyasins, including myself, had been coming together in the evenings in Pune to read our favourite Shakespeare play, taking on the roles of the mischievous fairies, the star-crossed lovers. Because there were professional actors in our group, the standard was high, so I wrote to Bhagwan suggesting we go public with the play, touring India as a PR exercise.

Bhagwan gave the okay and off we went as the Rajneesh Shakespeare Company to Mumbai, Delhi, Surat, Ahmedabad. My personal role was Egeus, an angry Greek father and grumpy old man who refuses to allow his daughter to marry the man she loves.

"Full of vexation come I," proclaimed Subhuti-the-Greek, doing his best to portray an indignant old man, "With complaint against my child, my daughter Hermia . . ." It is Egeus' objection that triggers the whole night-long drama between the four young lovers, made more comical by the intervention of Oberon, King of the Fairies, and his mischievous servant Puck. Acting in this chauvinistic fatherly role, it made me wonder what kind of dad I would have been if I'd really had kids of my own.

Delhi was our last stop on the tour. The Indian Prime Minister made it clear she wasn't coming to our performance. But she'd dropped in at the theatre during rehearsal to watch us. Then she invited us all to a meeting at her official residence in Safdarjang Road,

New Delhi – the same place where four years later she was assassinated by her own bodyguards.

A little political history may be required here: Indira Gandhi had
been successfully guided into Indian politics by her father, Jawarhalal
Nehru, who was the first Prime Minister after independence in 1947.
Indira proved to be as politically astute as her father, and had ruled
India from 1966 until 1975. Then, faced with mounting opposition
and charges of corruption, she had instituted a State of Emergency in
India from 1975–77.

She lost the next election and was jailed by the next government,
led by an ultra-conservative Gandhian called Morarji Desai, who also
strongly opposed Bhagwan and his ashram. Desai made no secret of
the fact that he considered Bhagwan a threat to traditional Hindu
values, and demonstrated his hostility by taking away the ashram's
tax-free status as a charitable institution.

Bhagwan made matters worse by ridiculing Morarji Desai as an idiot
and poking fun at his bizarre habit of drinking his own urine as a daily
health measure. In an effort to calm things down, Krishna Prem, my
colleague in the press office, travelled to New Delhi and asked for an
interview with the PM, which was granted but which resolved nothing.

"He kept saying to me, 'I don't believe you,'" related Krishna Prem,
on returning to Pune, then confided in me that he'd tried to convince
Morarji Desai that 75 percent of our people in our ashram were
celibate.

I laughed in astonishment. "That explains why he didn't believe
you," I told him. "Morarji Desai may be an idiot, but he's not stupid!"

While Mrs Gandhi was being held in custody, Bhagwan had been
one of the very few people in the country to publicly support her. In
1980, following fresh elections, she was brought back into power with
a landslide majority. Now she was doing her best to undo the previous government's actions against us and – in a cautious but genuine
way – demonstrating to the public that she liked us.

We were sitting in a big marquee on the PM's lawn, about 30 of us,
while outside, milling around, were dozens of people impatiently
waiting for the chance to speak to her, all with some urgent request,
some pressing favour to ask.

"But when do you rest?" asked one sannyasin, as the PM explained
her busy daily schedule.

"I'm resting now," she replied with a smile, a response that drew admiring applause from her audience. This was, on the face of it, a shining example of "meditation in the marketplace" – the ability to stay relaxed and conscious while going about daily tasks.

It was the kind of thing Bhagwan talked about all the time, because, as I've already indicated, he was against the traditional idea of sannyas: giving up your possessions, your home, your wife and children, and devoting yourself to the spiritual life as a wandering beggar, or sadhu. In Bhagwan's vision, you didn't turn your back on the world, which he considered cowardly, but instead brought the qualities of meditation into your daily life.

This was one reason why he was so controversial in his home country. He invited us to wear the bright orange colour of traditional sannyas, while drinking beer in local restaurants, smoking, joking, laughing and walking hand-in-hand with girlfriends. Small wonder, then, that Morarji Desai and other conservatives hated him.

There was a lull in the conversation with Mrs Gandhi, which was used by a Scottish friend of mine to regale the PM with a joke told by Bhagwan in one of his discourses. It was about a butcher's shop in a town of cannibals, where human brains were on sale by the kilo. The most expensive by far was the brain of a politician. Why? Because it had never been used.

As I realised which joke he was telling, a sinking feeling in my stomach registered my dismay. The one politician in the country who was willing to help Bhagwan's work was, by implication, being humiliated. I searched my own brain for a way out.

As the joke ended and the laughter faded, I called out loudly, "Bhagwan told that joke during the previous administration!"

This brought a huge laugh, because everyone present was well aware that the previous government had been led by Morarji Desai.

So the situation was rescued. But this was typical of us. Along with Bhagwan, we shared a reckless disregard for people in power. Which may have been fine in India, where people feared and respected spiritual mystics, but, as we would very shortly discover, certainly didn't play well in Washington DC.

Bhagwan's Private Life

"Can a lazy man become enlightened?" asked an English therapist, who'd recently joined the Rajneesh caravanserai in Pune.

"*Only* a lazy man can become enlightened," responded Bhagwan. He certainly practised what he preached. When he wasn't giving discourse, or darshan, or meeting with his secretaries, he was sitting alone in his room, doing nothing.

Just to give you an idea what this means, I'll tell you about an expensive Swiss watch that was given to him. It had a delicate self-winding mechanism designed to use ordinary, day-to-day movements of the body to continually rewind itself. It didn't need a battery, or an old-fashioned hand-winding mechanism. When it was placed on Bhagwan's wrist, there was a problem: it stopped. He just didn't move enough. So he gave the watch away to one of his disciples. To me, this capacity to be still, silent and alone is the most rare and extraordinary quality of any human being. As I understand it, this is the gateway to enlightenment.

Once in a while, though, he'd invite a woman into his bedroom to make love. I didn't intend to write about this, but, in a bizarre paradox, there is a risk of Bhagwan being characterised in history as a celibate saint, even though he was known as *the sex guru*. In 2007, Suresh Kumar, chairman of Compact Disc India, based in Chandigarh, announced that his company's film production division would be making a movie titled *The Guru of Sex* about the life of Bhagwan Shree Rajneesh. *Gandhi* actor Sir Ben Kingsley was being sought to play the lead role. Mr Kumar said there would be a startling revelation at the end of the film that Rajneesh himself was celibate – a finding based on statements made by the mystic in his own discourses.

Mr Kumar was wrong, but he can be forgiven for his mistake. I recall a joke made by Bhagwan, sometime in the late seventies, that gives such an impression. Responding in discourse to a hostile question about gurus who seduce other people's wives, Bhagwan said, "As far as your wife is concerned, don't be worried! When I take my bath I take my bath with my dress on so that I do not have to look at the unemployed! Don't be worried at all – I hate to look at the unemployed!"

However, a few years later, answering questions at an international press conference in Oregon, Bhagwan was asked directly, "Are you celibate?" He said, "No," but then qualified his answer, adding that if his body was in good health, he would still be sexually active. In other words: he wasn't celibate, but wasn't active either.

In July 1985, Howard Sattler from Australia's 6PR Radio was conducting a one-on-one interview with Bhagwan. Half-way through their conversation, Bhagwan was again condemning the practice of celibacy.

"Have you ever been celibate?" asked Sattler.

Bhagwan replied: "Right now I am celibate, but if my health gets better, I am not going to be celibate. I have never been celibate. I do not do anything against nature. Right now, I am celibate, not because celibacy has any value, but just because I am sick. I don't have any energy to make love to a woman and do all the gymnastics, no. I have enough energy to talk to my people, to talk to you. If I get healthy again, I promise you, I will not be celibate."

Sattler commented: "Don't promise me, promise them," indicating a nearby audience of female sannyasins, "All these ladies about the place tell me that you're a great lover."

"I am!" Bhagwan agreed.

But the word "lover" has many meanings, especially in spiritual circles, where every disciple – male and female alike – is regarded as a lover of the master. So, the journalist probed further:

"How do they know that?" Sattler asked.

"Many of them must have loved me. I must have loved them."

"Does that mean you've had sex with them?"

"Certainly. How do you love if you don't have sex with them?"

With a smile, Bhagwan added: "I don't know why but women are always willing. I have never met a woman who was not willing."

This was as explicit as Bhagwan ever got. However, once again he added that he wasn't active. Why he chose to give this impression is anyone's guess. My own feeling is that he did it to spare his disciples unnecessary torture. The guys, like me, would have become depressed by comparing ourselves to a man who always scored and never got rejected, while the women would have gone crazy with jealousy when others were chosen, desperately hoping that they too might one day be invited into his bedroom.

So, for the history books and for the film-makers, let's get it straight: Bhagwan was a sexually active human being. There is no doubt about this. I have heard accounts from two women who made love with him. Neither of them would lie about such a thing. Nor were they the only ones. From what I gather, there were many more, both in Pune and on the Oregon Ranch. Vivek, the young Englishwoman who became Bhagwan's long-time caretaker, also became his lover, probably as early as 1971. Vivek never talked about it publicly, but, after her affair with Bhagwan had ended, she privately confided in one of her later lovers, an American sannyasin called Devakant, who subsequently wrote about it in his book, *In the Eye of the Hurricane*.

"She told me many intimate details of their relation," Devakant recalled, then added: "Suffice to say that their love affair and relation as man and woman was beautiful, deep, mysterious, natural and remarkable."

It seems safe to assume that Bhagwan's approach to love-making was much the same as anyone else's. He told one woman "I like your energy!", which is a pretty standard approach for any guy coming on to a woman.

Again, from what I've been told, the power of the experience for Bhagwan's lovers wasn't the sex itself. He didn't introduce them to elaborate Tantric rituals – that wasn't his style. It was the energy and love that radiated from an enlightened being that really blew them away, plus the sense of fun that was his unique contribution to the master–disciple relationship.

"He played with me!" confided one woman to me, giggling with happiness at the remembrance of her solo encounter with Bhagwan.

To be personally intimate with a man who is fully present, completely relaxed and at home in himself, is bound to be a memorable event. Even if you were just doing something apparently ordinary with him, like having a cup of tea, as many people did in the early seventies when Bhagwan was living in Mumbai, the sheer power of his presence might well transform it into a mind-blowing experience.

Forty years on, with the rise of the #MeToo movement, it could be argued that Bhagwan, by sleeping with his female disciples, was exploiting emotionally vulnerable women and abusing his position as a charismatic leader. Well, he was certainly charismatic and in a position of power, and I don't think any of the women whom he invited to his room objected, resisted, or were subjected to pressure, or bribed in any way. On the contrary, most of them seemed to have been delighted – but seen in today's light that isn't of course the whole story.

And there were exceptions, too. For example, I have read one memoir by a Canadian, who, as a young, self-styled "hippie girl" touring India, came to hear about Bhagwan and visited him in his room in Mumbai. Having been initiated into sannyas, she was invited to take off her clothes and lie face down on the bed. According to her own story, she went into shock, having only recently lost her virginity at the age of 19, and was terrified that Bhagwan would try to make love with her. But he didn't. He performed some energy work on her back, then told her to get dressed, advised her to take a more relaxed attitude to her sexuality and said goodbye.

So, I think it's fair to say that from Bhagwan's side there was never any sense of trying to force women into sex with him. For one thing, it wasn't his style. For another, he didn't need to. If he'd given the okay, there would have been a line of women outside his door 24/7. Again, seen from today's perspective this doesn't absolve him altogether, but at the time everyone was generally acting in good faith. No doubt some people will take the view that he should have abstained altogether, but after all, he was hailed as "the sex guru", offering the world a revolutionary cocktail of meditation and free love. It would have been odd if he hadn't practised what he preached.

One thing he did that impressed me, on a human level, deserves a mention: when he stopped sleeping with Vivek she soon found another lover, so Bhagwan had an additional room built on the roof of his house, so that her lover could be within easy reach of Vivek while she continued to work as the mystic's caretaker. How many guys do you know who would do that for their ex?

154

What also impressed me was that Bhagwan seemed to enjoy being alone even more than being with a woman. I remember sitting in the front row of darshan one night, listening to him talk to a Western couple about love, relationships and the rewards of intimacy. Then he surprised me by adding, "Relating, to me, is a secondary experience. The real joy is to be alone with oneself."

In that moment, it was as if Bhagwan was speaking Martian, so removed was his statement from my own experience, and I realised how much importance I was giving in my personal life to love and togetherness. Habitually, out of my cultural conditioning, I had been equating being alone with an empty, negative feeling of loneliness. Yet here was someone who cherished it more than any kind of relationship or friendship.

But I think the main reason Bhagwan didn't often talk about his private life was that he felt everyone is entitled to just that – a private life. His response to a question in 1977, asked during a discourse series on the sayings of Jesus, illustrates the point:

"Bhagwan, what did Jesus really do with Mary Magdalene?"

"No personal questions, please."

The Twilight Zone

Since we seem to be passing through a literary red light district, there are a few more sexual issues I'd like to discuss. This is motivated, in part, by reading a journalistic hatchet-job directed against Mooji, the popular British Jamaican spiritual teacher, who was recently attacked online by a professional anti-cult crusader. I've never met Mooji and know little about him, but reading the article felt like déjà vu to the max: allegations about Mooji's sex life, the blind devotion of his followers, mind control techniques, sessions of screaming and shouting . . .

It could have all been written about Bhagwan 40 years ago. In fact, it was. But it came back to me with renewed vigour because, a day after the Mooji exposé, I happened to catch up with a BBC News interview with Hugh Milne, who was Bhagwan's personal bodyguard in the 1970s.

The Netflix series *Wild Wild Country* provoked a global surge of interest in Bhagwan and his movement. As a follow-up, the BBC tracked down Milne and published his interview a few months later. After training as an osteopath in his native Scotland, Milne had travelled to India in 1973 to meet Bhagwan, having listened to audiotapes of the mystic's discourses. At that time, Bhagwan was living in his Mumbai apartment, where Milne asked for initiation as a sannyasin and received the name "Shiva", which was how we all later knew him.

The BBC interview, titled "The Scot who was the sex guru's bodyguard", describes how Bhagwan "began to sleep with Hugh's girlfriend and then sent him away to work on a farm in one of the hottest parts of India".

Naturally, this gives Milne's story a victim slant, but there's another angle to this saga that was not mentioned. In 1974, after returning from farm duty, Milne followed Bhagwan to the mystic's newly created ashram in Pune, where, after a short time, he was given the role of Bhagwan's bodyguard. This new, glamorous position changed everything.

Sitting next to Bhagwan every evening in darshan, guarding the mystic every morning on his arrival in Buddha Hall for discourse, Shiva gained instant status, and soon became one of the most desirable alpha males around. The entrance to Milne's sleeping quarters quickly became a metaphorical revolving door, spinning almost off its hinges, as Shiva enjoyed the enthusiastic attention of a veritable flood of Bhagwan's female sannyasins – even today, some 45 years later, some women, when remembering those times, still laughingly refer to him as "the ashram stud".

Further on in the BBC article, after describing the shift to Oregon, we learn of Milne's personal crisis when he sees Bhagwan's followers receiving "inhuman" treatment, working incredibly long hours and "falling apart" in their efforts to build the Ranch.

Strange. I helped to build the Ranch and, in spite of my slender frame and noticeable lack of physical strength, never fell apart. Neither did my friends. In fact, history tells us that the disciples of other mystics, like George Gurdjieff, for example, or various Tibetan, Chinese and Japanese spiritual masters, often faced far more arduous challenges.

For example, as I mentioned earlier, Zen Masters had a habit of whacking their disciples on the head with a stick in order to wake them up. One innovative Zen mystic actually threw a disciple out of a window, them jumped after him. The great Tibetan yogi Milarepa was forced by his master to build a tower seven times, each time being ordered to destroy it again. Relatively speaking, I'd say we got off lightly. But watching us all working hard apparently provoked a crisis of conscience in Milne, who then left the Ranch and tried to rebuild his "shattered life" while penning a book about Bhagwan titled *The God That Failed*.

My own view of Milne's crisis was more simple: after leaving Pune and arriving in Oregon, Milne was no longer Bhagwan's bodyguard, so he lost his special status and was obliged to be ordinary, like the rest of us. He couldn't handle the demotion, so he quit. This being the case, one of my friends, tongue in cheek, renamed his book *The Guard That Failed*.

Now I must turn to the late Tim Guest, another chronicler of the Bhagwan movement, who enjoyed literary success with *My Life in Orange*, published in 2004. Writing at the age of 27, Guest described how, when he was five years old, his mother became a Rajneesh disciple, dyed all her clothes orange and whisked him off to India to live in the Pune ashram.

Apart from Guest's personal difficulties with commune life – a feeling of losing his mother amid a sea of orange people – the most controversial part of his book deals with the sexual initiation of several underage girls by older male sannyasins in a Rajneesh commune in Germany, in Pune and on the Ranch.

There is little doubt that it happened, but, to my mind the context in Pune was different from the wider world outside the ashram. There were hundreds of young men and women, mostly in their twenties and thirties, exploring their sexuality with each other in a heady atmosphere of freedom, love and sensuality. The kids had their own area, but they were curious what the adults were up to and some of them would run around the ashram in the evening, peering in windows, giggling and laughing when they saw people making love – which was pretty often. As well as being curious, the kids enjoyed being a nuisance – like kids anywhere, I suppose – and knowing how tolerant we were, they were keen on pushing our boundaries.

Maybe on some occasions, in some huts and rooms, the girls ran in and joined in the fun and games and lines were crossed that should not have been; I heard stories to that effect. But my point is this: I wasn't aware of anyone out stalking or grooming children with prurient and predatory intent and there were no organised paedophilia gangs of any sort such as we are aware of today in the wider world.

Eventually, when the ashram managers got to hear about these antics, they told the children's parents to rein them in, which put an end to their evening exploits. It was a relief and confirmed my own feeling that it was okay to set limits.

In spite of his book's negative slant, Tim Guest ended up assuring his guilt-stricken mother that he felt lucky to have had such an unusual upbringing. A few years later, he wrote a second successful book, analysing virtual communities, and was about to get married, but, alas, he was also a recreational drug user and died of an accidental morphine overdose.

Did some kids get damaged by our wild lifestyle? Was it, for example, a contributing factor in Guest's death? It's hard to say. About 2,500 people die every year in the UK from illicit drug misuse, so blaming Guest's demise on his sannyasin background might be a bit of a stretch and is not that simple. I know two women, now in their mid-thirties – one with kids, one without – who were raised in Rajneesh communes, never suffered any form of sexual abuse, never got hooked on drugs, and to this day seem perfectly normal. Of course, such people never get talked about. They aren't news.

I've heard several stories of family breakups, when one parent left for India. But then, by the time they are 16, half of the children in the UK will witness the breakup of their parents. The difference in these cases was that, after a few weeks or months, the absent parent would usually reappear on the scene in bright orange, with a mala and a new name. Naturally, the "sex cult" got the blame for the breakup.

Meanwhile, Bhagwan was pointing to a very different type of childhood damage that was, and still is, practised everywhere. The mystic focused on how children all over the world are indoctrinated with religious and national beliefs, reducing them from individuals to obedient servants of society's vested interests.

"The greatest slavery is that of the child," he explained in a 1981 discourse. "The educator, from the kindergarten to the university, is in the service of the establishment. His whole purpose is to cripple every child in such a way that he adjusts to the established society."

Bhagwan has a point. People take it for granted that it's perfectly okay to impose Christian, Islamic, Jewish, Marxist, Buddhist, or Hindu beliefs on their children, without asking permission. And every child is automatically stamped with a national identity. We don't consider it to be slavery, but with such forcible control of vulnerable young minds, what else is it?

In this chapter, since we're cruising through a sexual twilight zone, I'd better mention the male therapists, who were leading ashram groups and giving individual sessions, and who frequently made love with their female clients and participants. This happened freely and openly in the early Pune years and nobody thought much about it, since everyone was a willing participant.

Female group leaders also played around and I remember one extraordinary experience of making love with one of them during a Tantra-like session in a therapy group, where everyone was pairing off. The two of us sort of rolled across the floor towards each other and met in naked embrace. After a while, as I lay on top of her, rivers of fiery energy started running up and down my body, like some kind of whole-body orgasm, completely beyond my expectations or control. Naturally, I got hooked and wanted to start an affair. But fidelity wasn't on this group leader's agenda and I had to let her go. Also, I have to say, during our brief encounters after the group, the connection wasn't the same. Like so many energy events in Bhagwan's ashram, it was a spontaneous and mysterious happening, not a regular occurrence.

As I recall, at some point, around 1980, a clear instruction came from Bhagwan that therapists should stop sexually exploiting their group participants, which put a brake on the anything-goes, free-love attitudes that had been permitted until then. Gradually, over time, it became accepted that sannyasin therapists should embrace the same professional ethics as were practised elsewhere and those who did not, and who were found out, were suspended or transferred to other work.

More sexual gossip? Well, yes, when they ran out of money, some attractive female sannyasins took the train down to Mumbai and, having donned cocktail dresses and make-up, cruised the bars of the five-star hotels, looking for Indian and Western businessmen, or wealthy Arabs visiting from the nearby Gulf States. One or two nights were usually enough to replenish financial supplies and back they came to the ashram. As for me, I was jealous. It didn't seem fair. How come women could make money so easily, while this impoverished English gent could not? The only possibility would have been to look for wealthy clients with other sexual preferences and this was not my cup of tea. In any case, as a commune member, with food and shelter supplied, I didn't really need the cash.

By the way, I'm aware that, when writing about these controversial issues, there is an element that is hard for me to convey: the sheer exhilaration of riding a wave of energy and love that blew away all the rules. Looking back, it's easy to frown with disapproval at some of the things that happened and, while not excusing them, it's helpful to understand the atmosphere of rebelliousness in which they occurred.

When you blow up the walls of a prison in order to escape, you risk that some people may get hurt by falling debris.

Exit Sanjay, Enter Rajiv

Britain has a Royal Family that wields considerable social influence but has no actual power. India, on the other hand, has a Royal Family that has been exercising real power for more than 50 years – ever since independence.

I refer, of course, to the dynasty started by India's first Prime Minister, Jawaharlal Nehru. As I already explained, he passed the political baton to his daughter, Indira Gandhi. She worked hand-in-glove with her younger son, Sanjay. When he died in a plane crash, she handed the baton to her other son, Rajiv, and was grooming him for power when she was assassinated. Seven years later, Rajiv was also assassinated, and so his Italian-born wife Sonia took on the job. Now her son Rahul is leading the Congress Party, while Sonia's daughter Priyanka is said to be her mother's closest advisor.

Briefly, I had a front-row seat to watch the dynasty in action during one of its critical moments. In 1980, I was accompanying Laxmi on regular visits to Delhi. We had developed a close working relationship over the previous three years, because it was my job to write the ashram's press releases and her job to screen and sign them.

Laxmi knew I understood politics, which is why she took me with her to Delhi. She was seeking help from Indira's government: finding land for a new ashram, changing our tax status and other stuff. I was her *gofer*, which, for non-American readers, is a term applied to an all-purpose, low-ranking, assistant-cum-secretary-cum-errand-boy: "go fer this . . . go fer that . . ." etc.

Laxmi and I stayed at the Taj Hotel, sharing a room with twin beds. But there was no hanky panky. I never really thought of Laxmi as a woman, partly because her energy was so fiery and dynamic, and partly because she seemed to have dissolved utterly into her role as a disciple – oh yes, and she was also my boss.

Our tax status was a big issue. As I understood the situation, the legally constituted foundation that supported Bhagwan's work had been granted tax-free status several years earlier – perhaps as early as his years in Mumbai. But this had been taken away by the government of Morarji Desai. Now we were trying to get it back, but even though Mrs Gandhi had given us a green light, her civil servants in the tax department were dragging their feet, requesting a signed order from the PM, which, being a cautious politician, she was reluctant to give.

I'm pretty sure our books were cooked – they had to be, I presumed, for our rapidly expanding ashram to survive and prosper in such a bureaucratic and corrupt country. So I'm guessing that much of the revenue, which was mostly in the form of cash, went undeclared.

One other factor: most officially sanctioned charities in India seemed to rely purely on donations, whereas our finances were a mix of charges and donations. That's another reason why the civil servants were cautious about granting tax-free status.

We'd met Mrs Gandhi before, but on this particular visit our tax status didn't turn out to be the priority – it was a few weeks earlier, in June 1980, that her son Sanjay had been killed, recklessly attempting to loop the loop with his new plane when flying it for the first time, losing control, crashing and killing himself and his instructor. Laxmi and I had been completing one of our Delhi trips, leaving the downtown area for the airport, when the little plane roared low over our heads. We didn't know it crashed, or who was flying it, until we arrived back at the ashram in Pune.

Now we were sitting in Mrs Gandhi's drawing room in her bungalow in Safdarjang Road, while Laxmi, who never seemed awed or intimidated by anyone – well, maybe by *one* fellow – was lecturing the PM on the subject of her elder son.

"Now Sanjay is gone, it will be good if Rajiv starts helping you," Laxmi advised.

"I have asked him, but he is reluctant," explained Mrs Gandhi. "Better he hears it from you."

Mrs Gandhi called for her elder son and soon the fresh-faced, slightly overweight, 36-year-old pilot, looking smart in his Indian Airlines uniform, was sitting next to his mother, listening to Laxmi.

Laxmi lectured Rajiv for several minutes on the importance of having men in power who aren't actually hungry for power. Ambitious and cunning men are dangerous, she explained. Men like Rajiv are more trustworthy, more reliable, more responsible. It was his clear duty, Laxmi added, to help his mother in her time of need. Sanjay had been his mother's ally and closest advisor during the so-called "Emergency" of 1975–7, when Indira suspended the democratic process. He'd quickly acquired a reputation for ruthlessness, terrorising civil servants and politicians alike, and exerting massive influence over his mother.

His brother was just the opposite, at least in the early stages. Rajiv didn't like politics and blamed Sanjay for Indira's crushing defeat at the polls when democracy was restored in 1977. Now Indira was back in power once more and Rajiv was under pressure to give up his career as a commercial pilot to join her.

"Come to Pune and take advice of Bhagwan," said Laxmi, concluding her lecture.

Rajiv listened carefully, nodding and smiling at this little orange-clothed woman who seemed so certain of her opinions. I felt touched by the sight of Mrs Gandhi, who was sitting on the sofa, listening to the conversation. She seemed lonely and unreachable, a very different woman from our earlier meetings. It was as if some part of her had given up on life after Sanjay's death, as if she was doing her job mechanically, with no real enthusiasm to continue.

I knew then that even if Rajiv agreed to help his mother, it wouldn't be the same as with Sanjay. The younger son hadn't been merely a support for the PM. He was, in a way, her soul mate. They may have had their differences, but they shared a powerful bond: together, they lived and breathed politics. Rajiv, as history tells us, took up the family profession. Subsequently, both he and his mother were assassinated, but the Gandhi dynasty lives on.

Some time in 1988, when Rajiv was PM, doing miserably in terms of public support and reeling under the impact of a corruption scandal, Bhagwan commented: "Rajiv Gandhi should go back to being an airline pilot." Bhagwan's basic criticism, as usual, was that none of the country's leaders was doing anything to change the rotten, ancient prejudices that were keeping India in the Dark Ages. Rajiv Gandhi was talking about modernisation and technology, he conceded, but without addressing the underlying problems.

It was ironic, I thought, that Laxmi had been one of those who pushed Rajiv into politics, against his will, while Bhagwan was now advising him to get out of it.

The PM might have been consoled by the thought that Bhagwan would probably have criticised him anyway, no matter what he did, simply for being a politician. Why? Because from the mystic's perspective, politics is as far from meditation as a human being can get. A politician depends entirely on others for his sense of self-worth. A meditator depends only on himself.

"Dogs and politicians not allowed," warned a sign outside our meditation hall, underlining the point.

"What would you do if you were Prime Minister of India?" someone asked Bhagwan, in a discourse question.

His reply:

"I would resign immediately."

Mother Teresa

Sometime towards the end of 1980, Bhagwan and Mother Teresa had a little discussion. In one of his morning discourses, Bhagwan referred to a letter, published in the Indian press, from a European couple who'd been visiting Mother Teresa's orphanage in Calcutta with the intention of adopting a child.

Everything was going well, they wrote, until Mother Teresa discovered they were Protestants and not Catholics. Then she slammed the door in their faces, saying no orphans were available.

Bhagwan said this was typical of religious hypocrites like Mother Teresa, whose real mission in life was not to help others but to impose her faith on as many people as possible. He went on to describe her and Pope John Paul II as "great criminals" because they opposed birth control and abortion, thereby guaranteeing overpopulation in poor countries and condemning millions of people to hardship and suffering.

His comments were widely reported in the Indian press, prompting Mother Teresa to write to him personally. She denied there had been any discrimination against Protestants, adding: "About the adjectives you use against me, I forgive you with great love."

Bhagwan refused to be forgiven, saying, "Just old Catholic stupidity – they go on forgiving!" Then he explained: "Love need not forgive, because in the first place it is not angered. To forgive somebody you first have to be angry; it is a prerequisite. I don't forgive Mother Teresa at all because I am not angry with her at all. It is said that Buddha never forgave anyone for the simple reason that he was never angry. How can you forgive without anger? She must have been angry. This is what I call unconsciousness: she is not aware of what she is writing – she is not aware what I am going to do with her letter!"

Laxmi sent a letter to Mother Teresa, reporting Bhagwan's words, and it seemed she got the point. According to what we heard, she was so angry she ripped the letter into little pieces.

A year earlier, when Mother Teresa was given the Nobel Prize, Bhagwan described people like her as "charlatans" and "deceivers", seeking social recognition through exploiting the poor: "Their purpose is to function in this society like a lubricant, so that the wheels of society, the wheels of exploitation, oppression, can go on moving smoothly."

It was impossible to imagine that a man like Jesus would ever be given a Nobel Prize when he was alive, commented Bhagwan. Yet others, in the name of Jesus, could easily do so by perverting his original message.

Then, with a wicked sense of humour, he complimented Mother Teresa on her mathematical skills: "First create orphans . . . if you are against abortion there are bound to be orphans . . . then open an orphanage and win the Nobel Prize. Great arithmetic!"

Princely People

Prince Charles is a nice man but not, in my opinion, very much of a prince. He just doesn't have the vibe. He carries the title, but lacks the princely bearing. To find such a man, one needs to follow the interwoven royal dynasties of Europe to Charles' cousin, Prince Welf of Hanover.

Welf was tall, handsome and had a natural grace in the way he walked and the way he talked. He had arrived in Pune in 1975 with his wife and daughter, and soon became a sannyasin. His new name was Vimalkirti. Walking around the ashram with his long blond hair, dressed in a flowing orange robe, Welf looked like an elf-king from Rivendel, in Tolkien's other-worldly masterpiece *The Lord of the Rings*.

He was, in reality, the great-grandson of the last German emperor. Others may have been impressed by such aristocratic breeding, but Vimalkirti himself was not. He'd turned his back on the whole blue-blood scene and, after living in a German commune and exploring personal growth through therapy groups, he'd travelled overland with his wife and daughter to India. Hearing about Bhagwan, he visited the ashram and astonished his aristocratic relatives by taking sannyas and joining the community of the notorious "sex guru".

Once, when I interviewed him for a newspaper article, Vimalkirti told me that ever since he was a child he'd been plagued by the need to control his behaviour in every detail. "It was a constant refrain from my parents and relations," he explained. "They kept telling me, 'Watch what you do, others are looking at you.'"

Anonymity in the ashram seemed like heaven and, after travelling back and forth between India and Germany a couple of times, he settled in Pune and joined the ashram's workforce. Soon, he found himself in the kitchen, washing pots. Unlike me, he loved it.

But in November 1980, when Prince Charles came on a royal visit to India, Vimalkirti and his family – his wife Turiya and his daughter Tania – travelled to Mumbai in their orange robes to meet him. According to Vimalkirti, Charles was shocked by the blazing orange trio that walked into his hotel suite, but later in the meeting admitted that he envied his cousin's connection to a spiritual mystic. Privately, through Vimalkirti, he sent a question to Bhagwan.

I've forgotten his question, but I remember the answer. Bhagwan told Charles, very simply: "England will never understand you." The prophecy proved true. From his love of talking to plants to the dramas and tragedies of his personal life, Charles has had a very rough ride at the hands of the British media and public.

At the same Mumbai meeting, Charles told Vimalkirti, quite candidly, that he himself would be drawn to the lifestyle of his cousin but for one all-important reason: he wanted to be king.

How ironic. The encounter between Charles and Vimalkirti happened in the late seventies. Forty years have passed since then, so much water has gone down the Ganges, and yet Charles has still not fulfilled his ambition. Four decades of continuous self-control – doing everything that Vimalkirti hated – and no crown to show for it.

Vimalkirti died one year later from a brain aneurism, a hereditary weakness in the Hanover family. Immediately after it happened, Bhagwan surprised everyone by saying that the former prince had died as an enlightened, awakened being.

Not being enlightened myself, I couldn't tell. But what impressed me about Vimalkirti was that whereas most of us crave public recognition and scramble for ever-higher social status, he was totally uninterested in such things. He'd had enough of life as a prince. He wanted to experience it as a nobody. He wanted to be happy just being himself.

I'd say that's a pretty enlightened attitude.

Mrs G and Me

Mrs Gandhi was an intelligent woman, but she was also a careful politician. She admired Bhagwan but wouldn't risk public controversy, so nothing happened in regard to our repeated requests for her help in acquiring government land for our new commune.

One evening, I think it must have been early in 1981, I was hanging out at the ashram back gate with an English-born sannyasin called Devaraj. He was a qualified doctor who'd practised in London and was now part of Bhagwan's personal staff, having taken on the role of the mystic's doctor.

Devaraj was tall, with a mass of greying hair and a full beard, sharp blue eyes and a penchant for intellectual discussion. He loved to talk, pretty much about anything, had a good sense of humour and once in a while I enjoyed his company.

We were smoking *beedis*, those small, thin cigarettes filled with tobacco flakes and wrapped in a leaf, tied together with string, that were indigenous to Indian culture. They were harsh on the lungs but hugely popular throughout the country, due to their virtue of being far cheaper than cigarettes.

So, we were shooting the breeze about this and that, as English eggheads are prone to do, when, at that moment, a helicopter flew overhead carrying Mrs Gandhi to Pune airport. It so happened that Mrs Gandhi had been visiting the city that day and we knew that, if she possessed any courage, she would have used the opportunity to visit Bhagwan and his ashram. But she didn't.

Devaraj and I agreed that Mrs Gandhi needed an electric cattle-prod on her buttocks if she was ever going to assist us with a new commune – something that was becoming increasingly urgent. The tiny ashram in Koregaon Park was by now bursting at the seams with people from all over the world and most of them were living outside, in the surrounding neighbourhood. Bhagwan had made it clear that in order to create a really powerful energy field for meditation, a commune was required that would be big enough for everyone to live and work inside.

So that night the two of us went to the press office where I worked, and composed this dynamite letter to Mrs Gandhi. As I said before, I was a political journalist, accustomed to writing hard-hitting, provocative stuff, and this talent has always remained with me.

It's hard to recall now exactly what we wrote, but I remember focusing on a particular habit that Mrs Gandhi had. She liked to say that her father, Jawaharlal Nehru, had 400 million problems, and that three decades later she had 700 million problems – referring, of course, to the ever-growing population of the country. We took her statement and made a projection into the future, saying that if one of her grandchildren continued the dynasty and became Prime Minister, he would have . . . what? 1.5 billion problems?

Was this the legacy she wanted to leave to future generations? Wasn't it about time that she actually did something to change the course of events, like, for example, supporting Bhagwan and his work? That's the kind of angle we took.

Of course, we said, his views were so controversial – like compulsory birth control, for example – that she could not publicly endorse them. That would be political suicide. But, we argued, she could at least use her prime ministerial influence to help create his commune.

We finished the letter and sent it in to Bhagwan for his approval. We didn't use the normal route through the ashram's front office because we didn't want Laxmi to know what we were doing – I'll explain why shortly.

Instead, Devaraj gave it to Vivek, and she took it in. The only comment Bhagwan made was for Devaraj and myself to add our degree qualifications at the end of the letter. A former academic himself, Bhagwan was always big on that kind of thing because he knew that higher education impressed the Indian mind.

Our next task was to get the letter to Mrs Gandhi, which proved surprisingly easy. We gave it to one of the ashram's therapists, who was flying to New Delhi to lead a workshop with the staff at the German Embassy, instructing him to hand-deliver the letter to Maneka Gandhi, by now the widow of Sanjay. Maneka knew me and would personally pass it on to the Prime Minister. By this time, Mrs Gandhi was back in the capital and so was Laxmi. I'd been sick, so this time I couldn't go with her.

The letter flew like an arrow into Mrs Gandhi's hands. It went so fast! I knew it went fast, because the next thing that happened was that Laxmi was on the phone from Delhi, screaming at me. Apparently, Mrs Gandhi was really upset, had called Laxmi at the Taj Hotel, and poor Laxmi didn't know what the Prime Minister was talking about.

"Yes . . . well . . . er, sometimes our sannyasins like to express themselves . . ." Laxmi stuttered.

"But who has time to read it!" the PM shouted, having obviously just done so.

In a way, the whole thing unfolded the way I'd hoped. By keeping the letter secret, I figured Laxmi could protest her innocence to the PM when the shit hit the fan, which it truly did. I don't think Mrs Gandhi had been spoken to like that in her whole life.

But what I hadn't factored in was the inevitable fall-out on me. I took the call in Laxmi's office, in Krishna House, where her two personal secretaries, a young Indian woman called Sheela and an older European woman, were looking at me as if I needed psychiatric treatment. With Laxmi screaming in my ear and their four eyes boring holes in my head, it was really quite a scene.

My co-conspirator in the intrigue, Devaraj, as a member of Bhagwan's household staff, had an umbrella of protection around him. But I was standing naked in the line of fire. When I fell back on my last line of defence, saying, "Well . . . Bhagwan told us to send it," Sheela was ready. "We already checked with him," she snapped. "He says: tell Subhuti, it's just his mind." In other words, my whole scenario of believing it would be helpful to provoke Mrs Gandhi as a way of giving us more help was a figment of my imagination, with no substance.

This was my first real face-to-face encounter with Sheela. I'd seen her around, of course, and knew she was married to an American sannyasin who'd been diagnosed with Hodgkinson's Disease and who, after taking up residence in the ashram, defied his American doctor's bleak prognosis by living considerably longer than they'd predicted.

Sheela was a good-looking woman with a casual manner and easy laugh, but with a tendency to become very belligerent when – as in this case – she was in a position of authority and dealing with wayward sannyasins like myself. She had this look, which she could turn on apparently at will, which to me seemed to convey a grim message like, "Buddy, you've just committed the greatest mistake in the world and now I'm gonna make you pay for it."

In this way, I felt a clear difference between Laxmi and Sheela. For Laxmi, nothing was personal. It was all about "the work" and doing Bhagwan's business. For Sheela, almost everything was personal. As I was to discover later, she bore grudges, enjoyed wielding power and dealt harshly with those who crossed her.

To this day, I don't know whether Bhagwan really said "Tell Subhuti it's just his mind," or whether Sheela made it up, but I wouldn't put it past him to pull the rug out from under me. After all, this type of unpredictable switch was just one more tool in his bag of tricks to pop our ego balloons.

I basically went through the shredding machine, and emerged from Krishna House in what can only be described as an altered state of consciousness. I staggered slowly back to the press office and sat down at my desk, not knowing whether I had done right or wrong.

At that precise moment, Bhagwan's voice came booming into the press office saying, "Subhuti, you are right!" A taped discourse was being played in the adjacent Buddha Hall, and he was answering a question of mine from several years ago. The timing was just perfect and I cracked up laughing.

Voice of Bhagwan

I was in the doghouse after my letter to Mrs Gandhi, but it didn't last long. In the spring of 1981, Bhagwan stopped giving discourses and went into silence. India, as I mentioned earlier, has a tradition of silent sages, but this was a little different because Bhagwan's silence was only for the public. Privately, he continued to meet and talk with his secretary and staff.

Bhagwan gave no hint as to how long his silence would last, but simultaneously he created a new commune department called Voice of Bhagwan and appointed me as its head. So, in my own eyes at least, I went from "bad boy" to an "ashram superstar" in record time. This kind of thing was always happening around Bhagwan, which is why people likened life in Pune to a rollercoaster ride. Personally, I felt more like a yoyo, being bounced up and down on a mystical string. One thing was for sure: it wasn't boring.

A few more people were chosen for the department – about four of us in all. Our job was to "channel" new books, writing as if it was Bhagwan himself speaking. This was surprising, to say the least, but not totally bizarre, because I'd already acquired some experience in this field.

Writing letters to newspaper editors, attacking people who attacked Bhagwan, was like that. I'd tune into what Bhagwan might say to them, then use my journalistic skills to shape it into a stinging rebuke. Also, on a couple of occasions, when magazines asked for Bhagwan's comments on specific issues, he turned the job over to me, telling me to write it for him. I'm not sure if he ever read what I wrote, but he never once objected to the finished product, so I assumed I was doing a good job.

The first sentence was always the most important. It had to have the bite, the original angle, the insight, that characterised his style. Once that was on the page, the rest flowed easily enough.

For example, the *Illustrated Weekly of India*, one of the country's leading magazines, asked Bhagwan to contribute to a special edition in which many well-known public figures gave their views on the theme of "Indian Renewal". But he didn't feel like going over the topic again – he'd spoken on India's problems so many times – so I got the job.

Bhagwan's take on India was always the same: the nation's ancient social structure and traditions were destroying its ability to have any kind of future. So I kicked off in similar style: "An Indian renewal is not possible unless it is preceded by an Indian funeral . . ."

That's how the article went. It was new and yet it was old. He'd already said it, but not in these exact words. The piece was published under Bhagwan's name.

Then BBC television wanted to ask Bhagwan his views on religion. By this time he was in silence, so he passed the job to me. He was really pulling back from public life now – he'd also handed over sannyas initiation to one of the ashram's therapists.

The ashram's video cameraman was a friend of mine, a thirty-something former Etonian called Mutribo. In those days, before Oregon, I didn't know him well, but we'd cooperated on a couple of ashram projects and I liked his sense of humour, as well as his colourful stories about how to survive as a schoolboy in the UK's most prestigious private school.

Mutribo set me on a chair in a small auditorium, switched on the lights and cued me to start. I spoke a few sentences, dried up, then used the opportunity to check the video playback. Mutribo, shooting as if it was Bhagwan in discourse, had zoomed in for a close-up and my face looked like a frozen mask of fear.

"Not so close," I pleaded. "Keep a bit of distance."

We tried again and this time the words flowed okay. My closing line: "Until now, religion has been a plastic rose. Now, at last, the real rose has arrived."

Bhagwan didn't bother to look at it. He accepted the word of his secretary that it was passable. But the BBC was pissed off. They didn't want to screen some Anglo-Saxon substitute. They wanted the real thing, so the clip was never used – can't say I was sorry about that.

One odd aspect to the video project: Bhagwan had instructed me to talk as if I was him, but not to imitate his hand gestures, which were virtually his trademark. In every discourse, he talked with his hands as well as his mouth; they were constantly moving while he spoke. But when I spoke like him, the hands followed! I couldn't keep them still.

Our department was given a beautiful place to work: upstairs in Bhagwan's house, on a big balcony overlooking his garden, which was overflowing with trees and lush greenery. In the ashram's early days, this was where he'd given his morning discourses. We sat at our old-fashioned typewriters – this was long before PCs and Windows – banging away, producing our channelled Bhagwan books. Predictably enough, I favoured politics and got busy trashing the political mind and its lust for power.

To be honest, I don't think any of those books had the same quality. They might have fooled some people, but they didn't fool me. The "X" factor was missing. Yet, at the same time, it was a fascinating challenge to get myself "out of the way" and let Bhagwan's words flow through. Some of my colleagues in the press office scowled their disapproval at my new role, clearly of the opinion that I shouldn't be doing it.

"It's not Bhagwan," sniffed a German woman, haughtily, as if I'd desecrated a holy scripture.

"Hey, it's not my idea!" I replied. "If he asked you to do it, would you say no?"

But she needn't have worried. Not a single book was completed. Nothing was published. As suddenly as it had been born, our department vanished, but not because we'd done anything wrong.

One morning, in the beginning of June, a member of Bhagwan's personal staff came up onto the balcony and said, "You're invited to come downstairs and watch Bhagwan leave."

That was the first we knew of his departure for the United States.

PART THREE

Wild Wild West

Home of Our Own

You'd think it would be possible somewhere, on a planet the size of this one, for a bunch of people to hang out together, even if they are a little crazy. You'd think there'd be at least one country with sufficient faith in its own strength to grant a subversive mystic a little piece of its turf.

But there wasn't. Not for us. Which is why Bhagwan never wanted to leave India. He didn't want to leave for the simple reason that they couldn't deport him – not from his own country. He explained this, answering one of my discourse questions.

I asked him, "Why won't you leave India? Those idiots in Delhi will be the last people to understand your work." (This was during Morarji Desai's reign as PM.)

"It is difficult for me to leave India," he replied, then pointed out how some of his sannyasins were experiencing difficulties with governments in various countries.

"If I leave India that will be the situation again and again. Whenever my people will gather in one country, there will be trouble. And here they can create trouble for you – that can be managed easily – but they cannot create trouble for me. At least they cannot throw me out of the country! So I cannot leave India. And I know the Indian politicians will be the last people in the world to understand what is going on here. They will not even be the last – they will never understand."

Three years later, he did leave. Why? Because he couldn't create what he wanted in India. He wanted a place where we could all live, work and meditate inside the ashram walls, whereas in Pune we were spilling out into the Koregaon Park suburb and beyond, into other parts of the city.

He wanted a pressure cooker situation where he could close the lid on us, put the pot on the stove and turn up the heat – his basic

method of working with his disciples. This may sound over-simpli-
fied, even crude, but such situations create intensity, and without
intensity, according to Bhagwan, nothing happens by way of
transformation.

"Nothing else is needed – no method, no technique," he once
explained. "If the intensity is great then that will do the work. In fact,
all the methods and techniques only help your intensity. That intensity cuts the knot, that intensity becomes a sword. In a single stroke
you are no more the old person, you become the new person."

If Bhagwan could have had his way, I'm sure we'd have all ended
up in the Kashmir Valley, living in a big commune together. He loved
Kashmir, with its spectacular scenery and temperate climate, but
Kashmir didn't love him – they shut the door in his face as early as the
sixties – and perhaps it's just as well, because the Islamic fundamental-
ists who routinely launch terror attacks across that state would surely
have targeted us by now.

It wasn't only Kashmir. Finding a place anywhere in India proved
difficult, because of Bhagwan's notoriety. Nevertheless, at one point,
we did come very close to moving to Kutch, a rural area by the sea in
Gujarat. It even got to the point where we all forked out 80 rupees
for the train ride, but there was one overriding factor that killed it:
the site was way too close to the border with Pakistan to allow a
bunch of anarchistic sannyasins to set up residence.

So when Sheela eased Laxmi out of the driving seat and invited
Bhagwan to the US, where no one could prevent us from purchasing
land, he made a snap decision – well, he *always* made snap decisions,
so that's no surprise – and said "Okay, let's go."

Sheela's coup was staged during Laxmi's absence. Bhagwan's
diminutive secretary was in North India, negotiating with ministers
in the state government of Himachal Pradesh for land close to the
Himalayas. They weren't too thrilled about having Bhagwan as a
neighbour, but they liked the potential spending power of the
hundreds of foreigners surrounding him. A deal was possible, but it
was taking time.

With Laxmi away so much – almost continuously over a period of
several weeks – Sheela was functioning as her stand-in, meeting
Bhagwan every day and passing on his guidance to the commune. At
the same time, so I heard later, Sheela was gathering a number of

signatures from the coordinators of commune departments, supporting her claim to make her temporary position permanent.

Personally, I doubt if the coup would have happened if a trip to
America and the prospect of easily finding land for a new commune
hadn't been part of the package. There was one other important
factor that may have influenced Bhagwan's decision to go: his health
was deteriorating. The mystic suffered from a number of chronic
ailments, including a bad back, asthma and allergies. I noticed his
back problem one morning in Buddha Hall. He wasn't giving
discourses anymore, but he was siting silently with us for about an
hour, and one day, when he tried to get up to leave at the end, he had
considerable difficulty standing up.

India has a harsh climate. Mostly it's either too hot, too cold, or
too wet for human comfort, and Sheela repeatedly told Bhagwan he'd
stand a better chance of staying healthy in the US. So, one fine day,
on 1 June 1981, off he went.

Naturally, when she heard Bhagwan was leaving, Laxmi flew down
to Mumbai to see him before he got on the plane. He told her to stay
behind, to keep on looking for a place in India, a sure sign that he
didn't expect to be staying in America very long.

But she didn't — stay behind, that is. Even though Sheela had
replaced her as the mystic's secretary, Laxmi followed Bhagwan to
Oregon. I can't say I blame her. I wouldn't have wanted to be left
behind either. But it may have cost us dear. When Laxmi flew to
America, the project in Himachal Pradesh fell through. If she'd
persisted, as Bhagwan wanted, the story of our adventure with him
might have had a very different ending.

New Jersey Interlude

On 29 July 1981, the eyes of the Western world were focused far away from Pune. They were mesmerised with royal romance, gazing at the balcony of Buckingham Palace, London, where Prince Charles was standing next to his blushing 20-year-old bride, Lady Diana Spencer.

"Give her a kiss! Give her a kiss!" chanted the crowd and would not be denied. For even though a Royal Family is supposed to stand above the common masses, their superiority exists only at the whim of those below, and they dare not disobey.

In any case, the bride was far from reluctant. Hopelessly in love with her new husband, Diana gazed softly into his eyes and said, "Why ever not?" So Prince Charles leaned forward and softly kissed Diana's receptive, open lips. The crowd went wild. The nation swooned in a collective orgasm. A global audience of no fewer than 750 million people participated in this fairytale romance of a prince marrying his princess.

Alas, I missed the moment. At the time, I was knocking down illegal structures inside the ashram. There were lots of them to demolish. As more and more people had squeezed into the ashram, more and more buildings were needed for beds, kitchens, offices, storage and utilities. Asking Pune Corporation for planning permission was a joke – they wouldn't even repair the road outside our gate – so we just did it anyway. Now it all had to go, quickly, while there were still enough sannyasins around to complete the job.

So I didn't pay much attention to what was going on in London, until a couple of days later when I unexpectedly found myself at Heathrow Airport on my way from Mumbai to New York City. Waiting in the transit lounge, I could pick up any paper and see news and photos about the Royal Couple, the Royal Wedding and the Royal Honeymoon, while world leaders were falling over themselves to wish them a long and happy marriage. We all know how that turned out.

Bhagwan's trip to the US, a couple of months earlier, had attracted only a fraction of the media attention bestowed on Charles and Diana, but was reported nevertheless. Several British newspapers mentioned his departure from India and alleged he was "fleeing" to avoid being arrested for tax evasion – the creative imagination of journalists never ceases to amaze me. The ashram's tax status was still unresolved, but it wasn't even close to criminal proceedings. The only danger posed to Bhagwan, as he travelled from Koregaon Park to Mumbai airport, was that a plaintiff in another case might subpoena him and force him to remain in India. Hurting people's religious feelings was – and still is – an offence in India, and since Bhagwan did it in almost every discourse, there was always some kind of court case brewing along those lines.

As for my own journey, I hadn't figured on following the mystic so soon. But one day, while busy dismantling the ashram's boutique, I was called to the office, handed my flight ticket and then sent up to Krishna House roof to the ashram's sewing department to get a pair of maroon-coloured jeans and a purple, hand-made bomber jacket. No more robes for this sannyasin. Not in the Big Apple.

Bhagwan, meanwhile, had been staying for the past two months in a large mansion on a hilltop in Montclair, New Jersey. It was known locally as Kip's Castle and was a replica of a medieval Norman castle, the whimsical creation of a wealthy American industrialist in the early 1900s. Over the years, it had fallen into a state of dilapidation, but had been swiftly and thoroughly refurbished by a sannyasin team of handymen, flown in from India ahead of time to prepare for the mystic's arrival.

Bhagwan expressed no interest in touring New York City, even though his health was rapidly improving and he was fit enough to do so. Ensconced on the second floor of his new residence, he had a splendid view of the Manhattan skyline from his window. But he refused all invitations to go there. This distinguished him from the 40 million-plus foreign and American tourists who flock to New York every year to pay homage to the world's richest and most powerful city, to gaze upon the Statue of Liberty, ascend the Empire State Building, sit in Broadway theatres and stroll down 42nd Street.

A first-time visitor to the States, Bhagwan's only interest in going out of his room was to drive a Rolls-Royce at high speed on the local freeways. He loved speed, so a radar detector was hastily fitted to reduce the odds against him getting a ticket.

Bleary-eyed and jet-lagged, I caught up with him on my second day in the US, after spending the night sleeping on a mattress in the mansion's atelier. One of Sheela's aides shook me awake and said, "Subhuti, you're on the drive this morning."

It was my first ride in a Roller, but I wasn't in much of a mood to appreciate it, because I was still so tired from the long trip from India. Sheela's new American boyfriend Jay acted as co-pilot for Bhagwan, sitting in the front passenger seat and advising on exit ramps, routes and speed limits. Vivek was sitting in the back with "guest-of-the-day". Today it was me.

I don't remember where we went, how fast he drove, or how long we were out.

I do remember that, at some point, Bhagwan asked, "How many people are still in the ashram?"

Somewhat sluggishly, I realised he was talking to me. I also realised I didn't know the answer. Numbers were hard to gauge because people had been leaving Pune in a steady stream once it had become clear that Bhagwan wasn't coming back. Sannyasins who remained were wearing locally printed T-shirts that proclaimed "Last Mango in Pune", a tongue-in-cheek spoof, viewing the end of our ashram through the lens of Bertolucci's erotic film *Last Tango in Paris*. The sannyasin community was scattering in a modern-day diaspora, but would, I knew, coalesce once more. I never doubted that we would all end up together again with Bhagwan, somewhere on the planet. It was just a question of where and when.

"About thirty," I replied. It was my best guess.

Local residents in New Jersey learned of our arrival via their local TV news networks, who interviewed us in a fairly neutral way. They didn't know much about Bhagwan, except that he was a newly arrived Indian guru living in a big mansion just outside the town of Montclair, and that his followers had opened an office to distribute books, audio and videotapes in the US.

As news spread, we were welcomed in the time-honoured manner expected of mainstream attitudes towards strange, new, minority groups. Pellets from a BB gun smashed the window of our office in the commercial area, a "cherry bomb" exploding firework was detonated at 2:00am outside our mansion, and an old lady complained to a local television news station that she'd seen a sannyasin couple "rolling around" on the lawn behind our office. God knows how long she'd been peering out of her window to catch that.

I got my own initiation when a rattle of small stones, hurled against my window, announced the arrival of a local gang of youths at approximately 11:30 one night. Other sannyasins got the finger and jeering insults from passing cars. the *New York Times*, which until that moment I had revered as a lighthouse of good journalism, responded to these incidents with the headline "Cult Causing Trouble in Montclair."

As far as I could see, it was exactly the other way around. Montclair was causing trouble for the cult. But it didn't matter, really, because next day I was given a plane ticket to Oregon. Why? Because, in order to keep Bhagwan in the US, Sheela needed two things: permanent resident status for the mystic and land for a new commune.

To solve the first problem, an application was made for Bhagwan to stay as a "religious teacher", which was an approved category under US immigration law. To solve the second problem, an urgent search was made through various states, until Sheela found a big cattle ranch for sale in central Oregon, with an asking price of $6 million. Quickly, she obtained enough support from wealthy American sannyasins to make the first down-payment and the Ranch was ours.

The Big Muddy Ranch was big. It was 64,229 acres of wild, remote, over-grazed and undeveloped country, located on a plateau about half-way between the Ochoco Mountains to the east and the much larger Cascade Mountains to the west. Although the coast of Oregon was known for its rainy, misty climate, the Cascades siphoned off most of the moisture, leaving central Oregon dry and arid. It was timber and cattle country, sparsely populated – apart from a couple of towns – with empty roads, big ranches and a scattering of ghost towns.

The Big Muddy itself was shaped in a semicircle, with hills all around the periphery and a deep valley in the centre, which gave the place a protected feeling, since the only access was via a long, narrow, unpaved public road that snaked down into the valley. The road was a hangover from the gold rush days in eastern Oregon in the 1860s, when stagecoaches ferried ore from the gold fields to The Dalles, the nearest big town, located on the Columbia River.

The eastern boundary of our Ranch was effectively blocked by the John Day River and there was no bridge for miles, although vehicles could ford the river in summertime. The semicircle of hills also meant the Ranch had its own water catchment area, but most of the time there wasn't much water to catch. When it did rain, however, the Ranch lived up to its name and muddy reputation.

As far as buildings were concerned, there was a small cluster of them, standing in the middle of the Ranch's central valley, where the joining of two creeks and their flood plains created several hundred acres of level ground. There, in the middle of it all, stood one lonely ranch house, a smaller bunkhouse, a yard with a few garages and stables, and that was about it. All we had to do was transform it as quickly as possible into a home for a few thousand people.

Simple, right?

He's Not Here

I was squatting in the gap between two halves of a new trailer home, using a hydraulic jack to inch them towards each other. As soon as they were touching, we were going to bolt the two sections together, then build a couple of rows of breeze block pillars underneath, as a foundation for the whole house to sit on.

True, I wasn't one of the world's experts at high-speed home-building, but I was doing a fair job, along with other sannyasins who were learning new trades faster than an Indian sadhu can smoke a chillum. It was certainly a dramatic change from our laid-back life-style in Pune.

We were living in tents, tucked away in a small canyon off the main valley that we immediately dubbed "Tent City". The new trailer homes weren't for us. They were part of Sheela's effort to get as many sannyasins onto the Ranch as quickly as possible, by purchasing dozens of ready-made units from a company in southern Oregon. Big trucks would come roaring along the Ranch's dirt roads, each with a half-trailer in tow, hauling them onto the sites that we'd hastily levelled with newly purchased bulldozers and backhoes.

Once we'd joined a house together and blocked the foundations, an interior crew would come in, lay down carpet in all the rooms, then bring in mattresses, sheets, blankets and pillows. Everyone slept on the floor. Meanwhile, the Ranch's primitive water system was being extended, to connect the new bathrooms, showers and toilets. Electric power supply was also hooked up and long trenches started appearing across the fields of the main valley, as we buried the connecting pipes and cables in the ground. Septic tanks were also sunk into the soil for waste disposal, later to be replaced by a compre-hensive sewage system.

Acquiring construction skills happened in two ways: either there was a sannyasin who knew what to do and could show the rest of us, or we hired local handymen, learned from them and then took over. Wherever the law required the presence of a certified professional, such as an electrician, we would hire one local guy on a permanent basis and give him half a dozen of our own "apprentices" to assist with his work.

As soon as a trailer home was ready, another 20 or so sannyasins would be invited to the Ranch and fill up all the rooms. They, in turn, would immediately join us in the work crews, trying to piece together this new community, here in the middle of nowhere, as rapidly as possible. We were working 12-hour days, from 7:30am until 7:30pm, but we were warmly clothed and well fed at the bunkhouse, which now functioned as a kitchen downstairs and a dormitory upstairs.

Bhagwan arrived at the end of August 1981, as soon as a trailer home could be prepared for him in a small, secluded canyon, a little distance away from the ranch house. By this time there were 50–60 of us living on the Ranch and we all stopped work to welcome him. While waiting for the mystic to come, I met Laxmi, who'd recently arrived from New Jersey. We strolled around to the back of Bhagwan's new house for a private chat, renewing our connection. To my surprise, she was still talking as if she had authority.

"You must start writing press releases again, swami," Laxmi told me.

This sounded odd to me. Press releases? I was scrambling around under trailer homes without a headline in my head. But then I sensed her reluctance to let go of her old function and needed to make my own position clear.

"Laxmi, anything you want me to do has to go through Sheela first," I told her, as we turned around and walked to the front of the building. In response, Laxmi gave a little sigh, shrugged her shoulders, looked grim and said nothing. My attitude wasn't personal. I had no particular desire to replace Laxmi with Sheela, but Bhagwan was free to choose anyone he liked as his secretary and obviously he'd made a switch.

It was the beginning of a rough time for Laxmi. Not only had she refused to stay in India, she now seemed convinced that the mystic should not stay on the Ranch and, whenever the opportunity arose, was telling visiting Indian sannyasins that the Big Muddy "is not fitting for Bhagwan," suggesting that Ashland, in southern Oregon, was a better site for the new commune. This undermined Sheela's urgent and ongoing need for support and funding, bringing the two women into continual conflict.

I wasn't party to these arguments, but I'm told that on a couple of occasions – in both New Jersey and on the Ranch – Bhagwan invited the two women to his room, trying to make peace between them, while making it clear that Sheela was now his secretary and giving her his authority. However, the conflict continued and eventually Laxmi was told to leave the Ranch.

Bhagwan was flown in a Lear jet from New Jersey to Redmond, Oregon, then driven in a green Rolls-Royce to his hastily completed trailer home, with a lawn of freshly laid turf in front, surrounded by newly planted trees. It had all been thrown together in a matter of weeks. We hard-working sannyasins sat on Bhagwan's lawn, giggling and laughing as he exited the Rolls. He beamed a delighted smile, sat in silence with us for a few minutes, then disappeared inside.

We now had the distinction of knowing where he was, but few others did.

"He's not here, he's travelling."

That was the message sent out from the Ranch as rumours concerning "the new commune" and Bhagwan's whereabouts in America began to fly around the global sannyasin network. Not wishing to alarm her neighbours, the last thing Sheela wanted was a long caravan of sannyasins driving through central Oregon, asking directions to "the guru's ranch".

Meanwhile, my daily task of joining half-trailers together continued. We were working on a new site, located on a smallish plateau above the main valley, and I was making final adjustments when the roar of pickups distracted me. I crawled out from under the trailer to see Sheela arriving on the site with about a dozen local ranchers and townsfolk.

This was tour time; one of our periodic bids to keep on friendly terms with our neighbours and show them that, contrary to rumours beginning to circulate through central Oregon, we weren't spending our time indulging in sex orgies or stockpiling weapons.

"That doesn't look straight to me," offered an old lady, dubiously eyeballing my handiwork.

"I'm working on it," I replied cheerfully.

Sheela rolled her eyes in mock despair. In the beginning, she really did think she could carry the locals with her. But the continuous swelling of our numbers and the steady flow of trucks carrying all kinds of goods along the narrow, normally deserted road leading to our Ranch were beginning to make our neighbours suspicious, then nervous.

Behind their concerns lay the spectre of Jonestown. Three years before we arrived in Oregon, more than 900 members of the People's Temple were either murdered or committed suicide, on orders from their leader Reverend Jim Jones, in their isolated settlement in Guyana. Nearly all of the victims were Americans and the traumatic event sent a deep shockwave of horror through the country, creating a long-lasting distrust of any kind of cult. We may not have been a cult – Bhagwan always denied it – but we certainly looked like one. We all wore the same colour clothes, which had gravitated from orange to red during our shift from India to the US, and we all followed the same spiritual mystic. This, in itself, was enough to generate suspicion in the locals.

For example, when one elderly lady in small town near our Ranch was asked why she disliked us, when we seemed so open and friendly, she replied, "I expect the people at Jonestown seemed friendly until they drank the Kool-Aid."

By the way, it's an intriguing question but I never did discover why we made the shift from orange to red clothing. I don't think Bhagwan instigated it. In the early seventies, when he began to initiate people as disciples, his vision was for us to look like traditional Indian sannyasins, who always wore plain, bright orange.

In Pune, the mystic broadened the spectrum to include all the "colours of the sunrise" as a symbol of vitality, energy and potential for growth. Then, mysteriously, or perhaps just accidentally, we shifted exclusively to red, after arriving in the US. If there was any intention behind it, then perhaps the time-honoured notion of "showing a red rag to a bull" might have had something to do with it, thereby provoking the locals into angry reaction against us.

As for me, I arrived in Oregon with romantic notions about America, in the sense that I'd bought the Hollywood hype about it being a land of unlimited opportunity, and certainly the speed with which Sheela had managed to buy such a huge property was impressive when compared with our difficulties in India. But, alas, any notions about the US being a free and open society were gradually chipped away as opposition to our community grew.

I might also have entertained vague ideas about taking part in a brave experiment – "to provoke God" as Bhagwan had put it – but in Oregon the reality in those early days had more to do with adapting to a basic physical lifestyle: working long hours, learning new trades, keeping warm, eating and sleeping.

Many sannyasins seemed more enthusiastic about the Ranch than I was able to be, and were totally gung-ho about turning it into our new commune. I have to confess I didn't think we were going to make it, not because of local opposition, but because the Big Muddy was so huge, the project so vast, the financing too daunting.

However, no one was asking my opinion and since I'd signed on for the duration – "forever" so to speak – I kept my mouth shut, got on with my work and gratefully noted each time there was food on the bunkhouse tables.

The bunkhouse was our first kitchen, but it was way too small for us to eat inside, so we picked up our food inside and ate at wooden tables in the yard outside. The meals were vegetarian, of course, and there was plenty to eat, but flies were a problem that first summer – we had to eat with one hand while continuously waving the other to keep them off our plates.

The only mealtime that proved stressful was breakfast. Porridge, cereal, bread and butter, jam, boiled eggs . . . everything was okay, but fried eggs were the breakfast of choice and there just wasn't enough time to cook them for everyone before work started. I remember one morning arriving at the kitchen stove and seeing three eggs left. Perfect! The guy in front of me would take two and I'd get the last one. But after sliding two eggs onto his plate, the guy slowly and deliberately took the third one also, then looked at me with a gunfighter's stare, daring me to object. We were, after all, in the Wild West.

He was a tall man, muscular, morose by nature, lacking in humour and wearing a cowboy hat. He also drove a massive bulldozer. Clearly, in his view, in the pecking order of ranch hands a heavy-equipment man like himself took precedence over a mere member of the trailer-home setup crew, and he was therefore entitled to eat as many eggs as he wished. I opted for a second helping of porridge.

This kind of edgy, macho, cowboy attitude soon started to be adopted by guys on the Ranch, especially by those wearing cowboy hats and driving big machines. One actually called me a "greenhorn", behaving as if he was an old hand, whereas in reality he'd arrived just a few weeks ahead of me.

But the macho phase didn't last long. When Bhagwan put women in charge of all the departments, the cowboys had to undo their gun belts – figuratively speaking – and listen to the "moms", as the new female department heads were nicknamed.

I don't know if you've tried it, but it's hard to stay macho when your "mom" is telling you to pin your socks together before giving them for washing, and to leave your muddy boots outside the dining room. There is an old Western saying:

"A man's gotta do what a man's gotta do."

On the Big Muddy, it soon became:

"A man's gotta do . . . what his mom tells him."

There was another reason for the shift in attitude: very soon, women were also driving massive machines and taking charge of construction projects. The rapidly expanding Ranch became an equal-opportunity experience and women were making the most of it.

Marlboro Country

We were driving our Chevy pickup along a narrow winding road that marked the southern boundary of the Ranch. It was late October 1981, and we were patrolling as part of a ban on deer hunting we'd imposed on our property, much to the chagrin of local rednecks. Bumper stickers had started appearing in central Oregon showing a Rolls-Royce in the cross-hairs of a rifle and also the slogan "better dead than red" – giving new meaning to the old McCarthyite catch-phrase of America's anti-communist fifties.

One of Oregon's biggest daily newspapers provocatively published a photo of a big group of stags across the top of one of its news sections, with the headline "Bhagwan's Bucks". The caption explained that these stags were out of bounds to hunters, because they were on the Big Muddy Ranch – the guru's protected turf.

The terrain on the Ranch's southern boundary was typical of the dry side of the Cascade Mountains: rolling hills with rocky outcrops, sparse grazing land for cattle, dotted with hardy junipers that sucked the moisture from the semi-barren soil.

As our pickup crested a rise in the road, we had to pull over and park because the scenery before us was awesome. The land fell away before us for miles, all the way down to the John Day River, where dark reddish cliffs bordered the hidden watercourse, then rose again steeply to the hills beyond. There was little sign of human habitation . . . the land was big, wide and empty.

Maybe this is a good moment to explain that, even though our Ranch was big – almost 120 square miles – most construction happened in the central valley where there was a big area of flat ground. At that time our building boom was still in its infancy, but soon there would be an airstrip, a meditation hall, a garage for trucks, buses and cars, a shopping mall, office buildings, a reception centre and two canteens, all built by sannyasins. It was also the location of Jesus Grove, the trailer-home complex where Sheela and other Ranch managers were already living. Soon, too, we would start building houses ourselves rather than buying trailer homes, and these would be sited a little further down the valley, towards the John Day River. Dense clusters of wooden, A-frame-style sleeping huts would replace our Tent City in a side canyon. Close to the river itself would be our dairy, chicken and truck farms.

By now, the Big Muddy had been officially rechristened "Rajneeshpuram". But when, a little later, we succeeded in incorporating our own town on the property, the Ranch became "Rancho Rajneesh" and the town got the name "City of Rajneeshpuram". Bhagwan chose the names, already knowing, I suspect, how uneasy this would make his neighbours.

Away from the central valley, the Ranch was virtually untouched and here, on the southern boundary, the land was empty and very quiet. A couple of horses were standing motionless in a field to our right, in a place called, appropriately enough, "Horse Heaven". A pair of eagles glided above us, their wings motionless as they rode the thermals and the wind.

The sky was spectacular, packed with big, puffy, grey clouds that permitted the light to shine through only in a few brightly focused beams, as if announcing the impending arrival of a UFO, or the apocalypse, or the Second Coming.

I turned to look at my companion. "Wow, this is Marlboro Country!" I exclaimed and she nodded her agreement, reaching into her jacket pocket and offering me a pack.

So, even though neither of us were really smokers, we got out of the truck and lit up, leaning casually back on the warm hood, puffing slowly and enjoying the cowboy country landscape that surrounded us. It didn't matter to us that some of the actors who'd played Marlboro Man in the famous Philip Morris ads were dying of smoking-related diseases. We needed to experience this all-American moment for ourselves. We were laughing while we did it. We knew it was stupid, but we enjoyed acting out the nation's cowboy mythology.

To me, this was one of the most attractive aspects of being a sannyasin. We felt encouraged to experience just about everything life had to offer, whether it was hazardous to our health or not.

"Make as many mistakes as you can," Bhagwan had urged us. "Just be a little intelligent and don't make the same mistake twice."

Cowboy Across the River

John Bowerman was, and probably still is, a nice guy. Early in our Ranch saga, he rode his horse across the John Day River and came to see us. He was wearing a big cowboy hat, cowboy boots, blue jeans and a blue denim shirt with a loose rag of a scarf around his neck. He looked like something out of a Louis L'Amour novel about the Wild West.

John rode up to the old ranch house, introduced himself to Sheela, then sat down to lunch with us on wooden benches outside the cookhouse. He was a good-looking guy, in his late thirties, and son of Bill Bowerman, the legendary American track coach who is best remembered for co-founding Nike and ruining his wife's waffle iron while trying to create a new kind of sole for running shoes.

John owned a ranch on the other side of the John Day River, which formed the eastern boundary of our property. In summertime, the river was low and offered a fording place, where John had ridden across to greet us. At the end of the meal, John stood up and recited a poem about some misfit character who'd had a hard time fitting in with other folks. I don't remember any of it except the final line, when John declared:

"Because I'm wearing my red shirt tonight!"

Upon which, he theatrically ripped opened the buttons on his blue denim jacket and displayed a bright red T-shirt underneath. Of course, all we red-clad sannyasins applauded like crazy.

Later on, as the battle lines hardened between us and the locals, John withdrew to the other side of the river, but I kept in touch with him via a war of words, published weekly in a local newspaper called the *Madras Pioneer* – Madras being the nearest town of any size.

One week, John would write a complaint about our activities; next week, I would reply. For example, he protested that, at one planning meeting, we had occupied all the seats, forcing elderly women with "weak legs" to stand at the sides of the hall.

"They may have weak legs, but they sure have mighty strong tongues!" I retorted, referring to all the rumours and gossip about us that were eagerly broadcast in the neighbourhood.

On another occasion, he questioned the legitimacy of our land use – a hot topic in Oregon, which I'll discuss later on. In reply, I pointed out that John was so busy writing negative letters about us that he couldn't possibly have any time for ranching, which left him open to being sued for land use violation himself.

"I look forward to it," John shot back, saying he was probably the only person in central Oregon who hadn't been dragged into a lawsuit by us and he felt bad about being excluded.

This verbal sharp-shooting went on for months.

Since I was not an American, I needed a "nom de plume", graciously given to me by a sannyasin called Doug, who'd recently joined us. So, "Doug" I became. "The poison pens of the John Day" was how John described our correspondence, with humorous self-mockery.

John's father Bill also joined the fray, using some of his hard-earned cash from Nike to buy a huge field on the other side of the John Day River. Known as "the bread basket", it was used for growing wheat and had once been part of the Big Muddy. Bowerman feared we'd buy it in order to expand our territory across the river. In his haste to shut us out, so I was told, Bowerman paid about double what the field was worth. The locals might be united against us, but they weren't above exploiting the situation to make an extra buck.

A little later on, after starting our own newspaper, we published a cartoon sequence showing old Bill Bowerman jogging in a pair of Nike track shoes, looking tired, puffing and blowing, trying to keep up in a race with the Rajneeshees. In the end, he tripped over his own shoelaces and fell down.

John was upset. "Leave my father out of this," he complained, in the *Madras Pioneer*.

But, as "Doug" pointed out in the following week's newspaper, Bill was eager to fight us, so he had to take the fall-out. In this ongoing, rangeland war of words, no combatants were spared, no prisoners taken.

Farming a City

"You don't need a city to run a farm."

That was the slogan used by a militant group called 1000 Friends of Oregon who, a few months after our arrival, started flexing their muscles, offering free legal services to our neighbouring ranchers in order to challenge our right to build a new community.

1000 Friends was their name. But 1000 Friends weren't friendly. In fact, for years, they had been hated by almost every rancher and rural property owner in the state. Why? Because they took it upon themselves to enforce Oregon's restrictive land use laws, setting themselves up as a snoopy watchdog, opposing any additional building in the countryside. This included extensions to existing ranches, such as the so-called "mother-in-law" units needed for elderly relatives who couldn't live alone anymore.

They had been, as one rancher put it, "a major pain in the ass".

Now, suddenly, they were being seen as the good guys. Why? Because they chose to go head-to-head with us in a court battle over our colonisation of the Big Muddy Ranch, now renamed "Rancho Rajneesh".

Ammunition for the 1000 Friends attack machine had been provided by Tom McCall, one of Oregon's most celebrated governors, who in 1973 made a widely publicised speech against what he called "sagebrush divisions, coastal condomania and the ravenous rampages of suburbia".

What was that about . . . and what did it have to do with us?

Briefly, Oregon looked snootily down on its southern neighbour California for allowing unrestricted development in rural, coastal and forest areas, with a cabin up every creek and a trailer home in every canyon. Senate Bill 100, passed into law the same year as McCall's speech, imposed strict controls on land use in Oregon, intended to make sure that Golden State sprawl never happened here.

Eight years later, when we arrived, we soon discovered that the Ranch's rural zoning meant that, even though it was spread over 120 square miles, it could legally house only a couple of hundred residents, and by the end of 1981 we'd already surpassed that number. What to do? Sympathetic local planners suggested incorporating a "city" on the Ranch – "city", I should explain, in the American use of the term. We're not talking London, Paris or Tokyo here; just a legally incorporated town.

The state's own watchdog, the Land Conservation and Development Commission (LCDC), took a long, hard look at our proposed city and decided they weren't going to oppose it. According to them, Governor McCall and the legislators hadn't intended to stop new cities from being born, but to prevent unplanned, unregulated development. So they backed off and were ready to let our city go ahead.

That was when 1000 Friends of Oregon jumped in and took us to court.

"The incorporation of Rajneeshpuram was a wonderful deal for 1000 Friends," commented one county official, long after the saga ended. "They pointed to the Rajneeshees and said, 'Look at this danger we've got down there.' They used that to get membership. And membership, of course, means more money to them . . . more staff and more power in the state."

I never got used to being called a "Rajneeshee". It seemed like such a dumb term compared to "sannyasins", which is how we referred to ourselves in India. But the media got hold of it and wouldn't let go, so "Rajneeshees" we became. Collectively, we were also called "the Rajneesh", while Bhagwan became "the Bhagwan". Apparently, to the media, just calling him "Bhagwan" gave him too much credibility, or status . . . or *something*. I never really understood the difference, but "the Bhagwan" himself didn't seem to mind and so, to the local TV networks and newspapers, "the Bhagwan" he became.

Meanwhile, Oregon was beginning to buzz with all kinds of reactions to our rapidly growing community, both negative and positive. It wasn't more than a few months before Governor Vic Atiyeh made his own feelings plain.

"It is very clear that their presence has been extremely disturbing to the long-time residents," he told a meeting in Madras in March

1982. "Their presence is so different. If I moved into a neighbour-hood and they really didn't like me, I see no reason why I should stay."

When I read the governor's comments in a local paper, I remember thinking, "Gee, thanks, Vic. I'm sure the Native Americans would have appreciated a similar attitude from the white settlers who came busting into Oregon, slaughtering them and stealing their lands. At least we paid for ours." Sheela made a similar point in her statement to the media, travelling to Salem, the state capital, to hold a press conference on the issue. She called it "*Mayflower* mentality", a refer-ence, of course, to the first ship to bring English Puritans to America, and meaning "first come, mine forever". This immigrant mentality was not allowed to apply, she pointed out, to the indigenous people already living here.

Our zoning difficulties triggered a massive news story, which focused the full glare of America's media spotlight on Bhagwan and his followers for the first time. This is how it happened:

Before we could incorporate our own town on the Ranch, any business activity other than farming – such as our mail-order books-and-tapes business, relocated from New Jersey – had to be located someplace else, in an authorised commercial zone. The nearest was in a sleepy little town called Antelope, some 20 miles away, population 42 and declining.

So we moved into town and set up shop, but the sudden influx of red-clad newcomers alarmed the townsfolk. Seeing how the original residents would soon be outnumbered, Antelope council scheduled a disincorporation election that, if successful, would have scrapped the town's charter and dissolved the city back into Wasco County, in which both the town and our ranch were located. To block this move, Sheela got busy buying bungalows in Antelope, and there were many locals who were happy to sell. Some of them had been wanting to move out for years, but could find no buyers – living in this tiny town in the middle of nowhere wasn't on many people's bucket list.

As you can imagine, news of a strange cult trying to take over an all-American town ticked all the right boxes for a major national story, and on election day, 15 April 1982, Antelope was filled with journalists and cameramen, including all the major news networks. I'm told there were more reporters and cameramen than voters.

The election result was suitably shocking: the disincorporation bid failed. Sheela had succeeded in buying enough houses and filling each one with the maximum permitted number of residents – sannyasins of course – and registering them to vote. The motion was defeated by 55 votes to 42. When asked for her comment on the victory, Antelope's new mayor, a Harvard-educated American sannyasin named Karuna, dressed in red and a mala, observed diplomatically, "Well, I think it's a victory for Antelope."

It was a remark that deceived nobody. Next morning, the new reality facing Oregonians, waking up throughout the state, could be summarised thus:

The cult had won and the cult was here to stay.

Norma Paulus, Oregon's Secretary of State, glibly tried to brush aside her own responsibility in the affair by saying, "Anyone with a sleeping bag could vote in the Antelope election." Paulus had unwittingly helped Sheela's cause by liberalising Oregon's voting laws, making it easier and quicker for newcomers in a town to register to vote.

The journalists took it all in their stride. "Antelope, I spent a long weekend there one day," quipped one bored commentator, parodying a famous joke by American comedian W.C. Fields.

It was a tense situation, but not without humour. After taking over the town, the newly elected sannyasin councillors passed a resolution stating that each council meeting should begin and end with a joke. When renaming public institutions, they came up with "Jesus Christ Fire Station" and "Adolf Hitler Recycling Center".

The media loved us and some reporters were quite courageous in taking a stand. "I don't care what anybody says, there are good people on both sides of this dispute," declared one TV commentator. But they weren't allowed to play our game for long. They had to get serious even before we did. For example, a radio sports commentator, watching a football game in which Oregon State University triumphed over a visiting team, joked to his colleague, "Well, Ted, the Bhagwan smiled on the Beavers today," – Beavers being the local team's nickname. The implication that an Indian guru was capable of exerting mystical influence over the fate of an all-American bunch of jocks was too much for the Beavers' supporters. Their howls of protest forced the commentator to make a public apology.

A Portland TV news presenter, noting Antelope's public buildings had been named after Hitler and Jesus, remarked on camera, "Those Rajneeshees sure have a wacky sense of humour!" She had to eat humble pie and publicly backtrack the very next evening. According to Joe Public, it wasn't funny. It was a very serious situation. In fact, it got so serious that we ended up believing it, too.

As for me, I was just glad I wasn't asked to live in one of the Antelope bungalows Sheela had bought. Nobody wanted to be there, even though we organised a regular, free shuttle service driven by sannyasins throughout the day and evening, carrying people to and from the Ranch.

Antelope was virtually a ghost town. Apart from a small café, there was nothing going on. All the action was on the Big Muddy and everyone wanted to be part of it. As I recall, some enterprising Antelope-based sannyasins suddenly became interested in creating lasting romantic relationships, just so they could sleep on the Ranch.

The Good Housewife

"I'm a good housewife."

Sheela had an unusual way of expressing herself. We were standing together inside the cabin of an old twin-prop DC3, which Sheela had just purchased along with a second DC3 and a third plane – a Convair that, so legend had it, once belonged to Howard Hughes. Rajneesh Airlines, as the fleet was called, solved the problem of speedy transport to Portland, Oregon's biggest city, and to the capital Salem, which were both hours away by car.

Sheela's comment came out of the blue and it took me a few moments to realise that she was referring to her ability to take care of the Ranch. I guess that's how she saw it: playing mother and house-wife to a growing community of sannyasins, now several hundred strong. We were still building like crazy and some people were grumbling about no time off, so Sheela called a meeting in the dining area, just outside the cookhouse. She said this was Bhagwan's last effort to create a large commune and if it didn't work he would retire to the Himalayas with no more than ten specially selected disciples and work exclusively with them.

"And you can bet your ass it won't be you or me," Sheela snapped. That's what I loved about her in those days. She had no illusions about her own spiritual status. Bhagwan loved her, too, but used her talents in a different way. She excelled at irritating people. It got to the point where – so I'm told – Oregonians only had to see her face appear on the evening television news to scream, "Turn it off, for Chrissakes!"

Oregon's politicians did their best to avoid her but weren't always successful. Governor Atiyeh nearly had a heart attack when she showed up unexpectedly at a meeting in Salem and invited him to come to the Ranch, which by that time was surrounded by controversy.

"I will," he assured her, trying to remove his sweating hand from her firm grasp. But he never did. He knew it would be political suicide to pal up with us.

Mark Hatfield, Oregon's long-term Republican Senator, got ambushed by Sheela at a public hearing, also in Salem. The hearing was about the timber industry and Sheela wasn't scheduled to speak, so she waited in the corridor, close to the public toilets, correctly guessing that sooner or later Senator Hatfield would need to take a leak. Then she blocked his way and lectured him on defending the rights of religious minorities. It was their first and last meeting.

Her use of the English language was effective but odd. It always had a bite to it. When a radio interviewer asked Sheela if one of the Ranch residents had been living in Jonestown, she snapped, "I hope not because she'd be dead by now."

When asked about our territorial ambitions and how much of central Oregon we were planning to take over, she shrugged and said, "If I want it, I'll buy it."

When she faced off with Dave Frohnmayer, Oregon's State Attorney General, on the *Good Morning America* TV breakfast show, she promised beforehand that she wouldn't say "bullshit" – her reputation having preceded her. So instead she said Frohnmayer was guilty of "prostitution of public mind". Did anybody know what that meant? Did she?

More plainly, she dismissed Frohnmayer as "a communist, a fascist . . . and a jerk."

Bhagwan, who'd continued his public silence after coming to America, resisted all efforts to replace her as his spokesperson. At the very beginning of the Ranch, Bob Davis, Oregon's most senior and most effective lobbyist and a personal admirer of Bhagwan, came to our Ranch and told the mystic face to face: "I can get you anything you want, but Sheela has to go."

She stayed. So, from the outset, Bhagwan's priorities were clear. This wasn't about making friends, settling down, being good neighbours, building an alternative society, living in harmony with nature, or creating "an oasis in the desert" as a religious community.

This was about . . . well, what Bhagwan had always been about . . . building a pressure cooker situation, kicking ass, causing trouble and waking up. And I have to say, from this perspective, the Ranch was wildly successful.

Love is in the Air

It was a delicate moment, requiring subtle diplomacy. The young couple were enjoying making love in broad daylight, in the middle of our new meditation hall, while a local television news team from Portland was filming close by.

Awkwardly, I approached the lovebirds. The man was lying on his back, on the white linoleum floor, while the woman was sitting astride him. He was wearing a T-shirt and trousers. She was wearing a blouse top and a wide flared skirt that covered his hips. At first glance, it was just an affectionate moment between two clothed people. However, as I saw her reach underneath her skirt to guide him more accurately into her, it became obvious what was happening. Then she started slowly riding him, moving up and down, with an ecstatic look on her face.

I couldn't blame them for making love. That morning, love was in the air. The whole hall was awash with heartfelt feelings. It was early July 1982, the very first day of our "First Annual World Celebration" in which thousands of sannyasins from all over the world had converged on the Ranch to be with Bhagwan.

The fact that the festival happened at all was a near miracle. Bhagwan had told Sheela to organise the gathering of his global family of sannyasins, but the Ranch wasn't ready to deal with so many visitors. We had only just enough trailer homes and A-frame huts to accommodate ourselves, let alone this massive influx. So we ordered hundreds of tents, while hastily building hundreds of wooden platforms to put them on. The first wave of guests occupied the tents we'd managed to put up, then promptly joined in the task of erecting more tents so that the next wave would have somewhere to sleep. Portable toilets were trucked in. Communal shower units were built. Marquees were erected as eating areas.

Dozens of gas burner stoves were rented or purchased for cooking our meals. Sometimes, when the cooks couldn't manage, everyone was invited to sit down and make hundreds of sandwiches instead.

Our big, new meditation hall was supposed to be a giant greenhouse – that's how we got zoning permission to build it. And, to be fair, we did have the intention to convert it after the festival. We even bought glass panels for the roof, but a few months later when "Rajneeshpuram" became a city, we had the power to do our own zoning, so the hall stayed as it was.

The atmosphere at the festival was euphoric. I don't really know how many people showed up but, as I recall, we told the press it was a gathering of 5,000 sannyasins and other guests and nobody seemed to disagree. Everyone was so happy to see each other again. We'd left Pune not knowing when, or if, we'd be able to reconnect, yet here we were, hardly 12 months later, hugging and "hello-ing" in the middle of the Wild West.

So, on that first festival morning, when Bhagwan left the hall after meditating with us for about an hour, the place turned into a huge hug-fest. Most people were happy enough to greet each other standing, but one or two couples were lying down – some with more than hugging on their minds, like this particular couple.

"Excuse me," I said politely, in my best English manner, as I approached them. "I don't want to spoil your fun, but there's a local TV camera team over there. I'd really appreciate it if you would enjoy yourselves back in your tent."

The couple weren't angry. They took it as good fun. Slowly, they disengaged, the woman giving the man time to pull up his trousers under her skirt before she stood up. They wandered off, arm in arm. I couldn't believe the television team hadn't noticed. Perhaps it was just outside their frame of understanding – that people could be making love in such a situation, right under their noses, without a care in the world.

The media did, however, get a shock when they turned up to witness our first Dynamic Meditation in the new hall. Dynamic was, and still is, Bhagwan's trademark meditation technique, lasting one hour with five stages: fast breathing, emotional catharsis, jumping with arms raised, silence and dance. It was a warm July day, so hundreds of sannyasins in the hall stripped down to their underwear in preparation for the active meditation.

"Why are they taking off their clothes?" asked a startled newspaper reporter, standing next to me.

"If you ever do Dynamic you'll find out – just watch this," I replied, as more than 1,000 people kick-started the meditation with its vigorous breathing stage. Needless to say, the second stage, inviting spontaneous catharsis, turned the hall into a madhouse. People were screaming, yelling, crying, lying on the floor kicking and shouting. I don't think any of the press knew what to make of it. The jumping stage that followed looked more like a gymnastic workout than a meditation. It was only during the fourth stage, with its sudden command "Stop!" and ensuing silence, that a recognisable stillness and hush descended on the hall.

Mostly, the advisory dress code of keeping underwear on was respected. But one poor woman had stopped with one of her breasts hanging out of her bra. To our dismay, her photo was published the next day in an Oregon newspaper, which just shows how cheap journalism can be. One wardrobe malfunction among a thousand people and it's the one that gets into the paper.

Still, by and large, the First Annual World Celebration was a great success and the journalists were friendly and fair-minded. All kinds of gimmicky memorabilia were offered for sale to generate more income. It was a little tacky to have Bhagwan's face plastered all over plastic cups, coasters and T-shirts, but somebody came up with a bumper sticker that was an instant hit. It said:

Moses Invests, Jesus Saves, Bhagwan Spends.

When a small plane filled with rose petals scattered its contents along an endless line of sannyasins waiting to greet Bhagwan on his drive-by, even I had to stop worrying about the media and just let my heart open in awe at what we had created in such a short time.

Meanwhile, there was a flurry of interest in Bhagwan from American celebrities, which at first seemed promising but never amounted to much. Bette Midler, giving a concert in nearby Portland, spoke enthusiastically to her audience about our festival, although she didn't have time to visit herself. Shirley Maclaine contacted Bhagwan's staff, saying she wanted to come, but apparently her request for a front-row seat was turned down, so Maclaine nixed the trip.

Debra Winger was rumoured to be on her way, but unexpectedly landed a new movie role and had no time. Jerry Brown, Governor of California, had already asked for a secret audience with Bhagwan in New Jersey, but was told to be courageous and make it public – Brown backed off. There was gossip that Rod Stewart actually did visit the Ranch, incognito, with a sannyasin girlfriend, but afterwards never spoke publicly about it.

When the festival was over and all our guests had left, Bhagwan told Sheela to give us Ranch residents three days' rest and relaxation.

"They have earned it," he said.

The Rollers

It was a fun moment. I was driving a gold-coloured Rolls-Royce through the Ranch and sannyasins were waving cheerfully to me as I passed. They knew it wasn't Bhagwan – it was the wrong time of day for his drive-by – and they probably guessed where I was headed: to the car wash.

It was summertime and our Ranch was nothing if not dusty, so I had volunteered to clean this golden beast for its new owner, a wealthy Californian newcomer to the Ranch who'd picked it out from Bhagwan's growing fleet in return for a suitable donation.

One of the mystic's first Rolls-Royces on the Ranch was a big, white, armour-plated, bullet-proof Silver Wraith II. This car was no stranger to us. It had been purchased and used in India, shortly after a fanatic Hindu had thrown a knife at Bhagwan during one of his discourses. It was also used to drive Bhagwan from the Pune ashram to Mumbai international airport on his way to America, then shipped to the US to follow him. Soon the mystic was driving it off the Ranch in central Orgeon – and occasionally getting into trouble. Bhagwan liked to drive fast, even though our roads in those early days were still unpaved. One day, he was speeding out of the Ranch when he rounded a bend and collided with a large cement truck carrying a full load to our construction projects.

Normally, in such a collision, the car would be trashed, so the truck driver was startled when his own vehicle was the one that jolted backwards.

"By God, I never saw a truck bounce off a car before!" he exclaimed afterwards. The armour plating of the Rolls-Royce had proved its worth.

After experimenting with various models, Bhagwan settled on the Rolls-Royce Silver Spur, which, so he said, had a driver's seat whose shape exactly fitted the requirements of his bad back. Thereafter, a steady stream of Silver Spurs was being trucked into the Ranch, as Bhagwan's fleet began to grow.

There is a myth that still lingers to this day that Bhagwan wasn't really interested in collecting these fancy cars – that they were showered on him by grateful disciples. This is nonsense. Bhagwan wanted them, asked for them . . . and kept on asking for them. He knew it would drive people crazy and that was precisely the point.

In the tradition of Zen Buddhism, there are many "koans", which are basically unanswerable questions designed to frustrate the mind and bring a meditator to a state of inner silence and stillness. One of the best-known is: "Listen to the sound of one hand clapping." Another refers to the man who brought Gautam Buddha's message from India to China, asking, "What is the significance of Bodhidharma coming from the West?"

Allow me to introduce a new koan: "Why did Bhagwan have so many Rolls-Royces?" It's a fair bet that, in five hundred years' time, meditators will still be blowing their minds with that conundrum. Or writing PhDs about it. By November 1982, he had 21, and this was the point at which I realised it had to be a publicity stunt. It was one of those "aha!" moments when I suddenly felt in complete synchronicity with Bhagwan. I'm not saying it was the only reason, but it was the one that made most sense to me. That was when I wrote to Bhagwan, as editor of the *Rajneesh Times*, suggesting we line up the cars on the bridge over the creek outside his compound and take a photo. He gave the go-ahead and that's what we did.

It was a bit nerve-wracking. I remember one sannyasin showing up on a dirty farm tractor, thinking he could sneak across the bridge in the narrow space behind the cars. But I blocked his path.

"If your tractor scratches even one of those cars, my ass is grass!" I told him.

Fortunately, he got the point and drove the long way around.

I don't know why, but we only managed to get 19 cars on the bridge. The other two were left in the garage inside the compound. Still, it was enough to entertain the world, grabbing international headlines. We published the photo as a centrefold spread, with the title: "Yes, It's True, and Here They Are to Prove It!"

The story was taken up by newspapers and TV stations around the States and abroad. It was probably one of the most effective publicity stunts ever staged, although hardly the cheapest, and became our second massive media event after the Antelope takeover. From then on, Bhagwan was known in mainstream America as "the guru in Oregon with the Rolls-Royces".

By this time, Bhagwan was driving daily off the Ranch in one of his Silver Spurs, heading down the highway towards Madras, then turning around and coming back. On a couple of occasions, travelling too fast around a bend on a dirt road, he slid off into a ditch and had to be pulled out. Twice, he collected traffic tickets, one for speeding and one for improper passing.

As hostility towards us heightened, a team of sannyasins began to accompany him, following his Roller in a support vehicle, armed with a radar gun, a semi-automatic rifle and a medicine chest. Communication between the two cars was via Motorola radio.

One day, a female opponent of the Ranch, driving a pickup truck, swiftly overtook the security vehicle and pulled in front of Bhagwan's car. One of the riders in the support vehicle realised she was going to slam on the brakes and quickly warned Bhagwan by radio.

The woman hit the brakes as hard as she could, but Bhagwan was ready and came to a screeching stop no more than a couple of inches behind her. His self-appointed enemy then spun her car around in the road, flipped him the finger and drove off.

Bhagwan's comment? "I didn't know Rolls-Royce brakes were that good."

At around this time, a young Californian garage mechanic who specialised in auto body paint jobs arrived on the Ranch. When he told Bhagwan, "I can paint anything you want on a car," Bhagwan's eyes lit up and their partnership began.

Henceforth, Bhagwan's cars were transformed. No longer were they limited to the subdued colours recommended by the Rolls-Royce company itself. The golden Roller that I later drove was the first to emerge from the new paint shop inside Bhagwan's compound. Then came a steady stream of fantasy creations: cars covered with blue sky and clouds, a black car with white cranes flying along the sides, one with a thunderstorm and lightning flashes, ocean waves, orange flames, elaborate peacock-coloured prints, black kimono, crystal prism . . . Some of the designs were beautiful, some were really tacky, but all of them were a wonder to behold. Rolls-Royce executives in London must have shaken their heads and shuddered at the spectacle.

By the time our saga ended, there was a grand total of 93 cars in the compound – so many, in fact, that some had to stand outside in all weathers, an ignominious fate that had surely never happened before to a Rolls-Royce. Predictably enough, when Bhagwan came out of silence in 1984, almost every journalist who came to interview him asked the question: "Why do you have so many Rolls-Royces?"

His answer changed with every interviewer. Here's a selection:

"With 93 Rolls-Royces I shattered the pride of America."

"I am a rich man's guru. Blessed are the rich."

"I don't own a single Rolls-Royce. They belong to my sannyasins. I am the poorest man on earth. I don't have even a Honda!"

"I want to provoke your jealousy."

"Without those Rolls-Royces, no one would write about what is happening here."

The answer I liked best was also the most Zen-like:

"Just fooling around," he chuckled.

The Illusionist

I loved that movie. In 2006, actor Edward Norton brought to the world's silver screens a darkly handsome, brooding magician called Eisenheim the Illusionist. Living in Vienna at the beginning of the twentieth century, Eisenheim would sit alone on a theatre stage and conjure ghostly figures, whose utterances shook the Austro-Hungarian Empire to its very foundations.

Sometimes, I think of Bhagwan like that – an illusionist who impressed and frightened people with his magic show. I think of it especially when people ask me questions like, "How did the organisation become so rich?" Many people have wondered, and you can't blame them. When you look at the size of the Big Muddy Ranch, the number of Rolls-Royces, Bhagwan's collection of fancy watches . . . together, it looks like a fortune.

So how did it happen? The short answer is: it didn't.

Oh, there was money all right. But it passed through our hands at the speed of light, with demand always outstripping supply. It really was like a magic show, or a miracle – how the money arrived to pay the bills that were constantly being generated by the explosive growth of the City of Rajneeshpuram and the ever-growing Roller fleet. Credit was stretched everywhere, from the smallest *90-days-to-pay* retailers in Portland to the multi-million-dollar mortgage for the Ranch itself. The land was never bought outright, nor were the cars, but added to a line of credit that stretched from Oregon all the way back to Zurich.

The Rajneesh Car Collection Trust, The Rajneesh Investment Corporation, Rajneesh Financial Services . . . these were all legal entities, properly set up, but in practice were merely fancy names papered over a fast-moving current of cash – that's how I came to understand why they call money "currency". Like a foaming white-water stream, it flowed in from personal donations, property sales, discotheques, bonds, fund-raisers . . . even, so it was rumoured, from massage parlours, drug deals and gold-smuggling.

In the early Ranch days I recall walking one evening towards the canteen when Sheela drove by. Seeing me, she pulled up, lowered the window and said, "Subhuti, I need money." Directness was always her best suit. I dug in my pocket and gave her ten dollars – the sum total of my worldly assets. That was the way it went. Whoever had it gave it, no matter how puny the amount.

Fortunately, there were bigger sources available. The down-payment on the Ranch mortgage came from wealthy American disciples. Once we'd moved in, though, it was Europe that paid the bills. "The Ranch was built on Deutschmarks," commented one financial insider, saying that 80 percent of the money being channelled to Oregon was sourced in Germany. As I mentioned earlier, Germans formed the biggest group of Bhagwan's foreign disciples, and during the Pune years Rajneesh meditation centres had mushroomed in major cities like Berlin, Munich, Hamburg, Stuttgart, Dusseldorf and Hanover. There were big centres, too, in other European cities, such as Amsterdam, Milan, Copenhagen and Stockholm, as well as scores of smaller centres in towns and in the countryside. Anyone could start a centre and, in the first burst of enthusiasm after taking sannyas, many people did. Then the bigger centres morphed into communes, as sannyasins realised that it would be more fun to live together.

When the first round of donations for the Ranch were exhausted, sannyasins who had moved into communes were encouraged to sell the houses and apartments they'd left behind, then give the money to the Ranch. Later, on Sheela's instructions, many smaller communes were closed, their inhabitants were moved to big city communes, and the properties left behind were also sold to generate more money.

To make money, the city communes quickly developed a wide range of service industries to offer to the public, including building and construction, home decorating, plumbing, heating, wiring, painting . . . whatever could be managed with the skills on hand.

In 1984, responding to continuous demand for money in Oregon, Rajneesh communes in big German cities decided to open discotheques. Their style was distinctive: the staff commenced the evening by gathering on the dance floor, putting their hands together in a

Namaste and bowing to the customers. The discos were light, clean and well run. The *Bundespolizei* liked them because night-crime in those areas went down. They were popular and they were profitable. Unofficially, I heard that the Cologne disco alone boasted an annual turnover of more than a million dollars.

Many of these big communes also opened restaurants that offered a vegetarian menu and were almost always called "Zorba the Buddha", after Bhagwan's vision of synthesising the sensual pleasures of Zorba the Greek with the meditative depth of Gautam Buddha. Since no one was paid, it wasn't difficult for the discos and restaurants to turn a profit.

From Germany the money flowed to Zurich – whether by legitimate bank transfer or stashed in the trunks of cars I really can't say – and from there it flew to Oregon, where it was instantly spent.

I remember a few cameos from those times:

- The quaint initial fund-raiser that toured Europe, offering to tack your very own metal nameplate on a young tree – freshly planted on the Oregon Ranch – if you would "buy a tree for Bhagwan Shree".
- The young German woman who flew into Nairobi, Kenya, and opened her suitcase so that wealthy Indian sannyasins – Bhagwan had a big following among the Indian community living in Kenya – could throw in their gold jewellery and cash. Then she locked it and flew out the very next day.
- The Hollywood starlet who donated an expensive pearl necklace to Bhagwan, changed her mind the next day and asked for it back, only to be told: "A gift is a gift."
- The ritual greeting for Ranch newcomers who, when invited for a welcoming cup of tea on Sheela's porch, would be greeted with the question: "How much money do you have?"

For people with money, this last item was a tough issue. It didn't affect me, of course, because I was broke from the very beginning, but for wealthy people it was a testing moment. If they withheld, they might not be invited to live on the Ranch. If they gave all, they would have nothing to fall back on if, or when, the Ranch experiment ended.

People reacted in different ways. Understandably, most rich people were willing to give a percentage, but not their whole stash, and this was acceptable to Sheela. The funniest story I heard concerned a wealthy young man whose purse strings were controlled by his parents. In love with Bhagwan, he struggled hard to give as much as he could, but his parents stubbornly kept the bulk of his fortune intact. When later the Ranch blew apart and everyone left, he found himself immensely grateful to his parents – he still had his little pot of gold.

All in all, Ranch finance was a gamble, pushing the risk margin to the max, an international poker game played by a bunch of rookie card sharks. We were living on the financial edge, day by day, week by week, never knowing if enough cash would come in to cover our debts. But from the outside we appeared like a stable financial colossus with unlimited resources. Lehman Brothers would have been proud of us.

That's why I say Bhagwan was an illusionist. On several occasions, in discourse, he told us that as a child he loved nothing better than to sit all day with the street magicians in his village, watching their tricks. Maybe he learned it from them.

A word about those watches. Some of them were the real deal, hugely expensive designer pieces, crusted with jewels. But others were fakes, carefully crafted by a couple of sannyasin jewellers who were squirrelled away in some backroom on the Ranch, studying Piaget and other exclusive brands, figuring out how to make their bits of coloured glass look like diamonds, rubies and sapphires. I have to say, those jewellers did a great job. I could never figure out which of Bhagwan's watches were real and which were copies. It was all part of the grand illusion of limitless wealth.

"So, you don't own anything?" inquired a visiting journalist, interviewing Bhagwan on the Ranch in 1985, after the mystic had explained that all his cars and jewellery were the property of various Rajneesh trusts. The mystic nodded, spreading wide his empty hands. "I don't have anything," he affirmed.

"Yes, but it's costing your disciples a fortune to keep you in poverty!" retorted the journalist, borrowing a famous line once applied to the followers of Mahatma Gandhi. Bhagwan recognised the historical reference and laughed. "That's true, but they enjoy it and they love it. If I refuse, they will have heart attacks," he chuckled.

As for me, the only financial concern I had during the Ranch was whether I had enough change in my pocket to buy an ice cream after lunch. I was always flat broke. Whether in Pune in the seventies or in Oregon in the eighties, this particular sannyasin never donated a penny to the cause, because, once he'd quit his job at Westminster, he had no source of income.

So, even though both Sheela and Bhagwan have been accused from time to time of financial exploitation, pressuring wealthy disciples to give everything they had, it's only half the story. There were many sannyasins like myself who, from the very beginning, had no money, but were nevertheless welcomed into the communes. Many of Bhagwan's early Western disciples were hippies who'd been living in Goa, Manali or Rishikesh, and who gave up their freak lifestyle to become sannyasins and join the mystic's circus. As long as they worked along with the rest of us, they were accepted.

Much of the time, you didn't know if the guy sitting next to you in the meditation hall was a millionaire, a prince or a pauper.

The Rajneesh Times

Setting up trailer homes had been my first job on the Ranch. It was simple, enjoyable and free from political fall-out. In other words, as long as a house didn't fall apart once I'd put it together, nobody got on my case. So it was a relatively stress-free occupation.

That changed when I was asked to start a weekly community newspaper. It wasn't my idea. It was a by-product of incorporating our city, the City of Rajneeshpuram. The new council realised they were legally required to post official notices in a local newspaper and the nearest one was forty miles away in Madras.

Someone had the bright idea, "Hey, we've got our own city, why don't we have our own newspaper?"

Good idea, except no one knew how to make one. No one, that is, except a former British political journalist currently crawling under trailers, piling up breeze blocks.

That's how it began. I knew, from the outset, it was going to be a tough assignment because so much about the Ranch was illegal or sensitive. People from Europe were working without Green Cards, buildings zoned for farm use were being used as offices . . . it was a minefield. We had to write the stories, take the photos, check them for political ramifications and still get the paper to bed by Wednesday night each week. Thursday it would be printed in Bend, about 90 miles away, then trucked back to the Ranch and sold in the canteens that evening.

On Friday, our phones would start ringing, with calls from outraged Ranch managers, complaining about all the things that shouldn't have gone in the paper: that building shouldn't have been shown because it didn't have a permit . . . those people shouldn't be seen working because they were on tourist visas . . . it got so bad we started calling it "the Friday massacre".

More time was needed to check all the stories, but that's exactly what we didn't have. In order to be a legally recognised newspaper, we had to hit the Thursday deadline, or lose our status. If we lost our status, the city couldn't use us. So it was always a sweat.

In the beginning, I designed a tabloid-sized newspaper, like the British variety. This had the virtue of being small, so it didn't require much news to fill it – therefore less work for me. Had I been wise, I would have kept it like that, minimising my workload. Big pictures, small captions, lots of ads . . . I could have given myself a much easier time. But, well, you know the ways of the ego. Every newspaper in Oregon was broadsheet-sized, with sections, editorials, features . . . I wasn't about to be outdone. By the time I was finished, the only thing we didn't have was a sports section.

We had fun, though. When I saw a group of sannyasins riding through the Ranch on horseback, I asked them to pose for a photo. Not many people remember Zane Grey's classic Western novel *Riders of the Purple Sage*, but in the eighties an American country band was enjoying success using the name New Riders of the Purple Sage. I turned it around and, alluding to our red-coloured clothes, published the photo with the headline "New Purple Riders of the Sage".

On another occasion, just before our summer festival, I dressed an obliging sannyasin as a cowboy and put him on horseback, high on a ridge, looking down on hundreds of tents, erected for festival goers. "Strangers in Town?" asked the headline over the published photo. I'd always wanted to use that corny line from old western movies. Then I added, "Nope, it's our friends from around the world coming for the Second Annual World Celebration."

We hadn't been long in Oregon before someone in the news media suggested Bhagwan was anti-Semitic, probably because he'd pushed Sheela to tell an off-colour joke in one of her television interviews, and he'd also compared Hitler favourably with Mahatma Gandhi in a couple of Pune discourses, saying Hitler's violence was more straightforward, while Gandhi's was hidden and more cunning. I wanted to show that the anti-Semitism rumour was untrue, so I gathered all the American Jews living on the Ranch, about 20–30 of them, took a photo and published it under the headline "All the Jews That's Fit to Print", parodying the famous motto of the *New York Times*.

After the shockwave caused by the takeover of Antelope had died down, we published an edition with a banner headline on the front page screaming, "Rajneeshees Take Over Madras!" Madras was the next town and much bigger – around 5,000 people – so it was massive news. But the front-page story continued on page two, where an equally large headline announced "April Fool!" The date of publication was 1 April.

"It is not known if the citizens of Madras enjoyed the joke," quipped one highly amused TV news presenter, showing our newspaper on the late-night news.

Another favourite of mine was the day when our little post office took delivery of several swarms of bees. We photographed our post-mistress rather nervously holding one of the packages and used the headline: "Funny Bizzzzness at the Post Office".

Soon after we started the paper, Ronald Reagan came visiting Oregon. He was unpopular in the state at that time so, just to be different, we Rajneeshees decided to welcome him – this was in the early days, before the real conflict started. About 30 Ranch residents stood by the side of the highway, waving American flags and holding "welcome" placards. I was on the other side of the road with a photographer. The obvious shot was also the most tricky: catching the speeding presidential limo as it passed in front of our crowd. But the cameraman was good and got it right, so we had our front-page story.

Our affection for the president didn't last. Soon we were publishing a weekly column called "Reagan vs. Rajneesh", where we'd take a quote from Reagan – on God, religion, America, or whatever – and match it with a quote from Bhagwan. The general idea was to make Reagan look dumb. It wasn't difficult. Moreover, we'd registered our newspaper with the White House press office, which meant they were required to send us all of Reagan's speeches every week. So we were never short of material to send back to them – with Bhagwan's little barb attached.

We also had a weekly, full-page self-advertisement titled, "I never go anywhere without the *Rajneesh Times*". Sannyasins around the world sent in photos of people reading the paper in all kinds of unlikely situations: sailing yachts, hanging off mountains, standing in a creek up to their knees while wearing an office suit and holding an umbrella . . .

Someone sent us a photo of Reagan as a young actor with a chimpanzee sitting on his lap – the chimp, called Bonzo, had featured with him in several really dreadful Hollywood movies. So we got the designers to make it look as though they were both reading our newspaper, adding the hook line: "I never go anywhere without the *Rajneesh Times*". Of course, we sent a copy to the White House.

We had outrageous political cartoons. When Dave Frohnmayer, State Attorney General, started attacking our city, we portrayed him as a Republican elephant, with a German Nazi helmet on his head, dancing in a circus. Out of his mouth a bubble was saying: "I am not prejudiced against the Rajneeshees!" Out of his rear end, a big gas bubble declared: "Watch me stomp the Rajneeshees into the dirt and get elected governor!" The headline over the cartoon declared "Bimbo Breaks Wind!" Frohnmayer really did try to use his anti-Rajneesh stance in a subsequent campaign for the governorship. But even the Oregonians could see the guy was a jerk – Sheela's favourite term for him – and he failed to get elected.

It was through the newspaper that I began to sense how widespread the grassroots opposition was towards our community. For example, when a few brave politicians from the Oregon House of Representatives – the lower house of the State Legislative Assembly – showed up on the Ranch on a fact-finding mission, they soon caught the high-spirited atmosphere and began to enjoy themselves. They toured the Ranch, then gathered in a meeting hall for a question-and-answer session with sannyasin residents.

But they got a real shock a few days later after a photo appeared of them on the front page of the *Rajneesh Times*, sitting on a platform in our meeting hall, in front of a massive picture of a smiling Bhagwan, with the headline "Reps Say 'You're Okay'". Public reaction was overwhelmingly negative. All of the reps faced hostile questioning from their constituents and some even lost their seats at the next election because they appeared to side with us.

It was reliably reported that Frohnmayer himself parodied the situation at a Salem party, where he sang a variation of the famous 1972 song by Dr Hook, "On the Cover of the Rolling Stone". Adapting the lyrics, Frohnmayer sang: "Don't put my picture on the cover of the *Rajneesh Times*." Every Oregon politician soon realised that it was the kiss of death to do so.

There was a more serious aspect to public hostility, which became apparent in 1983 after we had purchased a hotel in downtown Portland, operating it as a kind of staging post for people arriving from abroad, and for Ranch sannyasins conducting business in the city.

In July that year, an American belonging to an Islamic militant group checked into the hotel and was rigging two explosive devices inside a room when one of them prematurely exploded. No one was hurt except the bomber himself, who lost several fingers. He was arrested, then jumped bail, but was eventually caught and imprisoned.

It was shortly after this incident that Sheela began to organise a paramilitary unit on the Ranch called the "Rajneesh Security Force". It consisted of about 20–30 carefully selected sannyasins who were considered trustworthy – I wasn't one of them – and who were armed with semi-automatic rifles and handguns. They were trained for combat by sannyasin ex-army vets, some of whom had seen service in Vietnam. To make the public aware of our heightened level of preparedness, a demonstration was staged of the force's skills, shooting at man-shaped targets on a newly created Ranch range, in front of half a dozen local television news teams.

"Do you have any tanks?" asked a journalist, half-jokingly, while interviewing a female member of our militia after she'd finished firing her rifle on the range.

"No, do you know where we can get some?" came the tongue-in-cheek reply.

I got my own taste of prejudice while getting the newspaper printed at the offices of the *Bend Bulletin*, central Oregon's biggest daily newspaper. One of the press room operatives made a point of wearing a baseball cap showing a Rolls-Royce in the cross-hairs of a rifle scope, but I said nothing until, one day, when he thought I was out of earshot, he called to another technician:

"Hey, look at all these pictures of Boogie-Woogie in their paper. They just love pictures of Boogie-Woogie!"

I stormed over and yelled at him, "You keep your remarks about Boogie-Woogie to yourself when I'm in the press room!"

I was so angry, I used the same term myself. Then I went to talk with Bob Chandler, the *Bulletin's* owner and editor. "I don't care what people think about Bhagwan," I told him. "But I want to be treated civilly when I come here to do business with you."

To his credit, Chandler fired the guy, although, out of compassion, hired him again after the Ranch ended.

Once, just for fun, we drove a Rolls-Royce to the *Bulletin*. After printing our paper, we returned to the parking lot to find a note tucked under the Roller's windshield wiper.

It said, "Go back to India."

It was to become a reality sooner than any of us realised.

In the meantime, running the paper was putting me in continual conflict with Sheela. We both agreed the paper was essentially a propaganda rag – one close friend even presented me with a copy of *Pravda*, the Russian state newspaper, as a tribute to my skills. But we collided over style. As far as I was concerned, she had zero taste and the subtlety of a warthog. One day, she called me into her office in Jesus Grove, the trailer-home compound where she lived and worked. She told me that she'd spoken with Bhagwan about her troubles with the paper, and he'd sent the message to me, "Do it the way Sheela wants."

Again, it was one of those moments when I didn't know if she'd really talked with him, or was just making it up. She looked tired, with dark rings under her eyes, and I felt sorry for her – having to cope not only with a hostile world outside the Ranch, but also with cantankerous sannyasins like me.

Then she described the puzzled and slightly disdainful expression on Bhagwan's face when, after hearing about our fights, he'd said to her, ". . . and all this fuss, just for the *Rajneesh Times*?" As if the newspaper was about as important as one speck of dust on the Big Muddy Ranch.

I laughed out loud. That felt real, exactly the way he'd say it. So from then on I did it her way. That is, until she kicked me off the newspaper. Before that final blow happened, however, there was the strange case of the "misfit mystic" and a few more journalistic anecdotes, which I simply must tell you about.

Misfit Mystic

"You cannot call him that. It's totally disrespectful!"

The woman in front of me was clearly upset and determined to straighten out the wayward journalist sitting in front of her.

A few minutes earlier, I'd been called to Jesus Grove, which usually meant trouble, and this occasion proved no exception. This time, it was an editorial for the *Rajneesh Times* that was causing problems.

The editorial had been written by me, then sent to Sheela's subordinates in Jesus Grove for approval. It wasn't well received. It began with a headline of "The Misfit Mystic". Underneath there was a lengthy explanation as to why Bhagwan could not be fitted into any category, any tradition, any spiritual belief system. He was a maverick, a misfit, incapable of categorisation or definition.

"You have to take it out. Write another editorial. This one's not going anywhere," said the woman, a forty-something European sannyasin who'd served under both Laxmi and Sheela as a dependable middle manager. Now she was on my case, big time.

But there was an "X factor" hidden in this editorial, which nobody except myself knew.

"I'm afraid I can't do that," I said, mildly.

"Of course, you can," she snapped. The woman was not accustomed to resistance from me. Normally, I wrote whatever these "moms" wanted. Not on this occasion. It was time to let her into the secret.

"You see, this editorial was dictated by Bhagwan himself and sent to us for publication," I explained, smiling innocently and secretly chuckling at the bombshell.

The manager went into shock. She didn't know what to do with it.

"Are you sure?" she stammered.

"Absolutely sure, you can check with Sheela, she brought it to us," I replied.

Her cheeks coloured in embarrassment.

"Well, at least you can change the title," she suggested.

I shook my head. "It's his title," I told her.

Game, set and match. The editorial was published exactly as it was.

I liked the editorial from another perspective as well: throughout Bhagwan's odyssey, journalists and commentators tried to fit him into a certain category, or tradition, as a way of explaining how he worked. Some suggested he was a Tantric Master, some that he was an exponent of Tantric Hinduism, or Advaita, or Zen Buddhism. I suppose he came closest to Zen, given his penchant for paradox and the unpredictable nature of his behaviour, but really he was just himself, a unique spiritual mystic who defied all categories.

The encounter with Sheela's lieutenant was an interesting moment for me, and not just because it gave me the opportunity to turn the tables on our increasingly authoritarian censors. It reminded me of the difference between the master–disciple relationship, which is purely a one-to-one personal connection, and the bureaucracy that surrounds a mystic when he attracts large numbers of people. It's the difference between an individual spiritual seeker and a church. As a church begins to form, we start to view its leaders as some kind of spiritual authority, whereas in fact they are just ordinary people like everyone else.

Here is the paradox that faces people like Bhagwan: the mystic said clearly that he was "against organisations because every organisation kills the truth". He went on to assert there was no organisation around him, just a functional body, like a post office, to manage daily affairs. But it was wishful thinking on his part. Or, rather, it was his hope for us to function in such a mature way. But it was not a reality and I think he knew it. The organisation existed, the more so because of his public silence, and I had just witnessed its attempt to distort his vision.

Bhagwan wasn't just talking about himself when he used the word "misfit". He emphasised that, in reality, it applies to all of us. We are all misfits. We are all unique individuals. We don't fit in anywhere and we don't belong to any organisation. Scary though it may be, that's our freedom and our dignity.

A Big Fish

"Sheela has caught a big fish," chuckled Bhagwan, as we sat on the floor around his chair. It was a rare moment. Bhagwan was in silence, as far as giving discourses was concerned, and he'd been inaccessible for most of his sannyasins except during his daily drive through the Ranch.

Now we were sitting in his private room inside his trailer home, laughing with him as he described how Sheela had acquired two letters, both written by Mark Hatfield, the long-serving Republican Senator for Oregon. Sometimes referred to as "Saint Mark", Hatfield liked to distinguish himself in public life by claiming to be a man of great ethical principles.

One letter was addressed to some of our opponents, sympathising with their difficulties in dealing with the threat posed by our Rajneeshee invasion and pledging his support. The other letter was addressed to a friend of Sheela, assuring her that he would defend our right to live in Oregon. The good senator's hypocrisy was well and truly exposed. It's hard for me to remember exactly when this happened, but I think it had to be either towards the end of 1982, or the beginning of 1983.

My task was simple. As editor of the *Rajneesh Times*, I decided to publish a special edition, showing photocopies of both letters and denouncing Senator Hatfield's two-faced politics. But Bhagwan didn't want to stop there. At this little meeting, called at his invitation, he offered us a new target.

"You use Hatfield to shoot at Reagan," he instructed.

So that was his real aim. He wanted the President of the United States to get directly involved in the dispute that was starting to boil between the Rajneeshees and the State of Oregon. For me, it wasn't much of a problem. All I had to do was write a headline asking, "Is

Reagan behind Hatfield's hostility?", followed by speculation as to why a conservative, right-wing president would want to get rid of an Indian guru and his red tribe.

But it was a more difficult challenge to sell the idea to the media. This task fell to Swami Prem Niren, a sharp-witted attorney who'd taken sannyas in Los Angeles and who'd been invited to the Ranch to join the legal team dealing with our growing stack of lawsuits. Niren was articulate in front of TV cameras. He was clean shaven, good-looking and, when he wore his black-rimmed glasses, reminded me of Clark Kent, Superman's mild-mannered normal identity. Unlike Kent, however, he exuded power as a lawyer and had verbally shredded a US immigration spokesperson while discussing Bhagwan's visa status on a TV chat show.

A press conference was called in our Portland hotel and the two Hatfield letters distributed to the crowd of journalists. So far so good. That "Saint Mark" was a hypocrite, nobody argued. But when Niren hinted that Reagan might be behind the Oregon senator's hostility towards us, he was met with scorn and scepticism. Naturally, the press wanted proof of this outlandish accusation. And we didn't have any – nothing tangible, anyway. Niren talked his way out of it, saying his sources were confidential, but the allegation was dismissed. One journalist – who up to that point had been friendly with us – privately cautioned us not to damage our credibility with such extravagant claims.

This showed me that you can't just take a suggestion from a mystic like Bhagwan and assume it will play out the way he wants. Mystics may be enlightened inside themselves – that's never a problem – but once they take on the task of helping others and start trying to influence events, they are as prone to miscalculation as anyone else. In other words, their efforts can misfire, or backfire, or light a fire . . . It's not in their hands to determine the outcome.

I am convinced that Reagan really was putting heat on public officials in the State of Oregon to get rid of Bhagwan, including personal talks with Hatfield. That was just about the only thing Hatfield and Reagan might agree on, because Hatfield was a rebellious, left-leaning Republican who often bucked the voting trend in the Senate. The two men didn't particularly like each other.

However, the main heat, as we shall see, was channelled through the Justice Department and the US Attorney's office. But evidence of the president's involvement remained scant. Reagan may not have been a very bright guy, but he was smart enough not to get involved in a public war of words with an unwelcome immigrant. The Gipper wanted to win this one without getting his hands dirty.

Nevertheless, it seemed for a while that the President would be compelled to make some kind of statement. Why? Because in 1983 Rajneesh lawyers initiated a class action conspiracy suit against the Reagan administration, claiming it was violating a religious minority's First Amendment rights. The lawyers made it clear they would subpoena both Reagan and his closest advisor, Edwin Meese, to testify. Had this happened, it would have proved embarrassing, because there was substance to the allegations.

In later interviews, conducted after Bhagwan had been deported, officials in the Justice Department and Immigration Service confirmed that continuous pressure was being applied by the White House for action against the mystic and his followers, which in a court of law could have been presented as evidence of First Amendment violation.

"I think they just wanted us to do their dirty work for them," commented Robert Weaver, who – as Deputy US Attorney in Portland – was on the receiving end of directives coming from Washington DC.

In the end, the lawsuit never happened. During the final days of Bhagwan's stay in the US, when the mystic's lawyers cut a deal with federal prosecutors, one of the demands made by the government's side was that the case against the Reagan administration had to be dropped – and it was.

Sheela's Court

As far as I know, I did not have a past life in the Palace of Versailles, at the time of *Le Roi Soleil* – the Sun King, as Louis XIV was called by his sycophantic admirers. But walking into Jesus Grove, Sheela's sprawling trailer-home complex, did inspire a sense of déjà vu.

It certainly wasn't the décor that gave me Versailles flashbacks. There was no ceremonial Hall of Mirrors, no elegant façade, nor lavish private apartments. On the contrary, Jesus Grove was a functional, modern, bare-bones-style residence. No, it was the sense of reverence for power and subservience to powerful people that gave me a certain uneasy "haven't we all done this before somewhere" kind of feeling.

For example, if I needed to see her about some issue, I'd walk into the lounge and wait while one of her lieutenants went into her bedroom to let her know I was there. Often, I'd be invited in and typically find her either in bed, or sitting on the loo, naked, in the middle of her morning bowel motion, dictating a message to some secretary. In Versailles, there were royal titles bestowed by King Louis, such as "Master of the Royal Bedchamber" and "Keeper of the Royal Chamber Pot" – I'm making these up, but they're similar to titles conferred by Louis on favoured courtiers. Well, there were no such titles in Jesus Grove, but Sheela's private life, at least some of it, somehow became a ritualised part of her working life. It was as normal to see her naked in the bathroom as it was to see her clothed, while continuing to do business.

Secretaries, heads of commune departments and political advisors surrounded her, coming and going according to need. She had her own Italian cook, rarely eating in the commune's canteens, her own laundry staff, and Motorola wireless handsets were strategically placed so that anyone on the Ranch could be reached at any moment.

Special radio channels with scramblers were used for confidential matters and the instruction "go to purple" was the signal to switch from the Ranch's public Motorola channels to the coded waveband.

Bhagwan had repeatedly invited Sheela to come and live in his own compound, where the rest of his personal staff were residing, but she always refused, citing as an excuse the remoteness of his bungalow and her need to stay in touch with the rest of the commune and the outside world. In other words, she preferred to build her own little kingdom.

Sheela's power, of course, derived from her role as Bhagwan's secretary and as the sole conduit for his messages to Ranch residents and sannyasins around the world. We assumed that whatever she told us to do came from him and, in the beginning at least, this was probably true. In the early days, too, she was more playful, happily collaborating in jokes for the *Rajneesh Times*, such as allowing herself to be dressed in a fancy red robe as our local "Pope". The implication being, of course, that Bhagwan was on the same level as JC.

But Sheela could become fiercely emotional. I remember one occasion when I was asked to attend a court hearing – giving evidence in a land use case about the incorporation of our city – and made a hash of it, allowing the opposing attorney to trick me into a damaging admission. When I sat down, I was expecting Sheela to scold at me, but instead she looked at the opposition with total fury and hissed, "Bastards!" As if she could have easily machine-gunned the whole courtroom, there and then.

Her reaction surprised me because even though I'd been outman-oeuvred, I didn't take it personally, or see these lawyers as monsters. To me, they were professionals doing their job. To Sheela, they were her sworn enemies.

The same day, flying back to the Ranch after dark, she looked out of the plane window at the lights below and exclaimed passionately: "Look! Now tell me that's not a city down there!"

"Sheela, don't take it so seriously," I said, hoping to calm her down. "If things don't work out here, we'll just find somewhere else to be with Bhagwan."

She scowled at me.

"We're not going anywhere," she retorted vehemently, then cited another lawsuit, this one brought by Oregon's State Attorney Dave

Frohnmayer, saying, "Frohnmayer thinks he can get us with violation of the separation of church and state, because . . ."

She let her comment hang in the air for a moment, which allowed me to quickly jump in: "Because it's true!"

Then I clapped my own hand over my mouth in mock horror, as if I'd made the biggest *faux pas* imaginable, and quickly looked around the plane in alarm, as if someone from the opposition might have heard me. It was intended as a joke, but wasn't received as one. Sheela gave me a withering look and gave up on me. After that, I don't think I was ever included in a court case again.

That was the difference between us. As far as I was concerned, the whole elaborate process of forming a city was a charade, a game we needed to play in order to be with Bhagwan. If it didn't work, so what? We'd simply pull up sticks and go to the Himalayas, or somewhere else.

I could envision it as a wonderful media opportunity: the whole tribe of Rajneeshees walking slowly and symbolically out of the Ranch, on foot, in a long line, along the county road, expelled – so we would say – by the bigotry and prejudice of Oregonians and the US government.

For Americans, it would evoke guilty memories of the infamous "Trail of Tears" when, in 1838, the Cherokee Nation was forcibly removed from its ancestral homeland in the south-eastern United States, to so-called "Indian Territory" west of the Mississippi.

But, clearly, such an epic scene wasn't part of Sheela's game. I began to understand how invested she was in the success and permanence of Rajneeshpuram. It was beginning to be obvious that she also had her own agenda, which didn't always mesh with Bhagwan's way of doing things. Their personalities were, to say the least, a volatile mix. Bhagwan was a risk-taker and a provocateur. He was already playing a dangerous game with the American authorities and he certainly didn't need a renegade secretary hiding things from him and pushing her own priorities. With the Ranch's future balanced finely on a razor's edge, that might be enough to bring the whole commune crashing down around our ears.

Apocalypse Now

"REPENT, YE SINNERS, FOR THE END IS NIGH!"

We are all familiar with the scene: a religious fanatic standing on a street corner, holding a sign that is prophesying imminent doom for humanity. It's one of the most common mainstream clichés about cults and sects, and variations on this theme have appeared in many magazines and newspapers as cartoons for humorous relief. So it was a bit of a shock to receive a message from Bhagwan, sometime in late 1983, that we should be prepared for an apocalypse in which all the world's major cities – the mystic named New York, Los Angeles, Tokyo and London – would be destroyed in a Third World War and only remote communities like our Oregon commune would survive.

I can't remember all the details, but I seem to recall that our survival plan would involve hollowing out several of the hills surrounding the Ranch's main valley, so that we could take refuge underground during the war itself, then re-emerge and carry on, the rest of humanity having meanwhile been annihilated. Bhagwan likened the project to building a "Noah's Ark of Consciousness", which, like the biblical original, would steer us safely through the global crisis.

One additional responsibility, Bhagwan mentioned, would be to collect the world's most precious art and other cultural treasures so that we could preserve them in one of our caverns. Just how we were going to acquire all those Van Gogh paintings and other masterpieces was left unclear.

Surprise or not, his announcement made one hell of a news story for the *Rajneesh Times* and we splashed it across the front page. It may have been indicative to the popular appeal of such woeful tidings that the copies we made available to the public outside the Ranch, in local towns and cities like Antelope, Madras, Redmond and Bend, immediately sold out. If the world was about to end, even our opponents wanted to know the details.

My job, as editor, wasn't to question the plausibility of Bhagwan's message, but rather to support it. That, after all, was why the newspaper was called the *Rajneesh Times*. It was, essentially, his baby, devoted to his vision. So, with his apocalypse warning on the front page, we designed a back page titled "The Center of the Cyclone" with a whirling, spiral motif. Bhagwan's face was in the middle and surrounding him, seemingly tossed by fate, were various gloom-and-doom headlines culled from America's daily newspapers.

Since the Russian Air Force had recently shot down a Korean Airlines jet, killing all 269 passengers and crew, and the Kremlin had then accused the Americans of deliberately sending the airliner into Soviet airspace as a spy plane to test Russia's air defences, this story featured prominently in our first back-page spread.

Indeed, for a while, as the airliner incident escalated into one of the most tense moments in the Cold War, with NATO and Soviet troops on high alert and Reagan making ill-timed comments about bombing Russia, it looked as though Bhagwan's warning might have come at the right time. Eventually, though, the crisis cooled off.

Another surprise followed shortly afterwards. During one of the celebration days on the Ranch, I had volunteered to be one of the guards, keeping the commune secure, while everyone else joined Bhagwan in the main meditation hall. He wasn't speaking, but he sat on the podium while a couple of thousand sannyasins got high on singing, dancing and meditating in his presence.

Shortly afterwards, as a reward, Sheela called us guards together and took us to Bhagwan's residence, where he laughingly gave us all cowboy hats as a thank you for our services. Then, settling back in his chair with a smile, he said: "You can ask one question, and one question only."

I was quick off the mark. "Bhagwan, can you tell us more about your vision of the apocalypse and how we may avoid it?"

He looked at me and, since it was my question, spent most of the time talking to me. What he said was not recorded, and my own recollections – which I typed out the very next day – were immediately destroyed by Sheela. I got her point: since Bhagwan was officially in silence, he couldn't possibly be giving discourses, even in private.

But he did a fair job in convincing us that it was going to happen.

"The Third World War cannot be avoided," he told us, "because all the conditions needed to create the war have already taken place . . ."

He talked about the struggle for global domination between Russia and America. He talked about the irreconcilable conflict over Jerusalem between Muslims, Jews and Christians. He talked about the arms race and also about the destruction of the environment. He must have talked for about half an hour, then stopped and beamed a warm, concluding smile at us.

"Good," he chuckled and we were dismissed.

The funny thing was that, even though this was a dire prediction, the atmosphere around Bhagwan was always warm, loving and a little bit jolly. So we left his room giggling and laughing, as if we'd just been given the best news ever. So much for Armageddon.

After a few months, our back-page apocalypse feature wore thin and was eventually dropped. Armageddon failed to manifest. Bhagwan issued no further warnings and we were spared the twin tasks of digging out caverns beneath the hills and stealing Van Gogh paintings.

At the end of the Ranch, in conversations with the media, Bhagwan admitted that his warning had been a strategy to encourage sannyasins to leave their home cities and come to Rajneeshpuram, where he could work on their spiritual growth more effectively. He didn't seem to mind that this exposed him as a trickster, even as a fraud. In that way, he was immensely pragmatic. If he wanted his sannyasins close by, then some excuse had to be found to convince them to come. As long as it worked, it was right.

This reminded me of a question that was once asked to Gautam Buddha.

A disciple asked, "What is truth?"

Buddha replied, "That which works."

I can hear Bhagwan saying, "Ditto."

As for me, I didn't mind being deceived, because I always had a certain basic trust in my relationship with Bhagwan. Even if he said something that seemed weird, bizarre or completely off-the-wall, I could usually feel that it served an underlying purpose; that, in the long term, it would have a positive impact on my spiritual development.

Moreover, with Bhagwan, there was always a sense of theatre to everything, so if Armageddon was the mystic's flavour of the month, I didn't have a problem with it. And after all, how many journalists have the opportunity to announce the coming of the apocalypse, right across the front page?

While on the subject of far-fetched news stories, I do need to mention a particularly tacky one, which I will call "the adoption revelation". One day on the Ranch, it was suddenly announced that, way back in 1936, when Bhagwan was only five years old, his father had given up his young son for adoption. To whom? Why, to none other than Sheela's father, Ambalal Patel, who, by the time this story broke, was also living on the Ranch. A document had been "discovered" to prove the adoption had taken place.

Why had this bizarre piece of history been unearthed? Well, coincidentally, there was a clause in US immigration law that permitted resident status to be granted to an unmarried son of a legally resident alien. Ambalal Patel, although born in Gujarat, India, was a legally resident alien in the United States. Bhagwan, of course, was unmarried – he'd opposed the institution all his life – and now was revealed to be Ambalal Patel's adopted son. Bingo! An application was immediately filed.

If ever I ran a story in the *Rajneesh Times* that defied belief, it was that one, and I wondered if we'd soon be reporting sightings of UFOs, or interviews with psychics claiming to be in communication with Elvis Presley, now six or seven years in his grave. Fortunately, the adoption application was sidelined. I'm told that an expert in the field of historical documents aired his doubts about its authenticity. But, in any case, it was deemed unnecessary when, a few months later, the US Immigration and Naturalization Service (INS) startled everyone by recognising Bhagwan's status as a religious teacher, which qualified him to stay in the country.

This looked like very good news. It wasn't. There was a Catch 22 in the process. Much later, I learned that the government forces arraigned against us had recognised that the debate over Bhagwan's religious status was too confusing and would never produce the desired result of denying Bhagwan entry to America.

It was the next step, called "adjustment of status", that offered a solution. Because if it could be proved that Bhagwan had arrived in the US with prior intent to stay, thereby committing immigration fraud, his resident status could still be denied. So, the mystic was granted recognition as a religious teacher, in order to initiate the next step.

This, unbeknown to us, became the focus of their efforts. In biblical terms, the apocalypse had been postponed, but our very own version of Judgement Day was fast approaching.

The Red Bead Game

She was beautiful, in an Italian sort of way, with long dark hair and deep brown eyes that shone with an inviting sparkle. She was also single and had, by some gift of the Ranch's bureaucracy, been assigned to our living room to sleep on a spare mattress for this one night, before being given a permanent space. I'd known her in Pune and felt an attraction then, but had not done anything about it. Now here she was, freshly arrived from Europe for a short stay on the Ranch and seemingly very pleased to see me. She was in no hurry to go to sleep, propping herself up on one arm to chat with me, while showing enough of her beautifully suntanned body to start my lower chakras whirling.

Our chemistry was more than physical. Like so many moments of this kind, it was an energy event: two polarities sending sparks of bio-electricity towards each other in a controlled combustion that seemed physical, sexual, emotional and heartful at the same time.

The next morning, as we both knew, she'd have to go to our medical centre Koran Grove and get a red bead to wear on her mala, which would announce that she was a new arrival and off limits in a sexual way until she'd been tested for STDs and gone through a short period of quarantine.

STDs had been troubling our community for years. That's the price we had to pay for the free sexual atmosphere and our general preference to use the pill, the coil and other birth control methods that didn't require the use of condoms. In Pune, with so many people living outside the ashram, it hadn't been possible to do anything about STDs except on an individual basis. If you felt some kind of genital irritation, you went to the medical centre, got yourself tested and diagnosed, then took a bunch of antibiotics and hoped your next partner was infection-free.

But here in Oregon, we were able to create a highly effective programme that allowed free sexuality while virtually wiping STDs off the campus. It was revolution, because I could vividly remember TV documentaries about the so-called "Summer of Love" in the Haight Ashbury district of San Francisco, in 1967, where the romantic idealism of a free sexual atmosphere had been plagued with the problem of rampant venereal diseases. Too often, the puritan-minded undertone of such documentaries was that sexual freedom cannot work as a social norm and would inevitably be punishable by some dreadful medical problem.

But in Oregon we managed to get the problem sorted. First, everyone inside the community was tested and treated if infected, creating an STD-free zone. Then all newcomers to the Ranch were asked to wear a red bead and were not allowed to make love with commune members until they'd also been tested and gone through quarantine.

It worked – well, it worked most of the time. At first, people inside the commune who left for a short visit were received back on trust. If they said they hadn't been with anyone on the outside, they didn't need to go through the procedure. But when a sudden outbreak hit the community and was traced back to an American guy who'd just returned from Hawaii, he reluctantly admitted he'd had sex on Maui but hadn't wanted to go through the hassle of quarantine. Trust was discarded in favour of compulsory testing for everyone who came in, whether returning from a short trip or not.

So you can imagine my dilemma. On the one hand, here was this Italianate beauty, saying "Yes, Subhuti" with her inviting eyes, while on the other hand there were strict sexual regulations – which I considered to be a sound practical idea and well worth supporting. But having missed several previous possible dates with her in Pune, I couldn't afford to wait. Who knew about tomorrow? Amorous connections on the Ranch were unpredictable and ever-changing. Walking out of the medical centre the next day, she might meet a handsome bulldozer driver or a rugged-looking cowboy on a horse and . . . yes, one more missed chance for Swami Anand Subhuti.

I simply had to take this opportunity and so, after a long embrace and a little kissing, I invited her to leave her living room mattress and come to my room. All rooms were shared, but my room-mate was working at the Rajneesh Hotel in Portland, so we had the space to ourselves. We enjoyed a night of delightful love-making and the next day I accompanied her to Koran Grove. I had a feeling I was heading for trouble and I was right.

"I also need a red bead," I told the nurse on duty. For a moment, she looked puzzled, then noticed the smile on the woman's face and the penny dropped. The nurse frowned her disapproval, letting me know that bending the rules in this cavalier way wasn't a good idea, and announced she would have to report this erring sannyasin to higher authorities.

So there was a lot of fuss and some embarrassment for me, but later on the rules were modified to cope with such situations, especially at festival time. This is how it worked: at the beginning of a festival, commune members could elect to "go out" of the STD-free zone and put on a red bead, joining everyone who was visiting for a few days. They could be with whoever they liked, except commune members, with no questions asked. At the end of the festival, they could be tested and return. The system worked nicely until the outbreak of the AIDS epidemic, which I'll come to shortly.

By the way, I was right about my Italianate lover. She disappeared into the Ranch dating scene and we never connected that way again.

The Raving Cult Member

Somewhere in the 300 hours of archive footage about our Oregon saga, I am pretty sure there is an embarrassing clip of me, acting for all the world like a raving cult member. Really, I had the best of intentions but, as many a wise man has observed, the road to hell is paved with them. This is how it happened:

While working on the *Rajneesh Times* I frequently came in contact with an Oregon-born freelance reporter who'd taken it upon himself to expose the "Rajneesh cult" for the threat he considered it to be. I will refer to him as "Mr X".

At county planning meetings, at state education hearings, at court cases . . . whenever and wherever the issue of the Rajneesh commune was on the agenda, sure enough, Mr X would show up, asking questions and taking notes for his next alarmist article about the danger we posed. Once, I even caught him trying to surreptitiously record a conversation between two members of our planning team during a recess in a county hearing. I warned them and Mr X quickly retreated, but, as always, he never quite disappeared from view.

Well, one fine day in the summer of 1983, one of the local television news affiliates was in the downtown area of the Ranch, filming the latest developments, when Mr X showed up. He began to challenge a member of our "Peace Force", the name we'd given to the legally constituted law enforcement agency created by our newly incorporated city – in other words, our local cops.

Immediately, the news team focused on their exchanges. There was no need for me to interfere. The Peace Force sannyasin was doing perfectly well by himself, answering Mr X's hostile questions calmly and politely. However, I thought this would be a wonderful opportunity to expose Mr X in front of the cameras, by asking him how much money he was earning from his appearances at various public meetings around Oregon, where concerns about the growing "Rajneesh threat" were being regularly discussed.

Of course I had to speak louder than him, in order to interrupt, so I guess I was almost shouting when I issued my challenge: "Just how much money are you making from all your hate-provoking speeches around the State of Oregon . . ." and so on. Mr X kept trying to ignore me, so I kept trying to out-shout him. Eventually, we both gave up and left the scene, going our separate ways. The next day, I had the opportunity to watch the news clip, recorded at our hotel in Portland and delivered to the Ranch, and was horrified to see the outcome.

The main problem was that it was impossible to hear what I was saying, so my bid to expose him got completely lost in our shouting match. Instead, I looked and sounded like some demented cult member, harassing a poor innocent Oregonian. He looked like a local hero, trying to do his job as an investigative journalist, while I looked like a madman.

I swear, invitations for Mr X to attend anti-Rajneesh meetings must have doubled after that clip was shown. If he was making money, his income must have shot up, thanks to me. I couldn't even blame the news channel, because all they did was show the clip, without comment.

Sheela didn't seem to mind. "Well, it got rid of him," was her only comment. But the poor guys engaged in our political dealings with state and county officials shook their heads and shuddered. I'd just made their already-difficult jobs even harder.

I don't think it changed anything; in the long term, we were doomed anyway. But it was certainly a humbling experience for me and a lesson as to just how easily an intention to expose a hostile opponent can have the reverse effect.

AIDS warning

Bhagwan wasn't much of a prophet. He said he would die on Master's Day, which he'd created as an annual event on 6 July. He actually died on 19 January. He said half of the population of India would be dying from starvation by the end of the twentieth century. It didn't work out that way. He assured his disciples he would live until the turn of the century. He died a full decade earlier, in 1990.

His lack of accuracy didn't bother me too much, because Bhagwan had often told us that he wasn't a prophet, that he was fallible like everyone else, and that the future is always unknown. So whenever he made a prediction, I assumed he was doing so in support of some other point he was trying to make.

But in the spring of 1984, Bhagwan got it right. Out of the blue, he suddenly announced that AIDS would become a global pandemic, affecting heterosexuals as well as homosexuals. His timely warning on AIDS saved my life and the lives of hundreds of sannyasins. He may have exaggerated the figures – he said up to two thirds of humanity might die from the disease – but his message was hugely beneficial to those who listened to him. At a time when experts were saying the AIDS threat was confined to homosexuals, haemophiliacs and intravenous drug users, Bhagwan could see the vast heterosexual population was next in line.

While the rest of America thought Bhagwan was scare-mongering and over-reacting, we implemented an AIDS prevention programme at the Ranch and in Rajneesh meditation centres around the world.

"If you can drop sex without repressing it, that is the safest way to avoid AIDS," Bhagwan declared. Well, very few people on the Ranch were ready for that, including me, so his next advice was what became important for us.

Free condoms were to be issued to everyone and, also part of Bhagwan's instructions, same-sex love-making was banned. This was rough on homosexuals, but reflected the fact that they carried a higher risk of infection, since at that time AIDS was devastating America's gay communities.

Gay men and lesbians were attracted to the mystic and had been living with us since the early days of the Pune ashram without any kind of discrimination; they were fully accepted. Although Bhagwan said in several discourses on the subject that he considered homosexuality to be a form of sexual perversion, he gave his support to individual gay disciples. For example, when one of his gay sannyasins wrote to him, saying he felt confused by what Bhagwan was saying, the mystic replied "No need to feel guilty, in your case, it is natural."

To another gay man, with a similar question, he assured him, "You need not feel guilty about it. One certainly has to go beyond sex, but that is as much applicable to heterosexuality as it is applicable to homosexuality. Heterosexuality or homosexuality are just styles of the same stupidity!"

Bhagwan didn't want anyone to feel guilty about anything. He saw guilt as a weapon in the hands of society's vested interests – the priests and politicians – to manipulate and control people by cutting their energy and making them feel bad about themselves. Freeing people from guilt was one of his main priorities.

As far as AIDS was concerned, Bhagwan's early warning worked well. It was a life-saver. "These things are easy to stop if you catch them in the beginning," Bhagwan had explained. "Later on, it is going to be much more difficult."

Remember that we, as a group, were highly exposed to sexually transmitted diseases. People were continually arriving from everywhere on the planet and there was an enthusiastic dating scene on the Ranch. Stable couples were a rarity. You could have three or four different partners in a week, although most liaisons tended to last longer. The red bead method of stopping STDs from entering the community couldn't cope with AIDS, because in the early days there was no test for it. Even when testing became possible, it was no guarantee, because the HIV virus might take weeks or months to show up. In short, it was a regarded as a mysterious, fatal disease that was not understood – AIDS research was still in its infancy – and that's why Bhagwan came out with his warning. Later, when AIDS testing became feasible, we found the HIV virus was already on the Ranch among a few gay men and a couple of AC/DC guys who swung both ways. No women tested positive for HIV. Those who had the virus were given a choice: either move to a special, isolated area of the Ranch, or leave. It was tough on them. But it was effective. As far as we knew, nobody contracted the HIV virus on the Ranch.

If the US and other countries had swiftly adopted similar preventive testing measures, the 35 million people worldwide who have died of AIDS would have been saved. The 14 million AIDS orphans living in Africa would still have parents. The 37 million people currently living with the HIV virus would still be healthy. But in the US even normal social safeguards for preventing life-threatening diseases were suspended for AIDS, such as patient referral, contact tracing and isolation. There was no emphasis on protecting the healthy, and the underlying mainstream attitude seemed to be that, if you got AIDS, it was either because you were gay, or fucking around, so you brought it on yourself by unnatural or promiscuous sexual behaviour.

For me, it was fascinating to understand how Bhagwan came to realise that AIDS was such a threat. During the seventies, he'd said several times in his discourses that, as the final culmination of life-negative religious attitudes, humanity has lost the will to live. Now, unconsciously, it is preparing for collective suicide on a global scale, either through nuclear warfare or destruction of the planet's eco-systems.

When AIDS erupted, Bhagwan focused on the fact that it attacked the human immune system. This, according to him, was a biological symptom of the same suicidal impulse, since a robust and healthy immune system is a clear indication of an individual's will to live.

No matter how Bhagwan arrived at his conclusion, the truth is that his announcement came at exactly the right moment. As the devastation caused by AIDS spread around the globe, we remained immune. We were tested every three months on the Ranch and this became a source of humour. Given Sheela's insistence that we should exhibit a 100 percent positive attitude in our daily work, we asked, "When is the only time you are allowed to be negative on the Ranch?"

Answer: when you take your AIDS test.

Moscow Rules

"Hey, Subhuti!"

On the face of it, this was an ordinary morning at Rancho Rajneesh. As usual, I was heading for breakfast at 7:00am, prior to starting work half an hour later. But everything about that morning was different. It was spring 1984 and I'd just been dismissed from the *Rajneesh Times* as part of a Ranch-wide purge that pushed dozens of old-time sannyasins out of key jobs and into relative obscurity. Sheela had grown tired of our independent views and our inability to understand the need for unquestioning obedience.

It was a shock, of course, but somehow in tune with my feelings at the time, because my sense of priorities was changing. All through my career as editor, Sheela's most effective way of keeping me in line had been to threaten to close the newspaper if I didn't cooperate. She knew how invested I was in running the *Rajneesh Times*, so it was an effective threat, but – like any form of manipulation – subject to the law of diminishing returns.

One day, when the by-now-familiar message was brought to me by one of her lieutenants, I surprised myself by replying, "You know, I really don't care if Sheela shuts us down. I'd just as soon go pick potatoes in the truck farm."

What made the statement so potent was that, in that moment, I meant it. I really did, and somehow the timing was in synchronicity with Sheela's general purge. Within a few days, I was informed by my coordinator that my services at the *Rajneesh Times* were no longer needed and told to report to the "Rajneesh Buddhafield Garage" for truck driving.

I didn't protest. Somehow, I could feel it was a blessing in disguise, but nevertheless, on that first morning, as I walked into the canteen next to RBG – as the garage was nicknamed – it felt like a savage blow. My view of myself as one of the key people, not only on the Ranch but in the development of Bhagwan's vision around the world, had been abruptly shattered. So when a group of guys sitting at the back of the cafeteria hailed me, I found myself wondering, "Why do they want me to sit with them? I'm nobody now."

It would take a while for me to understand that I could be appreciated not for what I was able to produce as a skilled journalist, but rather for who I happened to be as an ordinary human being.

"Take a pew, old chap," welcomed Mutribo, the video cameraman. He'd also just been purged from the Ranch's media unit. Others included Vimal, another Englishman with a fine sense of humour, and Milarepa, a musician and songwriter.

We trusted each other instantly. More than that, we decided, since we now had no say at all in the running of the Ranch, that we would devote ourselves exclusively to having a good time. To further this aim, we developed a special code language, known only to our brotherhood, including the key phrases: "ELP", "comfy chair" and "Moscow rules".

ELP stood for "Extremely Low Profile", describing the easiest way to live and work on the Ranch under Sheela's increasingly militant and paranoid regime: never stick your neck out, never attract unnecessary attention.

"Comfy chair" was a reference to the British TV comedy show *Monty Python's Flying Circus*, which ran a number of skits interrupted by the sudden arrival of a trio of hooded figures who cried, " Nobody expects the Spanish Inquisition!" As an ultimate form of torture, designed to terrorise victims and make them confess their heresy, the spokesman for the trio would command, "Bring the comfy chair!" At which even the other members of the trio would look terrified and aghast.

It so happened that, whenever erring sannyasins were called into Sheela's office to be verbally shredded by her team of willing lieutenants, they were invited to sit on a comfy sofa. This gave us a wonderful parody to play with: when somebody's behaviour was deemed not to be ELP – such as, for example, loudly objecting to some new rule or regulation – he was, inevitably, "heading for the comfy chair".

"Moscow rules" referred to the spy novels of John Le Carré, which we devoured hungrily at every opportunity. In Le Carré's sinister world of spy and counter-spy, British agents operating in Moscow had to observe a much stricter set of rules – Moscow rules – than in any other theatre of operation. Thus whenever we arranged to do something that was clearly against Ranch rules – skipping work for a swim in the lake, for example – we looked at each other over a cup of tea, smiled and whispered, "Okay, it's agreed, we'll do it, but remember, Moscow rules."

I loved being in that trusted circle as much as I loved the new, white Mac dump truck I was given to drive. It took me away from the seriousness and stress of the newspaper. It brought humour and playfulness back into my life, and reminded me I could feel good about myself without showing off my skills in a so-called important job.

As for my ongoing spiritual development, well, in some ways, it felt like it had been put on hold ever since leaving India. In Oregon, no time was scheduled for meditation in our community and I did precious little silent sitting on my own. But spiritual growth is a strange beast, not necessarily confined to people who follow a religious routine, or who appear to be behaving spiritually. One might sit in meditation every day in a monastery and get nowhere, because of personal attachment to one's self-image as a great meditator. On the other hand, one might suddenly feel peaceful, blissful and content, while engaged in a perfectly ordinary daily activity – like driving a truck.

Likewise, enlightenment, according to Bhagwan, was not something that could be methodically approached. It wasn't subject to the laws of cause and effect, so the idea of progressing towards it through a succession of stages – as Oscar Ichazo had taught in Arica – would never produce the desired result.

In fact, even to have a longing for enlightenment, I learned, created an impediment, because such longings were nothing but desires produced by the mind. It's hard to fathom but, since enlightenment was our essential nature, any effort to reach it only took us further away from it. We would be seeking it "there" when it was really "here".

So, any kind of approach needed to be very indirect. In this way, enlightenment was a wild card, a joker in the pack, a sudden crash of thunder.

Yes, you could meditate, but if you did so with great expectations of spiritual experiences, nothing was likely to happen. Rather, life needed to be lived in an ordinary way, although as consciously and as meditatively as possible, without hoping for enlightenment to occur. If your attitude was wrong, you could go on meditating for years without achieving it.

Bhagwan once told a very strange story, which I think is Indian in origin:

A yogi sat beneath a tree, meditating for 30 years, and eventually got upset, irritated and angry because in his view nothing was happening. He blamed his misfortune on the gods and left the tree. That evening, an ordinary peasant was walking by, when he saw the tree glowing with light. It was the energy that the yogi had created through his practice, but had then abandoned. The peasant felt magnetically attracted by the light and, without knowing anything about meditation, felt compelled to sit down beneath the tree and close his eyes. He became enlightened immediately.

This story conveys a truth about the enlightenment game: it's a very mysterious business. We might think, for example, that people living close to Bhagwan, or doing important jobs on the Ranch, were somehow more advanced, but in reality there was no spiritual hierarchy.

Moreover, one's own state of consciousness could change in an instant. Around Bhagwan, you could feel enlightened one moment, and the next moment feel like the most unconscious, unaware person on the planet.

To feel at home in oneself, relaxed and ordinary, taking each moment as it came, was perhaps the best attitude. This, indeed, fitted well with my job as a truck driver.

A Day in the Life

In 2013, nearly 30 years after the end of Rajneeshpuram, two film-making brothers, Maclain and Chapman Way, were in Oregon to make a documentary about an independent baseball team called the Portland Mavericks. While on location, several local people whom they were interviewing made remarks to them like, "Hey, if you guys enjoy making documentaries, you should have been here 30 years ago!"

That's how the Way brothers heard about "the Rajneesh invasion" and the conflict that ensued between the sect and the state. Still, they didn't think much about it until they stumbled on a treasure trove: 300 hours of archive footage about Bhagwan Shree Rajneesh and his followers.

The fact that this footage existed at all was a fluke, since in those days videotapes used by local television news affiliates were routinely recycled, over and over again, each time erasing the story that had been told the night before. But enough Oregon news channels real-ised the importance of the Rajneesh saga to preserve their tapes, which ultimately ended up in the hands of the Way brothers. The more footage they watched, the more intrigued they became and soon conceived the idea of a six-and-a-half-hour documentary series. Thus, the hit documentary *Wild Wild Country* was born.

Interviewed after Netflix launched the series, both brothers said they would have enjoyed living and working at the Ranch, while making it clear they wouldn't have been involved in criminal activities. Similar sentiments were echoed by Mark Duplass, one of the executive producers who helped the brothers make the series and sell it to Netflix.

"These were some of the greatest minds of their generation," reflected Duplass, in an interview about the Rajneesh community, "They were

Harvard graduates in city planning and engineering who came together, brought all their resources and built a city out of scratch."

He was particularly impressed by the green technology used in farming and protecting the environment, and by the promotion of women as leaders in the commune's key managerial positions, which he regarded as way ahead of its time.

So before I continue my story, I'd like to pay tribute to the ordinary sannyasins who lived and worked on the Ranch, and their astonishing achievement in creating a full-on township for 3,500 people in just over four years.

It was made possible, of course, by the love we felt towards Bhagwan, our desire to create facilities for everyone to stay with him, and our willingness to pour our total energy into the project without being paid a single dollar in return. The reward didn't come from a monthly pay-cheque, nor even from the finished product. It came during the process itself. For me, and I think for almost everyone, the buzz of being together, working during the day, dancing in the evening, making love at night, was the real return for our efforts.

So I never felt cheated by the collapse of the Ranch. I felt sad, of course. I felt angry, not only towards our opponents but also towards Sheela and Bhagwan. But I never felt robbed or in any way exploited. On the contrary, I felt grateful to have been part of such a unique experiment.

Here's a rough idea of how one of my days on the Ranch looked:

I lived in a trailer home, sharing a room with one other person, or maybe with three or four people if we'd had guests for the night. I'd wake up around 6:45am, jump in the shower, pull on my red clothes and get a bus ride to the canteen in time for breakfast shortly after 7:00am. There was time for porridge, or cornflakes, maybe toast and jam, with a cup of tea and a chance to joke around with some of my close friends. The main game among us, as I recall, was to see who could hold out longest before going for a second mug of tea, because whoever rose first from the table, mug in hand, was immediately presented with four or five other mugs to refill as well, amid much joking and teasing.

By 7:30am, we'd be at Rajneesh Buddhafield Garage, or RBG, where the taxis, pickups and trucks were parked for the night. We'd all gather together in the garage, sitting or kneeling on the floor, and recite the Three Refuges, which we'd adopted from traditional Buddhism:

Buddham Saranam Gachchami

Sangham Saranam Gachchami

Dhammam Saranam Gachchami

Roughly translated, this meant: I go to the feet of the Awakened One, I go to the feet of the Commune of the Awakened One, I go to the feet of the Absolute Truth of the Awakened One.

That done, we'd casually form into our functional groups: the sannyasins servicing the cars, those servicing the trucks and heavy equipment and the drivers going out to their various jobs. For a while, I was driving a Mac dump truck and there were usually about four or five of us, working as a team, with a coordinator directing us to the sites. These coordinators, who were usually men distinctive by the fact that they wore cowboy hats, had a Motorola slung in a holster on their belts and drove pickups. Women ran the garage administration, drove taxis and also operated some of the bulldozers and other heavy equipment.

Typically, we'd be instructed to drive to one of the gravel pits, where piles of gravel were heaped up into small mountains and a front-end loader would be parked nearby, waiting to fill our trucks with material that would be needed in a road-building or construction project somewhere else on the Ranch.

It was a simple and enjoyable routine: drive to the gravel pit, get loaded, drive to the site, dump the gravel, drive back to the pit. Often we'd have to wait, either to be loaded or to dump, and this would be a fine opportunity to continue reading a few chapters in another John Le Carré spy novel, passed on by a friend.

At 9:30 or 10:00am we'd stop work and rush off to the restaurant in the commune's shopping mall, where we'd enjoy a coffee break and, if we were feeling flush, eat fluffy omelettes, before returning to work. This was unofficial, really, because other work teams were accustomed to having their tea and coffee breaks on site, supplied by a portable tea wagon on the back of a pickup. The women who drove those pickups became known as "chai mamas" and were enthusiastically greeted wherever they went.

More driving and dumping followed until lunchtime and then, if it was summertime, we'd eat our meals quickly and board buses to take us to one of two lakes: either Krishnamurti Lake, which was our home-built reservoir, or the smaller, more remote Patanjali Lake, which was the nudist area. Naturally, the preferred scenery was at Patanjali Lake, where one could admire the women as well as take a leisurely swim around the little lake. But there were unexpected hazards. We'd stocked the lake with fish, and one guy, lingering near the shore, got the end of his penis nibbled by a curious, hungry trout. His sudden cry of alarm could be heard by everyone around the lake.

After a swim and a sunbathe, we'd arrive back in the downtown area of the Ranch in time for "drive-by", which was altogether different from the meaning this term acquired in Los Angeles. Our drive-by referred to Bhagwan's daily appearance in a Rolls-Royce. We would line up along one side of the road, watching and waiting as the mystic drove slowly past, giving us an Indian-style Namaste greeting with only one of his hands, while steering with the other. We'd return the salutation with both hands.

It became obvious to our truck-driving group that it would be more lively and fun to create a band – beating drums, slapping tambourines, playing horns – to celebrate his passing each day, and this soon became the norm. Often, Bhagwan would stop his car in front of us and wave both his hands in time to our beat, looking delighted and thoroughly enjoying this moment with us.

As soon as his car had passed, we would swing in behind it, playing all the way along the line until the end, at which point Bhagwan would take off at high speed, driving on a long, winding road that led to the Ranch's southern boundary. Then he'd turn around and drive back. This route was adopted as a safer alternative to driving off-Ranch, which by this time was deemed too risky as our war with Oregon began to heat up.

That was the only time we'd see Bhagwan. He played no further part in our daily lives except during festivals, and this, he told us later, was a deliberate move on his part, a challenge for us to see if we felt connected to him without his daily discourses.

More truck driving followed, then an afternoon tea break – usually on-site this time – then still more driving until 7:30pm rolled around, when we'd regroup at the garage, park our trucks, say another round of Gachchamis, then head for the canteen for supper. After supper, it was time to hit the disco, which doubled as a casino, so people could either dance, or drink, or gamble, depending on their preference. It was a fruitful place to connect with a member of the opposite sex and arrange a date for the night, or simply to have fun with friends.

One of the most memorable evenings during my time on the Ranch happened at the gambling tables, when a group of us truck drivers sat down together to play blackjack. The energy at the table was high and, as we started winning, it quickly rose higher, with much cheering and laughing, so that it seemed almost as if our energy was sucking the money across the table. The dealers, all approved by Sheela, looked increasingly desperate as our winnings mounted and they started swapping with each other, hoping the switch of dealers would break the energy. But it didn't. We just kept on winning.

Our total haul wasn't much by Las Vegas standards. I don't think we made more than a couple of hundred bucks, but since we started out with less than ten between us it was a major triumph. Next day, at the mall restaurant, it was omelettes all round, and we also paid a visit to the clothing store, where I bought myself a nice sunhat and others also found things to wear.

If we didn't have dates, then often we'd walk home together from the disco in the cool of the night, enjoying the peaceful nature around us, or else playing dumb boys' games, like trying to trip each other up without actually looking as if we were doing anything.

That was the day, the evening and the night. Of course, there were times when we all worked our asses off. For example, there was the so-called "townhouse crunch" – starting in 1983 and continuing into 1984 – when we had to build dozens of houses in a few weeks in order to beat a building moratorium that was going to be slapped on us by a hostile county government. Construction went on around the clock.

But it was all part of the chaos, fun, challenge and seemingly limitless energy that we felt during those hectic years. British colonialists, once upon a time, liked to refer to diplomatic manoeuvring with Imperial Russia over access to northern India as "The Great Game". For me, the same label could be applied to the creation of the Ranch. That was one of the greatest games I played in my life.

Out and About

During my career as a truck driver, I sometimes made off-Ranch trips, driving an articulated belly-dump to fill up with sand from a family-run gravel company near the town of Maupin in central Oregon. Exiting the Ranch, I'd always pass a white signboard, erected in the field of one of our God-fearing neighbours, which, in hand-painted black letters, warned our visitors: "Abandon hope all ye who enter herein."

Bhagwan chuckled when he heard about it. "Those fools don't know that they are preaching my thing," he said. To him, hope is a kind of postponement, always in the future. The real thing is to enjoy the present.

Further down the road, another local rancher had tied and spread-eagled several very dead coyotes to his fence, presumably as an indication of what he'd like to do to us. Those didn't bother me as much as the old guys, sitting in pickups on back-country roads, pointing a rifle or shotgun out of the driver's window. Were they waiting to shoot passing coyotes . . . or me? Once in a while, someone in a pickup would recognise my truck and give me the finger. One passenger wound down his window, climbed half-way out and sat on the door in order to raise his digit, just to be sure I got the message.

The family who ran the gravel and sand business were criticised for selling to us, but justified their action by citing poverty. "We like to eat in the winter," they explained. We were their best customer for cement-grade sand, which we needed for construction projects.

The wife thought she had my number. "We know what you do down there," she said one day with a knowing grin, "You put people on those low-protein diets so their brains can't function properly."

I shrugged. "Judging by the faces of folk in this area, I'd say the whole county is on a low-protein diet," I countered. She had to laugh.

One day, returning from Maupin to the Ranch, I found my turnoff from the highway blocked by the city garbage truck. The driver sat with his arms crossed, looking at me defiantly. But I guess he hadn't figured that I could turn at the next junction, because he looked astonished as I drove past at speed, waving cheerily.

It made for a longer trip, but the last thing I wanted was a confrontation on the highway. Out here in deepest central Oregon, I felt exposed, vulnerable and outnumbered, so I was glad that most of the locals saw fit to simply leave me alone. The fact that my trips were irregular, with no fixed schedule, also helped, I suspect, to keep me safe.

Maupin was named after a white settler called Howard Maupin, who had established the town of Antelope in 1863, operating a horse ranch and a stagecoach station on the road out to Canyon City and the gold fields of eastern Oregon. It was the same road that passed through the territory that would one day become the Big Muddy Ranch.

Maupin became famous for shooting a Paiute war leader called Chief Paulina, one of the last Native Americans in this part of Oregon to put up a fight against the white man's unrelenting encroachment on Indian lands. Chief Paulina was killed near Madras, not far from our Ranch, in 1867. It wasn't a fair fight. Paulina was bushwhacked by Maupin, who trailed the chief to his camp, crawled undetected into a concealed position in the brush, then shot him at long range with his Winchester rifle. Maupin then scalped the dead chief, taking his hair as a trophy and parading it through local towns before nailing it to his barn door in Antelope. When the survivors of Paulina's tribe heard about their chief's scalp being displayed in Antelope, the medicine men came to town one evening and cursed Maupin and his land forever.

When I heard about Maupin's slaying of Chief Paulina, it gave me chills and made me wonder if the Paiute leader would be the last Indian to be ambushed in our area.

But the bit about cursing Antelope made me smile. Maybe the arrival of another Indian leader and his red-clad tribe, which had so shocked and dismayed the townsfolk, disrupting their lifestyle, taking over their city, was the long-awaited fulfilment of the medicine men's curse.

Share-a-Home

I was driving past the canteen next to RBG in my dump truck, with a sinking feeling in my stomach. There was a long line of men, most of them wearing jeans, baseball caps and casual jackets, standing outside the canteen waiting for lunch. This line of "street people" was now a common sight and it was getting longer each day, as more and more of them arrived on the Ranch. It seemed to me they would soon outnumber the sannyasin population.

"That's enough, Sheela, for Christ's sake!" I said to myself, in the privacy of my cab. The days when I could have said it to her face were long gone.

But, in a way, I was lucky. I didn't want anything to do with this new "Share-a-Home" programme, in which homeless people were being bussed in from every major city in the United States. And I wasn't asked to. Most of the time, I was busy driving trucks while this bizarre scheme to take over Wasco County unfolded before my eyes. It was September 1984 and the county elections were less than two months away.

No one on our side admitted our agenda, but no one on their side was deceived. It was obvious: the unspoken aim of our apparently charitable invitation to America's homeless was to register as many street people as possible and sway the county election in our favour. To be honest, I didn't understand why Sheela felt the need to take over Wasco County. By now we had our own city, so to a degree we were self-governing. True, the legality of the City of Rajneeshpuram was being challenged in court, but, for the moment at least, we were a legally incorporated town. We also had Antelope, now renamed City of Rajneesh, where a new park for trailer homes was being constructed, expanding our presence there.

So why the county? Well, county officials could, to a certain extent, try to block our development plans, but there was another

257

possibility: I had a suspicion that Bhagwan might have put Sheela up to it, in order to keep the Rajneesh story on the front pages. Maybe he was already anticipating headlines like "Rajneeshees rename Wasco County as Rajneesh County," and chuckling over the furore it would cause.

Neither Sheela nor her close aides knew what they were taking on with the influx of street people, but they soon found out. The Ranch medical centre was immediately overwhelmed with sick people, suffering from AIDS, STDs, bronchitis, rashes, sores and also a great many with mental problems. This last category was the most trouble-some. Nobody had figured that America was solving its problem of what to do with psychologically disturbed people by leaving them on the streets, but it wasn't long before Sheela gained first-hand experience.

One afternoon, a guy started going berserk outside her office in Jesus Grove, swinging chairs around and threatening to crush people's heads with a rock. When Sheela came out to calm him down, he grabbed her by the throat and started to strangle her. Sheela was rescued by an American nurse with ethnic Filipino roots, called Puja, who had become one of her most trusted aides. According to testi-mony given later to federal investigators, Puja approached the man with a glass of water, which she'd laced with an anti-psychotic drug called Haldol, and persuaded him to have a drink. It knocked him out long enough to get him off the Ranch and back on the streets where he came from.

Most of those arriving on the Ranch seemed peaceful enough, but the ever-present threat of a sudden outbreak of violence was enough for Puja to begin injecting quantities of Haldol into the free beer given to the street people each evening, in the hope of keeping them calm. There's no evidence that it worked – most probably, it was too diluted to have any impact on the newcomers' behaviour.

To outside observers, the use of Haldol must have seemed shock-ingly unethical, which indeed it was, but more than that, it was an indication of the increasing sense of fear and desperation the Ranch leaders felt as they came to understand the threat of potential disorder and violence they had unleashed upon themselves, by inviting such huge numbers of street people into the commune. I have to say, I admired the guts of those ordinary sannyasins, both men and women, who looked after the dormitories and canteens, somehow managing to control these street people, who were 95 percent male.

But it's also true to say that some of these homeless men loved being on the Ranch, becoming enthusiastic workers and staying until the very end. Others received free medical treatment and cured their ailments. Not everyone was simply used and abused for the voting scheme.

Sheela held mass meetings with the street people, trying to weld them into a cohesive electoral force as voting day approached. It was at this point she uttered her notorious statement that became one of the most repeated video clips in all reports about the Ranch:

"I tell you, the county's so fucking bigoted it deserves to be taken over!"

A close second was her threat: "You tell your Governor, your Attorney General and all the bigoted pigs outside that if one person on Rancho Rajneesh is harmed, I will have 15 of their heads, and I mean it!"

The street people cheered and soon buses were being loaded to ferry them to The Dalles, the county's biggest town, where they would register to vote.

It never happened.

On 10 October, voter registration was halted by County Clerk Sue Proffitt because of "the probability of voter fraud". At the same time, two candidates sympathetic to the Rajneeshees were disqualified from running for the posts of Wasco County Commissioners, one because she failed to gather enough signatures to qualify, the other for suspicion of a fraudulent address.

Thwarted in her scheme, Sheela threatened to sue the county, but never did. Soon, large numbers of street people were being bussed off the Ranch and deposited in Portland and other nearby cities. By the end of 1984 only a handful remained. These, like I said, appreciated living on the Ranch and melted into the community.

The main casualty of the affair was one man who, having left the Ranch during wintry weather, was found near the roadside on snow-covered Mount Hood, having apparently got off a bus on the way to Portland. He died of exposure and may have become disoriented by overdosing on his medication, or mixing it with alcohol.

Afterwards, many commentators condemned our Share-a-Home episode as cynically exploitative, but that's too black-and-white for me. The intention was clear from the beginning: it was done in the hope of taking over the county, which didn't happen, and also creating massive publicity across America, which certainly did happen.

But there was more to it than that. The way the street people were welcomed, especially in the beginning, was caring and kind, and the free medical treatment they were given greatly benefitted them. So it was a mixed bag. Some were cured of dangerous diseases, while others – especially towards the end – got roughly handled.

For me, the Share-a-Home event did something to the purity of the Ranch. I don't judge it as good or bad, but somehow it polluted the atmosphere. To bus in hundreds of non-meditators and have them live among us may have been a test of our collective strength, but, even though we survived, it didn't feel good. As one of my friends commented, "The virgin has become a whore and no one wants her anymore."

Strictly speaking, it wasn't true. We still loved the Ranch and few of us were contemplating leaving. Nevertheless, it had tainted an otherwise beautiful atmosphere.

The Oval Office

I met him. I met the man who destroyed our city. I walked towards him as he stood outside the door of the Oval Office and raised my two hands in front of my chest, pressing my palms together in the classic Indian Namaste greeting as I looked him in the eyes.

I gave him plenty of time to see my mala, my necklace of wooden beads, with Bhagwan's face hanging from it in a locket. Then I shook his flabby, lifeless hand. Then we all went inside the Oval Office to have our photo taken.

I swear to God I am not making this up.

It was a bizarre occasion, the origins of which lie in a rural region of north-western Guyana in Central America. It was there, on 18 November 1978, that 909 members of the Peoples Temple Agricultural Project died from cyanide poisoning. I refer, of course, to the deaths at Jonestown.

At a nearby airstrip, Congressman Leo Ryan was also killed by Temple members, thereby becoming the first and only Congressman assassinated in the line of duty in the history of the United States. He'd flown down to Guyana from San Francisco to investigate complaints from his constituents that some of their family members were being held against their will in Jonestown.

After the killings, Ryan's daughter Pat campaigned lengthily and successfully for her late father to be awarded a Congressional Gold Medal, a decoration given – and I quote – "to an individual who performs an outstanding deed or act of service to the security, prosperity, and national interest of the United States". Winston Churchill received one posthumously in 1969, four years after his death. John Wayne got his in 1979, the same year he died. The Dalai Lama, alive and well in his 14th incarnation, was tapped in 2007.

Traditionally, the medal is awarded by the incumbent President of the United States. And so it was that, in the autumn of 1984, having attained the required signatures of two thirds of all members of the Senate and the House, Pat proudly led the Ryan family into the White House.

Where did I come in? Well, meanwhile, having divorced my Latin American wife, I'd married Shannon, Pat's sister, who was by that time a disciple of Bhagwan. To tell the truth, we wed so I could get a Green Card, but according to US immigration law you don't commit fraud unless the union is "solely" for that purpose. We kinda liked each other, so I figured it was legit. We tied the knot in Rajneeshpuram in a highly public ceremony, with no fewer than six TV news teams training their cameras on us. We were news. In the eyes of the media, the daughter of a man killed by a cult marrying into another cult was way too good a story to pass up.

That's why I say it was a bizarre occasion in the White House. For one thing, Ryan had been a liberal Democrat and was as far from Reagan's conservative views as one could imagine. For another, Pat was an active anti-cult campaigner, while her sister was walking into the Oval Office with a picture of her guru swinging from her neck.

Reagan didn't know what to say, so he said nothing. Maybe his scriptwriters couldn't get their heads around the paradoxes. Maybe the 72-year-old actor-president, just a decade away from being diagnosed with Alzheimer's, didn't know where Jonestown was, or who had died, or why a bunch of Democrats and two devotees of an Indian guru were standing in his office.

We lined up for the photo and somehow I managed to close my eyes in a blink exactly as the camera clicked. The incumbent President of the United States then presented the medal to Leo's mother, who reminded Reagan of those few occasions when he and the late Rep. Ryan had met, thereby extending the length of the ceremony from one minute to three.

In record time, it was over.

As Reagan stood awkwardly, waiting for us to leave, I wondered whether to walk over and say, "By the way, greetings from Bhagwan." But the suited guys with mean stares, radio earphones and tell-tale bulges in their jackets didn't look as though they'd let me. Besides, I liked Pat and didn't want to spoil her party.

Afterwards, on the lawn, Shannon told the waiting press corps: "I think my father would have understood and approved my decision to become a disciple of Bhagwan."

Hmm . . . not *tooooo* sure about that one, honey. But anyway, when the Ryan family appeared on the breakfast news on CNN the following morning, it was Shannon who was given the most air time. Pat was not amused.

The Hollywood Crowd

Sheela's downfall, when it finally came, began innocently enough with the arrival on the Ranch of the so-called "Hollywood Crowd". This was a group of wealthy sannyasins who'd been living in Beverly Hills, California, and who in 1983 left behind their luxurious homes in order to rough it with the rest of us in the wilds of central Oregon.

To me, they seemed like nice people who kept mostly to themselves and didn't seem interested in puffing themselves up or playing any power games. In fact, I have the feeling it was hard for them to live on the Ranch because they were used to Tinseltown luxury and this was in short supply in our neck of the woods.

However, one thing they did pulled them into the spotlight and set them on a collision course with Sheela. They informed Bhagwan that the rather plain and homely-looking material used to make his robes, sewn on the Ranch by his seamstresses, could be replaced with brilliant, fashionable fabrics from southern California's most exclusive clothing stores – Hollywood is, after all, Hollywood.

Bhagwan liked the idea and asked to see samples of the materials, which were shown to him by a Jewish-American woman in her late forties called Hasya. Prior to meeting Bhagwan and becoming a sannyasin, she was known as Françoise Ruddy, and in days gone by had divorced a billionaire businessman then married a film producer called Al Ruddy. According to her, it was she who'd handed him a novel titled *The Godfather* and persuaded him to produce it, winning him an Oscar for Best Picture.

"I produced the producer," murmured Hasya drily, while recalling her movie-mogul days during one of our conversations. I'd met her through my work on the newspaper and we thereafter stayed friends. She was graceful, attractive and intelligent. She was also very self-contained but with a lovely sense of humour, and smoked cigarettes continuously and elegantly like the Hollywood diva she used to be.

Eventually she had tired of the glamour lifestyle, become interested in meditation and travelled to India to meet Bhagwan in darshan, then joined the Hollywood Crowd in Beverley Hills before arriving on the Ranch. She was granted personal access to Bhagwan in his trailer home, in order to talk about robes and hats, and this created suspicion in Sheela, who was always watchful about any possible threat to her position.

I heard a rumour that his secretary was particularly upset about a million-dollar watch that Bhagwan had told Hasya he was interested in acquiring. Sheela, it seemed, thought the money could be better spent on the commune. Arguments began between the two factions, with Hasya saying "I can't say 'no' to Bhagwan," while Sheela was taking the opposite view: saying "no" to Bhagwan's outlandish requests was necessary. This, paradoxically, weakened Sheela's position, since her role as Bhagwan's secretary depended on her ability to do what he wanted.

But if the Hollywood Crowd made Sheela feel insecure, a parallel development must have shaken the ground beneath her feet, because in late October 1984, Bhagwan began speaking in public again. Out of the blue, during his lunchtime drive through the Ranch, he pulled up next to a waiting Portland television news team, powered down the window of his Rolls-Royce Silver Spur, and answered a question about his spiritual movement.

"Tell those guys this is the first and last religion," he said with a smile, then drove off.

Three days later, he began giving discourses every evening in Lao Tzu House, his trailer home, to a select gathering of about 30 disciples – therapists, Ranch managers and his personal staff – whom he called "The Chosen Few". If this sounds elitist, don't be surprised. Bhagwan was forever creating "in crowd" scenarios for us to chew on. Back in Pune, female disciples longed to be chosen as one of his energy mediums, while male sannyasins jockeyed for a place in the "samurai guard" team that kept Bhagwan's house secure.

During my brief career as "Voice of Bhagwan" I'd seen a piece of paper on which Bhagwan created a totally new structure for the ashram, including myself as "President of the Inner Circle of Mediums". But that was nothing compared to a list of 21 enlightened disciples that he issued in Oregon, only to dismiss the whole thing as a joke a few weeks later.

The night he broke his silence, Bhagwan came into the room looking like he'd returned from another galaxy. He sat in his chair, gazed into a mystical distance just above our heads and, after an eternal pause, said slowly, "It is a little difficult for me to speak again . . ."

It was always cold in that room. Very cold. So cold, in fact, that the regulars began calling themselves "The Frozen Few". I was an occasional guest and was warned ahead of time to wear several layers of clothing. As for the rest of the community, on Bhagwan's instructions they were shown a video of each of his discourses on the following evening, after dinner in the main meditation hall.

If Sheela didn't like Bhagwan reclaiming the spotlight – the news media were now focusing on him, not her – then worse was to come. On 19 December, Bhagwan said he would destroy any possibility of his religion being exploited by an organisation, adding, "That promise you can always remember: I will not leave you under a fascist regime."

The videotape of this discourse mysteriously disappeared – the "fascist regime" stole it – so it was never shown to the whole community. But 30 people had heard it and our extremely efficient bush telegraph spread the news like a prairie fire.

Still, as a truck driver minding his own business, I wasn't aware of a power shift developing in the way the Ranch was run. It was my politically astute colleague Mutribo who informed me. One morning, at RBG, he sprinted across the garage forecourt, jumped up on the running board of my rig, stuck his head in the passenger-side window and said excitedly, "Did you hear what Bhagwan said last night?"

I shook my head.

"He talked about Sheela and her group having an argument with Hasya and her group."

The news didn't strike me as earth-shattering, but it should have. This little tiff between two rival power groups was significant, Mutribo patiently explained to me, because instead of supporting Sheela – as he'd always done in the past – Bhagwan had treated the two factions equally. Sheela's power was diminishing, Mutribo assured me, and his analysis proved correct.

Lord Acton, the nineteenth-century historian and moralist, became immortal through a single observation: "Power tends to corrupt, and absolute power corrupts absolutely." Bhagwan disagreed. "Power never corrupts," he argued. "The corruption is already there. Power reveals the truth. Power provides the means for the corruption to become manifest."

All in all, I'm glad it wasn't me standing in Sheela's shoes. So much media attention, so many public battles, plus the adoration of thousands of sannyasins expressing their love to their master through you. It would be hard not to be carried away to la-la-land, floating skywards in a hot-air balloon of self-importance.

Bhagwan's next step in reclaiming centre stage happened a few months later, when he stopped giving evening discourses in his house and switched to giving morning discourses for the whole community in the Ranch's big meditation hall. Now he was really back in the spotlight and suddenly we all found ourselves promoted to "the chosen few".

I had little contact with Sheela, so I had no direct experience of how she was handling all this. But I did notice, around the summer of 1985, that her behaviour was becoming bizarre. At the annual summer festival, in July, she staged a weird piece of theatre for new arrivals, fabricating an argument with her closest aides, which was supposed to illustrate that power trips weren't allowed on the Ranch.

"Hey, come on guys, I have the power here!" Sheela exclaimed, as her lieutenants feebly made a show of trying to take it away from her. I noticed they weren't trying too hard, no doubt worrying that a convincing performance might prove fatal to their Ranch careers.

Around the same time, I was having dinner with a friend in the Ranch's à la carte restaurant, which had opened for business as part of our recently constructed shopping mall complex in what used to be the old ranch yard. My friend was paying. As usual, I didn't have a buck to my name. We'd just been served the main course when Sheela approached our table, clutching a bunch of forks in her hand, asking if she could taste our food. Apparently, she didn't trust the quality of the dishes created by Ranch chefs and this was her way of checking.

To me it seemed doubly odd: first, because managers of restaurants don't usually go around picking food off customers' plates; second, because after Bhagwan's AIDS warning we were urged to be super hygienic on the Ranch, whereas Sheela herself seemed quite happy to pick up any old germs from our half-eaten food.

But I wasn't about to argue. "Go ahead," I said and my friend also nodded.

Sheela skewered a couple of morsels on our plates, chewed on them, asked for our opinions – "yes, we like our food, thank you" – then moved on to the next table.

One more curious incident: as a trucker, with my bum almost continuously on the driver's seat, I was suffering from a sweat rash around my asshole. One day in the canteen, meeting Devaraj, Bhagwan's personal doctor, I asked him if he had any ointment that might help. Devaraj looked at me oddly and replied in the negative, but a few days later met me again and covertly slipped a small tube of cream into my hand, rather like a pusher making a drug deal.

"Don't tell anyone I gave it to you," he murmured, then walked away.

It wasn't until later, when I heard about Sheela's antipathy towards Bhagwan's personal staff, that I realised why Devaraj was so cautious. Following our increasingly strict Ranch protocol, I should have taken my anal condition to our medical centre for treatment, where other doctors were officially working. Devaraj wasn't part of this authorised medical team. Already taking heat from Sheela, he didn't want to give her another excuse for ragging on him.

Generally, though, I didn't give Sheela much thought. I knew she was under pressure, from the mounting opposition to our commune and also because of her desperate desire to please Bhagwan, but I assumed she considered herself capable of handling it.

One of the great virtues of driving trucks is that you tend *not* to get grand ideas about your social or spiritual status. And that's another reason why I wasn't particularly interested in keeping tabs on the political situation as it developed on the Ranch. I could still remember the stress of running the newspaper and was glad to be out of the game.

Somewhere, amid the hills of central Oregon, a battle was being fought – several battles, in fact. But, meanwhile, the sun was shining and the skies were blue. I was driving down an open road and I was happy.

Sheela Departs

At the end of the Ranch, it became clear to me that Sheela had no understanding of the relationship between a spiritual master and his disciples. She loved Bhagwan, but she loved him as a woman, not as a sannyasin. He loved her, but not in the way for which she longed. He never made love to her.

"I have made it a point never to sleep with my secretary," he told the media, with astonishing frankness, after Sheela had left. He never usually talked about his love life.

When the breaking point came, Sheela totally miscalculated how it would happen. In September 1985, I was driving a dump truck way out on the southern periphery of the Ranch, when I stopped off for a chat with a friend who was operating a bulldozer in a nearby quarry. He gave me the news: "Sheela's leaving the Ranch."

It was hard to believe, because her regime seemed so entrenched. I drove to the downtown area, parked and walked to Jesus Grove, where Sheela lived. She was sitting on her sofa, talking to a group of department managers, the people responsible for running the Ranch's various functions . . . kitchens, house cleaning, tool shops, truck farm and so on. She was trying to convince them to leave with her.

"I've had it," she said. "I can't take any more. Bhagwan doesn't care about the commune. He doesn't care about you. He's only interested in getting more and more Rolls-Royces, more and more diamond watches . . ."

She went on like this for a long time, referring contemptuously to "the Hollywood Crowd" who were going to take over from her. Curiously, I found the sight of Sheela badmouthing Bhagwan a refreshing spectacle. For years, she'd been harassing us, repeatedly insisting on 100 percent positivity from everyone. Now here she was, letting her own suppressed negativity spew out like a busted sewage pipe.

The trigger for her dramatic change – I found out later – was a mildly delivered public rebuke by Bhagwan in his morning discourse. I wasn't there that day. I think I must have been on an early work shift. Apparently, Sheela had written a letter to him, asking why she no longer felt excited when returning to the Ranch from her international trips. He explained that her ego was suffering, because, since he was speaking again, all the media attention was now focused on him – he no longer needed a spokeswoman.

That was enough. His devoted secretary was out of the door for good. As I saw it, Sheela's sudden turnaround was like the spiteful reaction that is so typical of modern-day divorce proceedings, when the loving couple suddenly start snarling and snapping at each other. Having played the faithful "housewife", Sheela vindictively wanted to wreck the family home by taking all the important managers with her.

But nobody felt like leaving, including me. I liked the Hollywood Crowd, and the prospect of having them in charge of the Ranch was appealing. Moreover, the choice of remaining with an enlightened mystic or leaving in the company of a former hotel waitress whom nobody liked anyway really wasn't a tough call.

In the end, only a handful of Sheela's closest personal aides went with her. Most of them, it turned out, were implicated in crimes and nearly all of them did jail time as a result. From what I was told later, Sheela thought she could take the meditation centres in Europe away from Bhagwan, or at least some of them, because of the royal treatment they'd given her when she'd been touring Germany, Italy, Holland and other countries.

On 14 September 1985, Sheela left America and landed in Switzerland, where she tried to set herself up in a Rajneesh centre in Zurich. Her stay didn't last more than a few hours. One phone call from Bhagwan's staff and it was all over. Not a single one of Bhagwan's meditation centres or communes in Europe was willing to support her.

It must have been a sobering moment when Sheela finally realised that all the power, all the attention and all the love that had been showered on her during the Ranch years had been borrowed from the man she'd been representing. As soon as she ceased to be his secretary, it evaporated.

That's why I say she didn't understand the master–disciple game. Otherwise, she could never, even in her wildest dreams, have imagined that anyone would see her as an alternative to Bhagwan. Nor would she have tried to leave the commune in a chaos.

"The commune is always in a chaos, nobody can disturb it," commented an unperturbed Bhagwan, when he heard about her intention. So that didn't work either. Defeated and isolated, she rented a house in a small village in the Black Forest and stayed there . . . until the cops came knocking at her door.

Whistle Blower

"I love to disturb people," Bhagwan told a journalist who interviewed him in the summer of 1985, "because only by disturbing them can I make them think."

He explained that he wanted people to connect with him emotionally, either positively or negatively, making it impossible for them to remain neutral or to forget him. "Nobody can remain hostile for long," he explained. "Hate can very easily turn into love, just as love can turn into hate. They are two sides of the same coin."

Bhagwan was soon to bring "disturbance" to a whole new level. After Sheela left, sannyasins who'd kept silent about her criminal activities started to come forward and Bhagwan went public with the whole can of worms in his daily discourses.

From September, he listed a host of crimes, including extensive wiretapping, attempts to kill members of his personal staff, a conspiracy to assassinate US Attorney Charles Turner, and a bid to influence a county election by spraying salmonella bacteria on salad bars in The Dalles, making about 700 people sick. To top it off, Bhagwan invited the FBI and the State Police to come to the Ranch and investigate his allegations.

Dumping my dump truck, I switched back to the *Rajneesh Times* as the story escalated and I soon realised how dangerous it was for Bhagwan to blow the whistle on Sheela. I'm not saying he shouldn't have done it. But I was certainly impressed by the fact that he did. From an ordinary man's perspective of avoiding trouble and staying out of jail, Bhagwan had nothing to gain and everything to lose by exposing her crimes. Her wrongdoing was bound to reflect on him, since he'd appointed her as his secretary and given her control over the Ranch.

From her side, Sheela had seemed confident that Bhagwan wouldn't risk exposing her illegal activities, calculating perhaps that he'd been sufficiently aware of them to be incriminated as an accomplice. The extent of his knowledge remains unclear. Clearly, he didn't instruct her to plant a bugging device in his own room, or encourage her to rub out members of his personal staff, but he'd allowed her to create a virtual police state and escalate the conflict with the world outside by fair means or foul.

Since all these crimes could have been hushed up with just one word from him, a cover-up would have been the obvious and safest course. But no, not with Bhagwan. He enthusiastically opened our very own Pandora's Box and soon the Ranch was crawling with cops, reporters and TV crews.

From Germany, Sheela struck back with allegations of her own, but these focused on his lavish taste in cars and watches, and his use of drugs like Valium and nitrous oxide, not on serious crimes, which she strenuously denied. "Sheela Brands Rajneesh 'Liar'" screamed the *Oregonian*, revelling in the war of words now flying between them.

Personally, I was surprised and disappointed by Bhagwan's use of drugs. According to my own assumptions of what enlightened people did, or did not, do, he shouldn't have needed them. But then again, I'd also assumed he would know when his room was being bugged and that he could outsmart the US government and keep us all safe for eternity. So much for my assumptions.

Bhagwan didn't seem to mind Sheela's allegations. When an Australian TV commentator asked to show him video clips of Sheela making a series of accusations against him, he agreed to respond on camera to each one. The answer I remember, the one that intrigued me most, was to her accusation, "Bhagwan, you exploit people." He immediately agreed saying, "Yes, it's true, because that is the only way they learn."

During another interview, Bhagwan called Sheela "a bitch", which I have to say seemed rather low-class for an enlightened mystic, and on another occasion he described her as "a real snake". But on the whole he was compassionate towards her, saying the real fault lay with the American government for its persecution of our community.

Many journalists were annoyed and frustrated by Bhagwan's refusal to take responsibility for Sheela's misdeeds. He did apologise, just once, saying in public discourse, "The fault is mine, I was in silence." But after that, he drove interviewers almost crazy by his unrepentant, unapologetic attitude. For me, it was fascinating, because it gave me fresh insight into the master–disciple relationship.

"I have chosen to be a master, that is my responsibility," he told one reporter who quizzed him on the issue. "They have chosen to be my disciples . . ." he paused, chuckled and waved a hand in a gesture of dismissal, ". . . that is not my responsibility!" In other words, the master offers his guidance, but what you do with it is entirely your own responsibility. So, at no time can a disciple make his master responsible for what he himself does.

As far as my own responsibility was concerned, I felt grateful that Sheela never tried to embrace me in her secret group of criminals, nor asked me to do anything illegal. The reason, I assume, is that she considered me too independent and too unreliable, with a built-in tendency to do what I think best, not what I'm told.

Many people, journalists and sannyasins alike, felt Bhagwan should have replaced Sheela much earlier in the game. I'm told he was warned repeatedly by Vivek, his personal caretaker, that Sheela was turning the Ranch into a police state and would destroy the commune.

Afterwards, he admitted that Vivek had been right, then added mysteriously, "But my wrong is my wrong." In other words: even when I'm wrong, I'm right – an original and intriguing attitude. Certainly, he never once said he regretted anything that happened on the Ranch, nor, come to think of it, anything that ever happened in his whole life.

Meanwhile, the police investigation had slowed and the crowd of journalists was starting to thin out. The new Ranch leadership did its best to persuade the media to stay.

"But why?" one cameraman asked me, after listening to their pleas, "The story's over."

"Because they think the feds are coming to get Bhagwan," I replied, "They're afraid the cops will use this investigation as a smokescreen to find excuses to grab him. And they think you are our best protection against a bloodbath."

The Incompetent Hit Squad

Really, one shouldn't laugh about such things. But, having a warped sense of humour, and having written several plays myself, I can't help thinking it would make a wonderful black comedy.

The stage for this theatrical drama was set by Sheela and her small group of conspirators who, departing from both reality and common sense, devised a whole series of criminal exploits aimed at relieving the ever-increasing pressure they were feeling from our opponents. When these events were first revealed, in the autumn of 1985, there were so many allegations and counter-allegations that I hardly knew what to think. But after leaving the Ranch, I tried to find out what really happened.

My snoopy, journalistic nature demanded answers.

The task wasn't difficult. A detailed investigation of the American government's efforts to deport Bhagwan and shut down our Oregon commune was published by author Max Brecher in his book *A Passage to America*. He interviewed all the main players, including politicians, cops, agents and officials.

On our side of the fence, the deeds done in the name of protecting Bhagwan were available in testimony delivered to the FBI by a number of Ranch residents who'd been involved in illegal activities and who chose to confess all in exchange for immunity agreements and plea bargains. These included the first mayor of Rajneeshpuram, Krishna Deva, who'd been a key member of Sheela's trusted circle, and a young Hispanic woman called Ava Avalos, who was the first to turn state's evidence. Avalos had arrived on the Ranch from San Diego in the summer of 1982, and her enthusiasm and organisational skills soon led her to become involved in Ranch management, then gradually in criminal activities. There were many more informers and they all told the same story: they had agreed to act illegally out of an overriding concern to protect Bhagwan and the community.

It was reading these confessions that conjured up visions in my mind of theatrical black humour. Because, even though the scenario was fraught with peril, and the conspirators serious in their intent, it is really a tale of almost comical ineptitude. So many things went wrong that I started to wonder whether, deep down in their hearts, any of these Ranch conspirators wished to succeed in their criminal endeavours. Or maybe Bhagwan was pulling strings, on some higher plane of existence, thwarting their every plan.

First, a little background:

According to testimony given by Ava Avalos, trouble began on the Ranch when Sheela became convinced that the mystic's personal staff were a danger to his health. In particular, she targeted his English doctor, Devaraj, whom she believed was conducting medical experiments with Bhagwan's body – mainly in the form of administering drugs – without the mystic's consent.

In fact, it was a half-truth. Experiments were being conducted, but on Bhagwan's own initiative. For example, when offered nitrous oxide during a dental procedure, Bhagwan reported seeing vivid images from his childhood, and subsequently dictated a number of books while under the influence of the gas. Apparently, he also experimented with steroids to relieve his asthma and valium to feel more comfortable in his body.

So the doctor was following the mystic's instructions. Nevertheless, Sheela was determined to replace Devaraj with a physician of her choice. According to Avalos' testimony, Sheela's trusted nurse Puja slipped a large dose of laxative into the poor fellow's coffee and, once he had been admitted as a patient to the medical centre, continued to add generous doses of laxatives to his meals. Even though the doctor was incapacitated, the plan failed. Throughout the mystic's time on the Oregon Ranch, Bhagwan resisted all attempts by Sheela to replace his personal staff, including his doctor, dentist, caretaker and others. This was a source of continuous frustration for his secretary. But Sheela's critics experienced similar frustration. In spite of repeated advice from a variety of people, sannyasins and non-sannyasins alike, Bhagwan steadfastly refused to replace Sheela as his secretary.

Meanwhile, outside the Ranch, the range war was starting to heat up. One obstacle was Dan Durow, Wasco County's planner, who was refusing to grant Ranch construction permits. His office was targeted. A hit team broke in at night, scattered Durow's files all over the floor, lit a fire, then legged it back to the Ranch. Next day, answering questions from journalists, Durow made a point of saying that files pertaining to Rajneeshpuram – the name given to our city – had been kept elsewhere and were undamaged.

Another bizarre scheme to destroy Durow's office required Rajneesh pilots, who were flying old, twin-propeller DC3s, to crash a plane into the building, parachuting out at the last moment. The pilots regarded the scheme not only as ridiculous but most probably suicidal for themselves. They refused.

Around the same time, a wealthy woman who had loaned Sheela a substantial amount of money began a court action in Portland, Oregon, to get it back. According to Avalos, a hit team was dispatched to her hotel with the intention of "bumping her off". The team was unable to discover the woman's room number, because the hotel's reception staff refused to give it to them. Avalos, watching the hotel's CCTV system through an office window, suddenly noticed that, far from stalking their target, the hit team was being stalked – by hotel security staff! She rushed to warn them and brought them quickly out of the hotel, speaking Spanish as a way to confuse suspicious hotel officials.

The *Oregonian* newspaper, which had followed the Rajneesh story from the very beginning, announced it was going to publish a 21-part investigative series about Bhagwan, Sheela and the Ranch. So a hit team was sent to destroy the newspaper's computers. Avalos describes the building of a special machine, nicknamed "Thumper", that allegedly had the power to fry any computer within range. But there was a problem: when completed, the machine proved to be so big and heavy it was impossible to transport and conceal.

As an alternative, a team of female "cleaners", complete with uniforms and cleaning equipment, was sent into the *Oregonian*'s office to locate the computers and destroy them.

But their uniforms were different from the company employees who had the cleaning contract. This was spotted and, once more, a quick retreat was needed.

As the conflict intensified, a bomb-making team began work on the Ranch. Most probably, this venture was conceived after the bombing of our hotel in Portland by an Islamic extremist. Chemicals were purchased for making bombs on the Ranch, but it soon became apparent that the project posed far more danger to the people trying to make these devices than any intended target. It was abandoned.

Meanwhile, Bhagwan's doctor had again been made ill and was admitted to the Ranch's medical centre, with the intention, this time, of permanently removing him from the scene. A hit team arrived at the centre, assuming the doctor had been sedated and would therefore be an easy target. When they looked in his room, however, he was wide awake. The plot was postponed. When, finally, a would-be assassin managed to stick a needle in the doctor's buttocks, during a crowded summer festival gathering in July 1984, the poor man fell ill but soon recovered in a local hospital.

A county commissioner called Ted Comini, who opposed Ranch development, was also targeted. When the hit team found out that Comini was in hospital in Portland for an ear operation, they dressed up as nurses and went to his hospital room with the intention of injecting unknown substances into the intravenous drip attached to his arm. There was only one problem: Comini hadn't been fitted with an IV drip. The plan was dropped.

Vivek was also marked for disposal. Armed with a master key, the hit squad slipped through the fence surrounding Bhagwan's compound and approached her door in the dead of night . . . only to find the key didn't work. Vivek had prudently changed the lock. The only casualty from this misadventure, it turned out, was a female member of the hit team who was carrying a cloth soaked in anaesthetic, which was supposed to be held against Vivek's face. The woman got so sick from the fumes that she had to lie in bed for days.

According to Avalos, during this time, Sheela told the team that "Bhagwan was not to know what was going on" and they were to lie if questioned by him.

Meanwhile, in a special laboratory known as "the Chinese laundry", Puja was cooking up a variety of chemical cocktails intended to "bump people off". In fact, although some people did become ill through these toxic substances – adrenaline and potassium chloride seemed to be her favourites – nothing ever worked the way it should. Everyone survived.

An attempt to influence the Wasco County elections in November 1984 by lacing salad bars in The Dalles with salmonella did succeed in making 700 people sick. But this was a rehearsal, held before election day. On the day itself, no attempt was made, most probably because the two pro-Rajneesh candidates had been disqualified and the imported street people were blocked from registering to vote.

This, by the way, was how we got classified by the US government as "bio-terrorists", a darkly sinister label that, since there were no fatalities, to me seemed a tad overstated. If you want to meet real bio-terrorists, I suggest you take a look at a whole gallery of American presidents and Congressmen who have denied global warming and refused to do anything to prevent climate change. That's a bio-terror-ist threat to the entire planet.

A scheme to eliminate Charles Turner, US Attorney for Oregon, was elaborately planned, with lengthy surveillance of his home and office, but it was never carried out. By that time, it seems, nobody in the hit squad was willing to pull the trigger.

The list of unsuccessful projects goes on, with many twists and turns, getting odder as time passed. For example, one man who'd been instrumental in bugging a large number of rooms on the Ranch was more than a little surprised, when using his bathroom one evening, to observe tell-tale signs that someone had placed a listening device in the wall of his room. The bugger had been bugged!

"The Rajneeshees were very incompetent in doing their dirty work," reflected Bernie Smith, Wasco County's attorney, afterwards. "They came up with the most grandiose schemes. They had all these plans to kill to hell everybody, but the truth is that no one was killed." Smith joked that one professional hit man from a New York gang could have achieved in five minutes what a whole team of Rajneeshnees failed to do in months.

Sheela denied all allegations made against her, but towards the end of 1985 was extradited from Germany to the US, where she pleaded guilty to a number of crimes, including the salmonella attack on restaurants in The Dalles and charges of attempted murder. She was sentenced to 20 years in prison, but was released after 39 months. On gaining her liberty, she immediately flew to Switzerland, where she felt safe from further prosecution. Years later, however, Sheela was convicted of conspiracy to assassinate Charles Turner, but was sentenced to time already served, so did not return to prison. She continues to live in Switzerland, managing two nursing homes. When interviewed by the BBC in 2019, following the success of *Wild Wild Country*, Sheela remained defiant, protesting her innocence and saying, "I have done no criminal act."

A very different story is told in *Breaking the Spell*, an in-depth account of Sheela's intrigues by her most loyal lieutenant from those days, Jane Stork, also known as Ma Shanti Bhadra and frequently referred to by sannyasins on the Ranch as "Shanti B". In her book, published in 2009, Shanti B recounted how, on 5 July 1985, Sheela had asked for a volunteer to get rid of Bhagwan's doctor:

There was silence in the room. No one spoke. The silence seemed interminable. Slowly, ever so slowly, sounds formed in my throat and a disembodied voice came out of me and said, "I will do it."

Shanti B agreed to inject the doctor with poison. She was also selected to be one of those who would try to assassinate US Attorney Charles Turner, because, in Sheela's own words, "she's a good shot".

Speaking of dark humour, my own reaction to these revelations was captured in a joke that went around the Ranch in the autumn of 1985: "We are the people our mothers warned us against." Beyond the joke, however, I felt a strange inevitability about the whole affair, as if we were acting according to a script, not unlike HBO's fantasy series *Game of Thrones*, which would one day capture the public's imagination.

It felt like that: a work of fiction, with stereotype combatants. I couldn't quite believe how predictable it all was: how the US government could be so predictably disturbed by us, how the American people could be so predictably upset with us, and how Sheela and her aides could feel so predictably threatened that we would end up looking exactly like the weird, dangerous cult we thought we would never be.

I'd assumed we were above it all, almost like puppeteers: fuelling people's fears, provoking their prejudices, fanning the flames of controversy, hitting the headlines, but all with a sense of theatre. As far as being a "Rajneeshee" was concerned, I never really saw myself fitting into this media-generated category, so it came as a surprise to me that others had taken their roles in the drama so seriously.

And what about Bhagwan? Was he surprised by all the revelations? When a journalist asked him this question, his reply was brief and to the point:

"Nothing surprises me," he answered.

The Questions

It was never clear to me, or indeed, to anybody, how much Bhagwan knew of Sheela's criminal activities. However, the issue needs to be addressed, so this is what I've learned:

It seems Bhagwan did come to know about the bugging in his house because suspicious members of his personal staff swept their own compound with an electronic detector, locating four of them, then informed the mystic.

Bhagwan's response? I'm paraphrasing, but it went something like: "If Sheela feels the need for such things, leave them where they are." Eventually, closer to the time of Sheela's departure, he started to suspect that his own room was also being bugged.

It's obvious that Bhagwan gave his consent to the takeover of the nearby town of Antelope, in 1982. He admitted as much in a press interview, where he explained that hostility from the locals left them with no choice:

"My people thought that the best way was to take over the government. What is the need of asking permission from these people when we have the government and we give the permission? – so they took over, there was no problem in it."

He also agreed to the influx of street people, in 1984:

"Last year we brought thousands of street people to share our homes with us, and the Oregon government got simply mad about it. They started thinking that we were going to take over the county or we were going to take over Oregon."

With good reason, one might add. To invite the media to believe that the timing of this influx before the November 1984 elections was just coincidental was a bit of a stretch, even for a master storyteller like Bhagwan.

One of Sheela's secretaries, Kate Strelley, authored her own analysis of events in a book published soon after the Ranch ended, titled *The*

Ultimate Game: The Rise and Fall of Bhagwan Shree Rajneesh. In it, Strelley reported that following Sheela's sudden departure, she was asked to help clean up the former secretary's personal files, some of which had been left behind. The content of these files was enough for her to conclude that "it was Bhagwan at the centre of things". But her book was short on detail and Strelley appeared to confound her own judgement by quoting Bhagwan as telling Sheela: "Whatever you have to do, do it. I just don't want to know what you do."

Following the attack on his personal doctor, Bhagwan had questioned Sheela, who retaliated by accusing the doctor of fabricating the story. I was later told that Sheela produced a bloody safety pin and showed it to Bhagwan, saying it was found by laundry workers in Devaraj's robe, and that he must have sat on it, thinking he'd been attacked with a syringe. The mystic then told his doctor to get more evidence and, when none was forthcoming, took no action against Sheela.

Federal prosecutors, at several court hearings, claimed that Bhagwan had authorised the assassination attempt on US Attorney Charles Turner. This accusation, it seems, was based on a conversation held between Sheela and Bhagwan, secretly taped by the secretary, in which Sheela said she was thinking of eliminating the federal official. Apparently, the mystic commented that if someone had shot Adolf Hitler when he was a young man, the world would have been a better place.

Shortly after Bhagwan's deportation from the US, when the Ranch was winding down, I spoke with Major Robert Moine, a senior officer in the Oregon State Police, who told me he'd read the transcript of this taped conversation. Moine expressed doubts about Bhagwan's involvement in the Turner plot.

"Did he really know what she was saying?" Moine queried. In our chat, he seemed more interested in the mystic's ability to unburden people of religious guilt – thereby helping them to enjoy life more fully – than with Bhagwan's own guilt as an alleged criminal. I think Moine was a closet Bhagwan fan.

In any case, in spite of all the sound and fury, claims and counter-claims, the only charges ever brought against Bhagwan by US prosecutors were related to immigration fraud.

What to make of it all? All I can say is "I don't know." But I would like to add this: whatever did, or did not happen, in the Oregon years,

Bhagwan's *modus operandi* throughout his life was that of a provoca-teur, not a mafia don. He wanted to wake people up, not bury them in the ground.

Alan Watts, the British philosopher and Zen teacher, once cautioned spiritual seekers that on the inward journey during the process of losing one's ego, "the consequences may not be behaviour along the lines of conventional morality."

Eloquently said! In other words, the desire to identify oneself as a "good person" may go down the tube. It's interesting to note that, before he was safely reinvented and sanitised by his followers as the ultimate good guy, JC held a similar attitude. In the Gospel of Philip, which is part of the Gnostic Gospels, Yeshua (Jesus) expresses his non-dualistic viewpoint thus:

Light and darkness, life and death, right and left
Are brothers and sisters. They are inseparable.
This is why goodness is not always good,
Violence not always violent . . .

Remembering this quote, I understood why I had been so inter-ested in discovering what had happened. I'd been trying to squeeze my understanding of events on the Oregon Ranch into the wrong box. I'd been struggling to find an explanation that would satisfy my own ideas about conventional morality.

Only one problem with that: it didn't work. Not with Bhagwan.

"I do not teach morality at all," he told us, on one occasion, explaining that ready-made ideas about good and bad, right and wrong, create as many problems as they solve.

"My whole effort is to make your morality spontaneous," he continued. "You should be conscious and alert and respond to each situation with absolute consciousness. Your action out of conscious-ness is moral, out of unconsciousness immoral . . . it may be the same action."

No fixed morality. No ready-made ideas of good and bad. It was a wild, wild vision of human freedom, with individual awareness as the only moral criterion. No wonder they wanted him out.

The Art of Whirling

I enjoy the mystical poetry of Mevlana Jalaludin Rumi and have a lot of respect for a guy who could whirl continuously for 36 hours without so much as a coffee break or a trip to the john, thereby attaining enlightenment, as Rumi apparently did.

If you've ever tried Sufi whirling, you'll understand the basic concept, which in my view has nothing to do with esoteric explanations such as symbolising the whirling cosmos, focusing on God and embracing all of humanity with love. Whirling throws you to your centre. That's the simple truth. The outside world, normally static and familiar, becomes a blur of fast-moving colours and shapes, disconnecting you from normality. With nothing to hold on to outside, you are pulled inside.

That's what happened to me at the end of the Ranch. I became a whirling dervish. Not out of choice, mind you, but simply because the world around me started moving so fast I couldn't hold onto anything.

By way of explanation, let me skip from Sufism to Buddhism and say a word about the Gachchamis. This is a Buddhist ritual, known as The Three Refuges, or The Three Jewels. As mentioned earlier, Bhagwan co-opted the ritual, suggesting that we should begin each working day by kneeling down, putting our hands in a Namaste and then slowly bowing down three times while reciting together:

Buddham Saranam Gachchami (I take refuge in the Buddha)
Sangham Saranam Gacchami (I take refuge in the commune)
Dhammam Saranam Gacchami (I take refuge in the ultimate truth).

Well, frankly, by October 1985, the local buddha wasn't looking too good, the commune was being shaken to its foundations and the ultimate truth seemed as elusive as ever. So from my perspective there wasn't much left in the way of refuge.

As an alternative, it seemed like a good idea to hang out with the press corps entrenched in the Ranch's hotel because it distanced me from the ongoing criminal investigation. I'd done nothing wrong, but unlike Bhagwan I felt guilt by association.

However, escaping into the role of a professional observer proved no solution for me. This wasn't the kind of disconnection Rumi and other dervishes were trying to experience. It didn't bring me closer to myself. Rather, it took me farther away. It sucked me into the world of instant analysis and banal headlines that reminded me why I'd left journalism in the first place. Naturally, other newsmen wanted to know my opinions. "Do you think Bhagwan knew about Sheela's crimes?" asked one TV newsman, thrusting a microphone in my face.

"I don't know what he knew," I replied. "But I haven't seen anything yet that makes me want to go back to Portland and work in some crummy office job from nine to five."

When the *Rajneesh Times* editorial team was invited to question Bhagwan at one of his meet-the-press sessions, I sat in front of him and did my very best to be a journalist rather than a sannyasin, by asking if it was okay to criticise the commune's management in the newspaper. In other words, reading between the lines, I was asking, "Is it okay to criticise you?"

It was the first time since my "apocalypse" question that we'd had this kind of direct, eyeball-to-eyeball connection, and while on the surface everything seemed mannerly – a straightforward press interview with a controversial figure – it soon began to feel like standing in the parking lot at the Fukushima nuclear reactor during melt-down.

It wasn't what he said. It was the effect of being so close to him again. I was getting sunburned at soul level and the SPF of my spiritual sunblock lotion was way too low. In response to my question, Bhagwan was neither angry, amused, nor indifferent. He just gave it to me straight: no criticism in the *Rajneesh Times*.

"If you simply want it to be a newspaper, then my name should be removed from it," he told me. "Then you can collect all kinds of stupid things that are happening around the world – murders, suicides, wars, and certainly you will be selling better . . ."

He then spent several minutes talking about how newspapers and television networks exploit news as a way of boosting their audiences and making money. I was sipping a glass of water while he replied, which was my best shot at behaving like a sceptical reporter instead of a devoted disciple. I managed to keep my cool-and-distant act going until Bhagwan started to address the issue itself.

"We are not concerned whether we sell to millions of people or not," he continued, explaining that the role of the *Rajneesh Times* was to support his vision. "Your freedom of expression is absolutely there, but you have accepted a vision," he told me. "Now you have to use your ability of expression to make that vision available to as many people as possible. That will be your creativity."

He paused, looking at me intently, as if assessing the questioner behind the question, then added: "But if my newspaper starts writing something against my own message, and you call it freedom of expression, then you are not being . . ."

Another long pause.

". . . a gentleman."

Bhagwan's use of this quaint and totally unexpected English-ism cracked me up and, in spite of myself, I smiled. Something clicked between us, which from my side I can only describe as a kind of mutual respect. It's hard to explain, but by asking his permission to criticise I'd somehow put myself in an inferior position, almost like an employee, whereas he was treating me like an equal. I'd expected him to say ". . . then you are not being a good disciple." But "gentleman"? That put me in a totally different category.

"Then you start a newspaper of your own and use your freedom of expression," he suggested, as if it was perfectly okay with him, either way. But the stand-off was over. It was clear to me that I wasn't about to trade in my sannyasin lifestyle for another tour of duty on Fleet Street. So I had to let go of that refuge, too.

That's when I understood the dervish perspective: while whirling, or being whirled, it's better to let go of everything . . . and keep on falling inside while everything outside is falling apart.

Turner's Gambit

Charles Turner felt humiliated. Other federal officials involved in the Rajneesh case were laughing at him and that did not feel good. Nevertheless, in spite of being ridiculed for the strategy he was proposing as a solution, Turner was convinced he had the answer: if "the Bhagwan" could be deported on charges of immigration fraud, the Rajneesh commune in central Oregon would collapse and the problem everyone was screaming about would go away.

Pressure was coming from all directions. Robert Krueger, head of Portland INS, confessed he was unable to throw Bhagwan out because the guru's immigration application was tied up in a lengthy review process. Dave Frohnmayer, Oregon's State Attorney General, was trying to use constitutional separation of church and state as a way of building a case against the incorporation of the City of Rajneeshpuram, but admitted it would probably take years. Meetings in Washington DC to discuss the situation included Senators Mark Hatfield and Bob Packwood, both representing Oregon, and the INS chief Alan Nelson, who said he was getting regular phone calls from the White House urging action.

Turner's assistant in Portland, Robert Weaver, said afterwards that in conversations with his head office in Washington, Bhagwan was always on a short list requiring urgent action, "because they were getting inundated with enquiries from the White House, from Capitol Hill, from constituencies – I know it was a matter of concern in the White House."

Even the Vatican, it seems, got into the game. A decade later, a short article appeared in an Indian newspaper stating that the Vatican had also been pressuring Washington to get Bhagwan out of the US. The driving force behind this lobby, the report stated, was none other than Cardinal Ratzinger, later to become Pope Benedict XVI, who at the time was Prefect of the Congregation for the Doctrine of the Faith, better known as the Inquisition. Much of this pressure was funnelled towards the US Attorney's office in Portland, because, quite simply, Turner was perceived as the man best positioned to get the job done.

So, here I need to qualify my accusation, made earlier in this book, that it was Reagan and his sidekick Meese who destroyed our city. Yes, of course, the right-wing president wanted this irritating guru gone. So did Meese. But the pressure wasn't coming only from the White House. In the end, it was coming from everywhere and it was channelled through Charles Turner.

The US Attorney for Oregon was not a reluctant participant. A strict born-again Christian, he described Bhagwan as "a man of consummate evil" and was also eager to get rid of him. What hurt Turner was how he'd been mocked by other federal officials. Later, when he was interviewed by author Max Brecher, the US Attorney was still bitter about the way he'd been abused by his colleagues.

"We were trying to develop this case [charging Bhagwan with immigration fraud] because we were using the criminal process to solve what was really a political problem," Turner told Brecher, who published the interview in his book.

"That was the court of last resort," the US Attorney continued. "When everybody else threw up their hands: 'What are we going to do with these people? How are we going to get them out of here?' They're totally entrenched. They're a political entity. They have money. They have power. They have organisation. They're sophisti-cated. They have people who are absolutely, completely, totally committed to what they are doing, zealous beyond anything I've ever encountered in my life. So, what are we going to do about it? Let's use the US Attorney's office to charge them with immigration fraud. And I didn't know whether there was a case."

Turner's strategy was simple: instead of trying to destroy an entrenched community, the state and federal authorities should focus instead on getting rid of its inspiration and its figurehead.

"I recognised early on that the thing to do, if they wanted to get rid of these people, was to deport the Bhagwan because he was the catalyst and the linchpin for this organisation," he explained. "If we could get rid of him, the whole thing would fall apart as a matter of course. And they ridiculed and laughed at me about that. But that's exactly what happened."

Turner seemed blissfully unaware during his candid interview that he was in effect admitting to a conspiracy: representatives of the world's most powerful government had decided to use the nation's criminal justice system to destroy a small spiritual community, without actually knowing if anything illegal had occurred. I'm not a lawyer, but this seems to me to be a clear violation of the Rajneesh community's First Amendment right to freedom of worship, nothing less than state-sponsored persecution of a religious minority.

The fact that Turner could make such a statement without fear of repercussions shows how safe the US government felt in moving against the Rajneesh commune. Nobody outside the community itself would object. Nobody would stand in their way. No section of the American public would raise its voice in protest.

Bhagwan had done his work well. Parodying Dale Carnegie's famous book *How to Win Friends and Influence People*, the mystic once commented that his own biography should be called *How to Make Enemies and Influence People*.

Turning the whole of society against us, he forced us to choose: either run back to the sheep pen, or stand alone, independent of all the support we had formerly relied on.

High noon was approaching and a showdown was imminent. Who was going to win this gunfight at our not-so-okay corral?

The Non-Massacre

Nobody died. That was the real miracle as the endgame played itself out at Rancho Rajneesh. This may sound like a non-news story, rather like a newspaper headline announcing: "No Earthquakes Today in California." But, in fact, it was a massive achievement. Why?

First reason: because the United States is, unfortunately, a trigger-happy country. Everyone knows about the recent spate of mass shootings, especially those aimed at schoolchildren, and the protests by African Americans against police killings of black people. But that's just the tip of the iceberg. More than 1,000 people are killed every month in gun-related incidents. It's an astonishing fact that more American civilians have been killed by guns in the past 50 years, totalling around 1.5 million, than all of the American soldiers in all of this nation's wars combined.

Second reason: because normal safeguards against excessive use of force in the United States do not seem to apply when it comes to groups perceived to be on the social fringe, especially those deemed to be dangerous cults. For example, in May 1985, just when our situation on the Ranch was beginning to boil, hundreds of Philadelphia police surrounded a city block where a "cult" called MOVE had its headquarters. MOVE was a black, back-to-Africa movement that was vociferous in its criticism of the United States, earning itself the ire of Philadelphia Mayor Wilson Goode.

"MOVE members were said to be loud, profane, unsanitary, disruptive, obnoxious," wrote Philip Weiss in the *New Republic*, a couple of months afterwards. "These are not capital offences. In fact, until a few weeks before the police assault, the mayor acknowledged he had no legal basis even to evict MOVE adherents. So they weren't evicted; they were murdered."

After evacuating surrounding houses, Mayor Goode ordered a helicopter to drop a bomb composed of high explosives on the

MOVE house, which was known to be stockpiled with gasoline. There was a tremendous explosion, followed by a fire that burned down an entire city block, causing about $5 million in damage.

Eleven MOVE members were killed, four of them children.

Gerald Arenberg, executive director of the American Federation of Police, declared that the Philadelphia police "broke every rule in the book". But newly appointed Attorney General Edwin Meese III disagreed. "The situation that gave rise to the tragedy was caused by the criminals, not the police," he told a Washington news conference.

For those of us living inside the Ranch, it wasn't a very encouraging sign.

In the spring of 1993, several years after our Oregon story had ended, armed members of the ATF – the Alcohol, Tobacco and Firearms Bureau – decided to raid a spiritual group called Branch Davidians, about a hundred of whom were living in a community outside Waco, Texas. Arrest and search warrants had been issued on suspicion of illegal possession of firearms and explosives.

During the bungled attempt to carry out a search, David Koresh, the leader of this religious sect, was shot and wounded in the arm. ATF agents then charged the building, but the assault was repulsed in a firefight that left four agents and six Davidians dead. In addition, another 16 ATF agents were wounded. The ATF's aggressive strategy had proved disastrous and the agency was quickly sidelined. Instead, control was handed over to a special unit of the FBI, who surrounded the ranch buildings and settled in for a long siege, hoping to wear the Davidians down.

It didn't work and so, after a 51-day stakeout, the FBI started destroying buildings with an armoured vehicle and pumping CS gas inside the main compound. A fire broke out that killed 79 Davidians, including women and children. Whether it was the group's death wish, or federal bungling, or a combination of the two, remains a debated issue.

In September 1985, a similar situation was building at Rancho Rajneesh. Rumours about impending federal indictments against Bhagwan, accusing him of immigration fraud, were circulating in the Oregon media. Attempts to work out terms for a peaceful surrender agreement, whereby Bhagwan and anyone else facing an indictment could voluntarily turn themselves in, were rebuffed by Turner.

According to some reports, SWAT teams were being readied and machine gun mounts were being fitted to National Guard helicopters. At least 15 armoured personnel carriers were strategically placed around the Ranch. Emotions were running high, especially among investigators at the Portland office of the INS (Immigration and Naturalization Service).

"Every time somebody got closely involved with the Bhagwan and the whole guru system, all of a sudden the burner got turned up in them," recalled Mike Inman, a former general counsel for the INS, who was involved at the time. "The INS investigators in Portland were really caught up in this, heavily, emotionally involved. They were really wanting to escalate this, far above and beyond what I wanted."

He recalled that when orders came down from Washington DC that the INS officers in Portland were not to take part in any raid on the Ranch, some of the agents were "kicking chairs" in frustration and rage.

Inman also recalled a conversation with Turner, quoting the US Attorney as telling him, "I want to storm the Bastille!" Meaning, apparently, that Turner wanted to stage a full-frontal attack on the Ranch in order to arrest Bhagwan – hardly a typical method for dealing with low-grade offences such as immigration fraud.

It was for this reason that I never felt much sympathy for Turner, even though he was on Sheela's hit list. Intentionally or unintentionally, the US Attorney seemed determined to push an already perilous situation even further in the direction of a bloody shoot-out.

Law enforcement officials were aware that Sheela had created a well-armed, professionally trained security force on the Ranch, which greatly increased the chances of a firefight. Governor Vic Atiyeh was feeling all of this heat and getting edgy. "I've taken about all of this that the governor of the state should take and that the people of Oregon should take," he declared.

So why didn't the inevitable happen? Why didn't the Seventh Cavalry wannabes come charging into the Ranch with guns blazing, hell-bent on bagging the Bhagwan? It didn't happen because Bhagwan pre-empted them. He suddenly left, taking all the heat with him.

Bagging the Bhagwan

Sometimes, even today, when I wake up early in the morning and cannot go back to sleep, I like to lie in bed and play a mind-game called "Gone Guru!" or "Get Him Out of Here!" It is designed like a board game, rather like Monopoly, Risk or Cluedo, and the aim is to get Bhagwan out of the United States without the mystic being arrested by federal agents.

It's not as easy as it might seem. Bhagwan's familiar figure, dressed in his hallmark robe and hat, was immediately noticeable wherever he went. The short runway at the Oregon Ranch wasn't long enough to take aircraft bigger than Lear jets, limiting his escape options, and the feds had agents concealed on the Ranch, watching for a breakout. Arrest warrants had already been issued and were held in Portland by Charles Turner.

Air Rajneesh had three planes on the Ranch: two ancient twin-propeller DC3s and a similar, third aircraft, a small Convair turbo-prop, which apparently had once belonged to the reclusive tycoon Howard Hughes. In theory, any of these planes could have taken Bhagwan on the long journey south to the Mexican border, without even one refuelling stop, and I heard later from one of the sannyasin pilots that this was discussed as an option. But apparently, at the critical moment prior to Bhagwan's departure, only the Convair was capable of such a long-distance flight and it had developed a cabin-pressure problem that would have made the trip uncomfortably noisy.

Even if Bhagwan had made it across the border, he lacked a transit visa and might well have been arrested by the Mexican authorities. Or, if he'd been secretly flown into the country, as was also discussed, he'd have to somehow continue his journey, either to the Caribbean or Central America – a long, tedious and hazardous trip.

A shorter trip to the Canadian border, although more practical and swift, would have run into a similar problem of lacking a transit visa. It's by no means clear that the Canadian authorities – at convenient airports such as Vancouver, Edmonton, or Calgary – would have permitted Bhagwan to board an international flight and make good his escape from North America.

My own solutions come down to two:

First, he could have been flown in the dead of night to nearby Redmond Airport and boarded a bigger plane there, perhaps with the false alibi that he was flying to Los Angeles to take part in a television talk show. Then, once airborne, the plane could have flown straight out over the Pacific Ocean, heading for Japan, Singapore or Hong Kong.

That might have worked. But my favourite strategy would have been to fly him to the nearby city of Portland, where he would call a press conference in the Rajneesh Hotel, dressed in fake handcuffs and chains, saying: "This is what the Reagan administration wants to do to me."

He could then have given them a deadline, saying he intended to leave the US by noon the following day, giving them 24 hours to arrest him, thereby forcing their hand. If they arrested him, at least it would have been on his terms, and a plea bargain could have been worked out – as it was eventually – so that he could officially leave the country.

In the end, a dubious option was chosen. On the afternoon of Sunday 27 October 1985, two Lear jets flew into the Ranch and were immediately spotted. John Bowerman, our cowboy neighbour across the John Day River, saw them fly over his ranch and called his friend Dave Frohnmayer, who passed the news on to Turner.

Bowerman wasn't the only one to notice the planes. As I learned later, there were federal agents on the Ranch, watching as Bhagwan boarded one of the jets and flew out. His personal staff flew in the other plane.

The two jets then flew eastwards across the United States, refuelling once on the way, and landed in Charlotte, North Carolina, where a reception committee of local police and federal agents was waiting for them – at Turner's request. Bhagwan was arrested at gunpoint and led away to prison.

Why Charlotte? Well, several members of the "Hollywood Crowd", who were now running things on the Ranch, had wealthy family connections in the city who could provide a comfortable house for him to stay in. From there, after resting, the plan was apparently to take him on to Bermuda, out of harm's way.

On the evening following Bhagwan's departure, I decided to have an early night, so instead of heading for the disco after supper, I went back to my house. As I came in, one of my room-mates, a German sannyasin called Bhagawati, was on the phone in the living room, papers and address books strewn around her on the sofa.

"Bhagwan's been arrested in North Carolina," she explained tensely, "We're contacting everyone we know in the media, internationally and here in the States."

Bhagawati, one of a team of sannyasins who liaised with journalists visiting the Ranch, explained that letting the world know about the arrest was their attempt to protect him from harm. The more global attention, the more careful the US government was likely to be.

To say the news came as a surprise was an understatement. I hadn't even heard that Bhagwan had left the Ranch. We didn't have television on the Ranch and, of course, there was no internet in those days, so news about Bhagwan was recorded at our hotel in Portland, then flown up to the Ranch, to be played for us on a TV monitor as we trooped into the canteen for breakfast, lunch or dinner.

The next day, we watched as Bhagwan, heavily chained and escorted by US marshals wielding sawn-off shotguns, was taken to a court hearing in Charlotte, the state capital.

"How do you feel, Bhagwan?" asked the media.

He chuckled. "I feel great!" he replied, trying to give them a Namaste greeting, even though his hands were chained to shackles on his feet, making it impossible. At least he was still then in his own robe and hat. A short while later, we saw him wearing a prison green jacket and blue jeans, being interviewed inside Charlotte's county jail by a succession of news channels.

Local TV stations in Oregon wanted our reaction. One morning, they gathered a group of us in the canteen and asked us how we felt about Bhagwan "fleeing" from the Ranch without informing us. I sensed that the TV reporters expected us to be angry with him, or to feel betrayed and abandoned.

As I recall, most Ranch residents adopted a "wait and see" attitude, which seemed sensible enough, and then one of the cooks said: "Well, we have to go on with making the lunch," and the meeting broke up.

Personally, I felt deeply split about Bhagwan's arrest. On the one hand, I experienced a kind of grim satisfaction at seeing him in jail, as if saying to him, "Well, you wanted to provoke the Reagan administration and you succeeded . . . happy now?" As if I'd had nothing to do with the whole provocation game. On the other hand, I felt a pain in my heart and there were tears in my eyes, so I wrote an article about the situation, beginning: "These tears are not for me, nor for Bhagwan, they are for the American Constitution . . ."

Meanwhile, in Charlotte, Bhagwan was in jail and Halloween was rapidly approaching, spawning a sudden popularity in "Bhagwan" costumes. Robes, hats and beards were sold, or hastily fashioned, adding a new twist to the annual masquerade.

"Charlotte Bagged the Bhagwan", proclaimed posters in North Carolina's capital. To the population at large, this was just a bit of harmless fun. But inside the jails of the United States, this was where it began to get nasty.

"Oklahoma City that's oh-so pretty . . ."

I can never hear the song "Route 66", sung by the Rolling Stones and other performers, without thinking of what happened to Bhagwan.

Barbara DeLaney, US Magistrate in Charlotte, ordered him to be remanded in custody and flown back to Portland to await trial for immigration fraud. Bhagwan was put aboard a federally owned plane used by the National Prisoner Transportation Service to take convicted prisoners from jail to jail. But he wasn't taken to Portland. He was flown to Oklahoma City.

Why Oklahoma? If you ask the feds, they'll probably tell you it was a routing decision: they were dropping Bhagwan there because they had other places to go before Portland. If you ask me, I refer you to the case of Karen Silkwood, whose story was portrayed onscreen by Meryl Streep in the movie *Silkwood*.

In 1974, Karen Silkwood was campaigning for better safety standards for workers at the Kerr-McGee plant near Oklahoma City, which produced weapons-grade uranium for the US government's nuclear defence programme. Far too frequently, the company's workers were getting contaminated. Kerr-McGee's owners were hostile to Silkwood's efforts, so she tried to stir up interest in the media. One evening, when she was driving with a sheaf of evidence to keep an appointment with a reporter from the *New York Times*, she was run off the road and killed. All her papers disappeared. At the post mortem, they found enough plutonium in her body to kill her anyway. It has been claimed that FBI or other federal agents collaborated with Kerr-McGee in arranging her death. There was certainly a close connection between Kerr-McGee and whoever was in power in Washington DC, as evidenced by John F. Kennedy's cynical and self-deprecating remark: "Every once in a while I have to go to Oklahoma to kiss Ronald Kerr's ass."

The relationship continued on many levels through the sixties, seventies and eighties, including the mysterious disappearance of 40 pounds of plutonium that may or may not have found its way into Israel's covert nuclear weapons programme.

What has all this to do with Bhagwan? Simply this: if the feds wanted to do harm to Bhagwan, then Oklahoma, with its murky history, was a more convenient place to do it than Portland, Oregon.

On the evening of 4 November 1985, Bhagwan arrived at Oklahoma City's Will Rogers Airport, named after the state's famous cowboy actor. He was taken to El Reno, a medium-security federal penitentiary about 30 miles outside the city. On the way, Bhagwan heard one US marshal say to another, "This guy is world famous, so don't do anything directly."

When they arrived at the jail, Bhagwan was told to book himself in under the name of "David Washington". He refused. The marshals said if he didn't, he'd have to stay outside in the cold all night. So Bhagwan told them to fill in the name and he'd sign it. They did. He signed with his familiar signature as Bhagwan Shree Rajneesh. A Xerox copy of that entry slip is in the possession of Bhagwan's disciples. It shows, bizarrely, the name of David Washington, followed by Bhagwan's elaborate, trademark signature in Hindi.

Then he was told he'd have to carry his own mattress to his cell. Nobody else wanted to touch it. He did, even though it looked filthy and damaged. There was no pillow, so he curled up one corner and slept like that. In the morning, for breakfast, he was given two slices of bread soaked in an odourless, tasteless sauce. Since he was hungry, he ate it.

Later, Bhagwan and some of his closest disciples became convinced that some kind of radioactive material had been inserted into the mattress; also, that some sort of toxic substance may have been mixed with his food.

At the Ranch, it took a while for Bhagwan's aides to figure out where he'd been taken. As soon as they got the information, they were frantic to do something. No poisoning was suspected at this stage, but people like Vivek, Devaraj and Hasya had expected the mystic to be flown straight to Portland and were worried that Bhagwan's delicate health – asthma, diabetes, a fragile back – might be suffering during his prolonged journey.

They called the lawyer who'd been conducting his defence in Charlotte, an attorney called Bill Diehl, and begged him to fly to Oklahoma City and see what the hell was going on. He agreed.

For a while, Diehl was stonewalled by federal officials, but dogged persistence paid off and he finally got to see Bhagwan at 1:30am on 7 November. Diehl's presence seemed to make Bhagwan's stay in Oklahoma City suddenly unnecessary, because at daybreak he was driven to Will Rogers Airport, where the federal prison plane promptly reappeared to fly him to Seattle – three nights and two days after arriving in Oklahoma. From Seattle he was flown in a smaller plane to Portland.

Meanwhile, a Portland TV station was conducting a phone-in poll, asking its viewers if Bhagwan was being treated fairly by the US government. At first, the "yes" vote led comfortably, but the sight of the mystic being taken in handcuffs off the plane at Portland Airport, wearing an ill-fitting trench coat as protection against the rain and looking very tired and fragile, tipped the scale in the other direction. The "no" vote won by a narrow margin.

The sight touched me, too. I think that was the only time in my years with Bhagwan that I ever felt sorry for him.

Innocently Guilty

The next day, against the wishes of the US Attorney's office, a federal judge in Portland released Bhagwan on bail, pending trial for immigration fraud. When the news reached the Ranch, by telephone, I was standing in our welcome centre with about a dozen sannyasins and a couple of TV camera crews. Everyone cheered and the TV crews started to capture the moment, but I ran to the side to avoid the cameras, because I didn't feel like cheering. I was too caught up in my conflicted emotions.

Soon Bhagwan returned to the Ranch and suddenly I was back in the PR business with my old colleague Krishna Prem from the days of the Pune ashram's press office. Along with Bhagawati, Hasya and everyone else, we felt an urgent need to keep Bhagwan in the public eye – especially abroad – since this would remind the White House of his international status and improve the chances of a fair trial process.

But how? Krishna Prem and I had the same idea: "Let's go to Geneva."

In the autumn of 1985, the Reagan administration was gearing up for the most important diplomatic event of the president's career: a summit meeting with Mikhail Gorbachev in Geneva, scheduled for 19–21 November.

History would look back on this moment as the turning point in the Cold War, and some American analysts would eulogise Reagan as the man who master-minded the defeat of communism. Personally, I never saw it that way, nor did Gorbachev himself. It was the Russian leader's attempts to revive a stagnant Soviet economy, by liberalising central control, that triggered a sudden surge of nationalism throughout the countries of the Soviet bloc – a surge that Gorbachev could have stopped by brute military force, but refused to do.

So to me, it seemed all Reagan had to do was smile and say "thank you" while his new pal Mikhail – hypnotised by his own glamorous image in the Western media – obligingly allowed the Soviet Empire to fall into pieces.

Goodbye communism, hello democracy.

Goodbye Vladimir Lenin, hello Vladimir Putin.

Anyway, we realised the summit meeting was going to be a massive media circus and we figured we could embarrass Reagan by going to Geneva and raising the "human rights" issue. How? By flooding the world's press with photos of Bhagwan in chains, surrounded by armed guards, being dragged through five jails in 12 days. Human rights had always been the West's trump card against the Soviets and this was a great opportunity to grab headlines by turning the tables. At the very least, the east European media would love us and Reagan's press aides would be fielding awkward questions.

We wrote the press release and were in the process of choosing photos and checking flights to Geneva when the project stalled. Bhagwan's new secretary, Hasya, who'd initially given the go-ahead, suddenly applied the brakes. A couple of days later she broke the news: Bhagwan wanted out.

"They are attacking my body and I will not be able to do my work," he told his advisors, then gave his lawyers permission to negotiate a plea bargain.

I could see his point. If he stayed to fight the charges, which seemed to lack any substantial evidence, he would have to appear daily in court, in downtown Portland, possibly for weeks, while the trial dragged on. Even if he won, there was no guarantee the feds wouldn't immediately come with another set of charges and he'd have to repeat the whole process again.

It reminded me of a wise comment made by one of the street people I'd temporarily befriended during the Share-a-Home programme. He'd been reading the *Rajneesh Times* and, unlike me, understood what Bhagwan was up against.

"You can fight all these people in Oregon and you can win, but you can't fight the US government, it's too powerful," he told me. "If they want to get you, eventually they will. Sooner or later, they'll get you." And so it proved to be. Besides which, there was the ever-present threat of some crackpot with a gun taking a shot at Bhagwan when entering or leaving the court. It was time to do a deal.

Niren, Bhagwan's personal attorney, who much later on was to feature prominently in *Wild Wild Country*, was one of the mystic's advisors in making this critical decision. But the same message was conveyed by a couple of American legal experts hired to help him: give the feds what they want and get out while you still can.

Charles Turner wouldn't accept a plea of *nole contendere* – no contest – because he needed a guilty tag to make sure Bhagwan could be deported from the United States. But Turner accepted an Alford Plea, a little-known device that allows a defendant to maintain his innocence while admitting there is sufficient evidence to convict him – don't ask me how that's possible. In court, Bhagwan entered his *guilty-but-innocent* Alford Plea to two charges of immigration fraud. He was given a ten-year suspended sentence, fined $400,000 and deported.

On the evening of 14 November, directly from Portland's federal district court, Bhagwan was given a presidential-style motorcade to Portland International Airport, his stretch-limo Rolls-Royce surrounded by a sea of police motorcycles with blue flashing lights. Highway ramps were blocked off. Media crews were chasing the convoy. It was quite an exit.

"I never want to come back," he'd told the judge. Then, with a wave and smile, he was gone.

One of the Portland TV news channels gave extended coverage to the take-off, while playing the well-known song by John Denver – the very same song that I had abused with my own lyrics when escaping from the Pune ashram all those years ago. Now the original version was being played as the TV cameras tracked Bhagwan's jet soaring into the night sky:

I'm leaving on a jet plane, don't know when I'll be back again . . .

The public wouldn't miss him. But the journalists would. What a story.

Five years later, Bhagwan would be dead at the age of 58, after suffering from inexplicable physical symptoms, including acute bone pain, sudden collapses, nerve damage and an extreme sensitivity to light that forced him to wear sunglasses when giving discourse.

Before he died, Bhagwan asserted that he had been poisoned during his jail stopover in Oklahoma. True or false? Well, short of a deathbed confession by a retired US marshal, nobody is ever going to prove anything. There is no smoking gun. No hard evidence.

Personally, though, I suspect foul play. If you ask me, it wasn't enough for the Reagan administration to get him out of the country. They wanted to teach this uppity little guru a lesson. They wanted an old-fashioned, Western necktie party. They wanted to read to him from the book, string him up and kick his horse from under him.

Why? For the same reason Howard Maupin shot and scalped Chief Paulina.

Because the only good Indian is a dead Indian.

Ranch Exodus

It was a scene out of the Bible. Like the Jews leaving Egypt. Like the Lost Tribe departing the Holy Land. I stood watching in amazement as thousands of sannyasins walked away from me, across the open fields, in a moving tide of humanity.

Then I knew, "Oh my God, it's over!"

It wasn't official, not yet. On the morning of 14 November, we'd all been called to Rajneesh Mandir, the Ranch's big meditation hall, where it was announced that Bhagwan was flying to Portland for a court hearing. We were invited to line the route to our little airport, to give him a send-off.

We didn't know he'd never come back. But as the entire community left the hall to line the road, I could feel it, or rather see it. We weren't just walking out of the hall. The Rajneesh tribe was walking out of Oregon and would scatter across the globe in a modern-day diaspora. The Ranch was finished.

Hours later, Bhagwan flew out of Portland, heading for India and the Himalayas, taking up residence in a small hotel near Manali. Those whose impulse was to immediately join him were disappointed to be told, "Don't follow him. He wants to be alone."

Meanwhile, back at the Ranch, our mayor-cum-lawyer Niren was at first telling the Portland news channels we'd be staying on. But the inward flow of money must have shrivelled to the merest trickle, because a few days later, one cold and snowy evening in late November, Niren called us to a meeting in the commune's big meditation hall.

"It's over," he announced. With a wry grin, he added, "They told me to keep it light."

Somebody howled like a lonely timber wolf, provoking scattered laughter in the crowd. There wasn't much else to say, so after a few minutes we turned our faces towards the bitter cold outside the hall and walked towards the mundane world we'd thought we'd left behind. By this time, there weren't so many of us remaining on the Ranch. People had been leaving in a steady stream and I don't think there could have been more than three or four hundred sannyasins left to hear Niren's message.

My path out of the hall took me right past a local cameraman called Tom who freelanced for Channel Two News in Portland. He was the only newsman still tracking a story that had made headlines on all the networks right through September and October.

"What's going on?" he asked me, adding, by way of explanation, "Nobody wants to talk to me."

I wasn't going to talk either and walked past him, but then something bitter and angry rose up inside and I stopped and turned around.

"I have something to say," I told him. Tom shouldered the camera, focused and signalled he was ready.

"Well," I said, addressing the unseen viewers, "Bhagwan has left and now we are all leaving. Are you satisfied now, Oregon?"

Then, to show my contempt, without looking as if I expected an answer, I just turned and walked away into the night. Tom was happy. He sold the footage and they ran it as the lead story on the evening news. "The people of Oregon needed to hear that," acknowledged one of Channel Two's newsroom editors.

But the PR team on the ranch who'd been working with the media all these months were upset by my sour performance and told me they'd taken me off their list of residents selected to talk with journalists.

What a joke.

"It's over! Don't you get it?" I yelled at one of them. "There is no list because there is no Ranch! It's O . . . V . . . E . . . R!"

People were leaving the Ranch quickly, but without panic. Volunteer cooks in the canteens kept the meals going. The electric bills may or may not have been paid, but the lights and heating still worked. Commune buses drove people to local airports and bus stations, dropping them off in mainstream America. Christian organisations in Portland set up a shelter, expecting dazed ex-cult members to emerge from years of brainwashing in urgent need of re-orientation and deprogramming. They must have been puzzled when nobody showed up.

Ironically, my own standard of living improved noticeably. Most people who'd deposited money with the commune's financial institutions couldn't get it back, but they were given credit for use on the Ranch, which they in turn gave generously to anyone who wanted it. So I was able to move into the Ranch hotel free of charge, stop working and start writing. I'd hoped to publish a "quick-and-dirty" page-turner about my experiences. But I was way too close to the action. Little did I know I'd have to wait 30 years to get the saga into focus.

Meanwhile, a huge sell-off started, as the entire assets of the Ranch went up for sale. Bargain hunters poured in to purchase everything from paving slabs to washing machines to bulldozers. All the trailer homes I'd so carefully crawled under, to connect their two halves and build their foundations, got sold along with everything else. Only the houses we'd built on fixed foundations remained.

One businessman ran up against an unexpected obstacle. His wife refused to let him come to the Ranch. "You're not going down there!" she snapped. Apparently, she genuinely feared he would be seduced by Rajneesh women, embraced by the sect and never come out again.

Where did the money go? Well, State Attorney General Frohnmayer slapped a RICO lawsuit on us to try to get his hands on it. This complex legislation – the Racketeer Influenced and Corrupt Organizations Act – was originally designed to stop money laundering and racketeering by the mafia. Other famous RICO targets included the Hells Angel Motorcycle Club, sex abuse by the Catholic priesthood, financier Michael Milken – the "junk bond king" – and pro-life activists who blocked access to abortion clinics.

For us, RICO didn't seem to change much. I can't recall if the case was ever decided. But I do know that, as the great sell-off continued, most of the money found its way out of the US and was used to finance Bhagwan's upcoming world tour in search of a new home. So I guess Frohnmayer only got a fraction of the loot.

I'm sure the Attorney General was hoping to get his hands on the Roller fleet, worth millions of dollars, but, by accident or design, the trustees of our Rajneesh Car Collection Trust were sannyasins who had no connection to any of the lawsuits. Frohnmayer had to watch helplessly as a Texas car dealer flew to Oregon and purchased the lot, trucking them out in a long convoy of haulage lorries.

As the Ranch population shrank and my credit ran out, I got a reasonable offer: join a skeleton crew that kept essential services going, in exchange for a free hotel room. Soon I was spending half the day rolling a big compactor over the land fill. I wasn't in a hurry to depart. When stories about Sheela's crimes had first erupted, I'd felt a strong impulse to leave in order to get some distance and perspective. But then everyone else left instead, Bhagwan included, so I got what I wanted, in an entirely unexpected way.

But the moment was approaching, I knew, when I'd lock the door of my hotel room, hand over the key and head out of town. The show was over. The curtain was down. And the script for the next episode of our drama had yet to be written.

Sure enough, one fine day in March 1986, I drove out of the Ranch in an old yellow school bus, part of the community's defunct transit system, which in its heyday had boasted the second-largest municipal bus fleet in Oregon. I'd agreed to drive the bus to Mill Valley, just north of San Francisco, for a guy who was planning to resell it, and he gave me a free ride as part of the deal.

When I reached the top of the Ranch, I pulled over and got out. From this vantage point, you could see the entire property, but no buildings, which were all hidden in the valleys. It was a vast empty landscape, timeless and endless, seemingly untouched by the intense dramas that had unfolded here.

Two years earlier, Arnold Schwarzenegger had entered movie mythology with his portrayal of The Terminator. The second movie in the series wouldn't be released for another five years, but a classic line from *Terminator 2* fitted the occasion so well, I'm sure I would have said it:

"Hasta la vista, baby!"

But not Schwarzenegger's other famous line, "I'll be back."

Oh no, good people of Oregon. Not me. I won't be back.

Leaving Normal

Let me backtrack for a moment to a scene in the Ranch's à la carte restaurant, shortly after the announcement that the commune was shutting down . . .

"Subhuti, old chap, this makes up for many previous transgressions on your part," observed Mutribo, smiling with deep satisfaction as he sipped a glass of Taittinger champagne, provided by me. None of us was paying the bill. We had connections with the maître d' and he was intent on giving free meals to all his friends. I'd acquired the champagne in a similar manner through the barman. As far as we were concerned, the *Titanic* was sinking and the first-class lounge was open to all-comers.

Zeno, a vivacious Jewish–American woman who'd worked with me as a designer on the *Rajneesh Times*, leaned back in her chair and surveyed the two British gentlemen seated before her.

"You know it's over when the Jews are leaving and only the English remain," she quipped, having booked a seat on tomorrow's bus for Portland. Thus we said goodbye to each other, knowing we'd meet again in some other corner of the planet.

Around this time, a friend of mine who'd been involved in our Ranch's farming projects told me that John Bowerman, our cowboy neighbour across the river, had invited him to lunch. He suggested I might like to go with him. The two men had kept a surreptitious connection through the conflict, even though John – after his initial gesture of friendliness – had sided with the other locals.

We drove around via the nearest bridge. It was the first time I'd actually been across the river – apart from swimming across one summer to sunbathe on an invitingly flat rock on the opposite bank – and it was a novel experience to see our huge truck farm, now deserted, from the eastern side.

While his wife was preparing pizza, I delved into John's fancy collection of leather-bound cowboy books and was soon deeply immersed in the adventures of William Cody, better known as Buffalo Bill. Clearly, John was seriously into cowboy mythology.

As we tucked in, John regaled us with stories about our conflict – told, of course, from the enemy's perspective. He said that, at the height of the tension, he was a in conversation with several guys who'd driven to his ranch. They were chatting by the roadside while watching our people working on the truck farm.

"Why don't we just go in there and shoot 'em up?" suggested one of the visitors, half-jokingly.

John shook his head and replied, in his dry, laconic drawl, "You wouldn't get half-way across the river."

Which was, I guess, a testimony of sorts to our security and preparedness. It was a nice insight into the kind of protection our increasingly hard-core reputation had given us. As our lunch came to an end, John justified his invitation to us by saying it was like under-cover trading that went on between the two sides in the American Civil War, during brief lulls in the fighting.

"The Confederate soldiers traded tobacco in exchange for coffee from the Union soldiers," he explained.

"Hey John, this war is over," I reminded him. "As far as I can see, you guys won. We're outa here."

We parted on good terms. Years later, John featured in *Wild Wild Country*. At the very end of the final episode, John was asked to sum up his feelings about it.

He thought for a moment, smiled and replied:

"I miss the fight."

Fall-out from the Ranch's spectacular demise continued for a while, on both public and personal levels. Publicly, the luckless Charles Turner was confronted by a disgruntled crowd of Oregonians at a meeting in Portland, who complained that "the Bhagwan" had got away too lightly. Turner protested he had no evidence to indict Rajneesh for anything but immigration fraud. But the crowd wasn't satisfied. It was their pride that had been broken, not just the law, and they were frustrated at not being able to take greater revenge.

"I have met all kinds of idiots," Bhagwan once commented, prior to leaving the US, "But the Oregonian idiot is a species unto itself." This was the kind of remark that endeared him to the locals.

Personally, I experienced a strange moment when being interviewed for a book by author Frances Fitzgerald from New York. I was telling Fitzgerald how amazing it had been to watch Oregon politicians ganging up against the commune, but she interrupted me, saying this had happened only after the commune's attempt, in the autumn of 1984, to rig the Wasco County election. I nodded, agreeing with her viewpoint that the State had acted legally, whereas we had not. It wasn't until after the interview that I came to my senses and realised she was wrong. The swelling tide of state and federal opposition had begun way before that incident.

For example, by the end of 1982 we'd built a dam across the Ranch's main valley, to enhance water supplies for our proposed city. Soon we had a 360-million-gallon reservoir, which we named Krishnamurti Lake. A few weeks later, some state agency introduced a new rule, saying the proximity of a reservoir couldn't be used as a criterion when considering the validity of applications for new cities. The rule was applied retroactively, a highly unconstitutional manoeuvre.

Stuff like this was happening all the time. Governor Atiyeh made his famous "welcome" speech – urging us to move on – as early as March 1982. So, why did I agree with Fitzgerald?

It wasn't just forgetfulness. It was an unconscious guilt reflex. The sight of Bhagwan in chains had got to me, too, and I was ready – at least in that moment – to sign a confession that we'd been wrong from the beginning.

Judas, old chap, I know how you must have felt.

PART FOUR

Back to Abnormal

The Waiting Room

O, rest ye, brother mariners, we will not wander more!
The Lotos-Eaters, by Alfred, Lord Tennyson

Purgatory, so Christians say, is a place where those not fast-tracked for immediate entry into heaven are obliged to go through a period of waiting and purification.

Limbo, on the other hand, is a sort of satellite, orbiting hell, where those who die in sin but also in friendship with the Lord await deliverance through JC's personal intervention.

Marin County, to me, was a kind of combination of the two. It was my waiting room. It was an easy, affluent place to chill while watching Bhagwan's travels, wondering if he'd succeed in setting up another commune or ashram.

Lying on a patio, next to a swimming pool, in the garden of a large mansion in Belvedere, I gazed across the sunlit waters of San Francisco Bay to the Golden Gate Bridge and the famous pointy-head Transamerica Pyramid skyscraper in the city beyond. Like I said, I'd driven a bus from the Ranch to Mill Valley. I was completely broke, so I grabbed the first job I could: selling potted plants in a garden centre at five bucks an hour.

"Was he a wonderful guy, or was it a real mess?"

The question came from my new employer, Nancy, the bright and breezy thirty-something manager of the garden centre. Once I'd got the job, I confessed to her that I'd come to the Bay Area from the recently defunct Rajneesh Ranch, guessing correctly that she liked me and wouldn't be fazed by my controversial past.

Nancy deserved an honest answer to her question and she got one.

"It was both," I replied.

After a few weeks scraping by on my low wages, I realised I could earn more money by hiring myself out to take care of the gardens of those who came to buy Nancy's plants.

"English gardener, quality work at reasonable rates." That was my ad in the *Marin Independent Journal* that landed me the job in Belvedere, one of California's richest cities. This was luxury by proxy. I came twice a week to tend the garden, but since the owners were rarely at home I usually had the place – and the pool – to myself.

Truth be told, I didn't have a green thumb. In this very garden, I'd committed the grossest of errors, chopping a branch from a decorative evergreen that, growing slowly over decades, had been carefully trained across the granite rocks of a beautiful waterfall. I'd destroyed the garden's central feature, but the old couple who owned the mansion forgave me. Instead of crucifying me on the waterfall, as I richly deserved, the husband chuckled and said, "We'll remember it as the English gardener's mistake."

His wife was an Anglophile, which is how I got the job. She loved nothing better than to see me swing open the gate and metaphorically bow down and tug my forelock – "good afternoon, m'am" – as she glided through in her Roller. I think she had ambitions to be the Queen of England, or at least of Belvedere.

Marin had everything: natural beauty, comfortable homes, temperate climate, easy access to the city and lots of service jobs for newly arrived refugees from Rajneeshpuram. Window cleaning, gardening, baby-sitting, household repairs, painting and decorating, taxi driving, garage mechanics . . . you name it, we did it.

Having been out of society for almost eight years, I had to grapple with a few changes, such as mastering ATM machines, which had mysteriously sprouted from bank walls during my seclusion, and learning to smile and say, "Have a nice day," when I didn't really mean it.

It was obvious that I couldn't function in California without a car, so I borrowed money from a friend to buy one. As a writer, I longed to be the proud owner of one of those new, revolutionary, beige-coloured boxes with tiny nine-inch video screens, called "Macintosh". Alas, they were outside my budget, so I settled for an Atari.

Aside from gardening, one of my first jobs catapulted me back into my old profession. Almost as a joke, I sent copies of the *Rajneesh Times* to the news editor of the *San Francisco Chronicle* and before I knew it, I was hired.

But there was a problem: I'm a writer and he wanted sub-editors. For the uninitiated, the "subs" are the guys who sit glued to computer screens in the newsroom, conjuring up headlines, adding captions to photos and cutting news stories to fit pages. Not my cup of tea. I did my best because I needed the money, but every night I left work with a headache. In the end, the news editor had to let me go. I was a lousy sub and we both knew it.

Life on the *Pacific Sun*, the North Bay's favourite freebie, was much more pleasant. I was required to turn in just one feature-length news story per fortnight. On the very first try, I hit the jackpot, exposing the conduct of a local police chief whose misdeeds had somehow been overlooked by the *Chronicle*, the *Journal* and other Bay Area dailies. After that, though, the quality of my stories slid downhill fast, because I just didn't want to work. I wanted to laze around, doing nothing, licking my wounds from Oregon. Journalism has been defined as "the last resort for the unemployable" and in Marin I certainly fitted the description.

Once, after my half-hearted investigation of a farmer who'd completely destroyed the local environment in rural West Marin for his own convenience, I was embarrassed to be informed I'd been awarded a prize for good news reporting – by the local farmers' association.

Journalism and gardening kept me afloat financially . . . but for what? That was the question I contemplated as I lay by the pool in Belvedere, drying off in the sun and listening to the bark of a lonely seal sitting on a marker buoy off Sausalito. I didn't want a career. I didn't want to buy a house, or start a family. Maybe all I needed was some spiritual R&R, a rest from the intensity of life with Bhagwan and the maelstrom that constantly blew around him.

I was in no hurry to reconnect. I was still upset with him about the way the Ranch had ended, even though I was actually happy to be out of Oregon. One day, in a fit of anger, I ceremoniously burned my mala – my necklace of wooden beads with Bhagwan's photo attached in a locket.

"Enough is enough," I told myself, as it disappeared in the flames.

Next day, to my surprise, I heard that Bhagwan had sent out a message around the world to all his sannyasins: it's time to drop the mala and red clothes.

"My God," I thought to myself, "You just can't win with this guy!"

When I wrote in the *Pacific Sun* about Rajneesh refugees coming to Marin from Oregon, a San Francisco television news station came to interview me. I must have bitched about Bhagwan and the Ranch, because, when the clip was screened, the TV anchor man ended his report by confidently predicting: "One thing is for sure, this guy will never leave home again for a cult."

Trust the media to jump to a wrong conclusion. In their eyes, I fitted nicely into the "prodigal son" category, a cult member who had seen the error of his ways and was now gratefully re-entering the mainstream. Such a comforting message for the viewing public!

In the East Bay, a sannyasin was monitoring the TV news stations and recording any items about Bhagwan, in order to send them to the mystic's staff. He was a friend of mine, so I immediately called him up.

"For Christ's sake, don't send that clip!" I begged him.

"No problem," he assured me. He knew how I was feeling. Just because I was pissed at Bhagwan didn't mean I was ready to reincarnate as Joe Normal.

But this little brush with television journalism provoked me to ponder: just why was I angry at Bhagwan? Although he never said he was infallible — indeed, he made a point of saying the opposite — I must have projected some kind of superman image onto him. I really did think he could outsmart the US government, the Oregon State government, the local religious fanatics and the rednecks. As an enlightened mystic, I thought, he would be able to stay ahead of the game and guide us in ways that would ensure we would always come out on top.

"Float like a butterfly, sting like a bee!" I'd always loved this remark by Muhammad Ali, describing his own skills as a boxer. It seemed to fit so well to Bhagwan's way of working — at least, up to the moment he appeared on all the major TV news networks in chains and prison clothes.

In addition, I felt Bhagwan had somehow robbed me of my moral righteousness. In my vision of the battle over the Ranch, even if I could imagine losing the fight with America, I was certain we'd come out of it as the good guys. We might go down, but we'd be seen as the real heroes. And what happened? Because of the salmonella attack on salad bars in The Dalles, we got permanently labelled as "bio-terrorists"!

So it was a shock for me to see my ideals destroyed. But seen from a wider perspective, this felt like a necessary stage in my own spiritual development, to see my projection onto Bhagwan of a super-daddy father-figure smashed into little pieces.

However, lest anyone be confused, I'm not suggesting even for a moment that Bhagwan deliberately went to jail in order to help his disciples overcome their superman projections on him. No way. He wasn't *that* compassionate! He wasn't into sacrifice and suffering at all. But, in the end, that's the way it played out, and although I was always keen to know where he was and what was happening around Bhagwan, I was happy enough to spend two years away from him, licking my wounds.

Marin was a good place to chill out. The yuppie population was obliged to work hard to maintain its lifestyle, but the sannyasins – sharing rent for big houses among four or five people – were not. We had time on our hands, so I could take off on long weekends to Mendocino County, where I'd stay in a cosy log cabin owned by Bill, an expat Irishman and former intelligence officer in the Irish Republican Army.

A rebel to the bone, Bill had become a sannyasin as a protest on the day the Reagan administration deported Bhagwan. He turned his house into a meditation centre, lived comfortably from growing marijuana and, while reclining with guests in his solar-heated hot tub, enjoyed telling tales about almost blowing up Margaret Thatcher, although he personally had retired and left the UK long before that happened.

My stay in Marin reminded me of the Tennyson poem cited earlier, *The Lotos-Eaters*, based on the classic Greek myth of Ulysses and his mariners. After the fall of Troy, during their epic journey home, they are blown ashore on an island off the coast of Africa, where the natives live in a state of sleepy, drugged intoxication, induced by eating lotuses. The tired sailors embrace the opium-like drug and decide not to continue their journey:

Surely, surely, slumber is more sweet than toil, the shore
Than labour in the deep mid-ocean, wind and wave and oar;
O, rest ye, brother mariners, we will not wander more.

I know Marin's residents won't like this, but for me their county was like that: a sleepy place filled with lotus blossoms; an invitation to give up the search for inner fulfilment and settle for outer comfort in yuppie paradise.

But then, in the beginning of 1987, Bhagwan landed back in Pune and the word went forth: he wasn't moving again. It was an invitation to rejoin the circus. Still, I might not have got out of Marin had I not fallen in love with a thirty-something Austrian woman who breezed into Mill Valley, shared my bed, stayed several months, then one day announced that she was on her way to India.

Once more, I packed my bags . . . and headed East.

Trauma with Side-Benefits

The end of the Ranch had been a traumatic experience, but it was *not* a tragedy – not for me, anyway. True, it was shocking to watch the community fall apart, but it was a relief to leave Oregon and a joy to return to India.

The transition didn't happen all at once. First, like I said, I stayed almost two years in California, watching from a distance as Bhagwan travelled the world in search of a new home. It wasn't easy for him. The full story has been documented elsewhere, so let's just say that wherever he landed – Nepal, Greece, Ireland, Uruguay, Portugal – that nation's government came under pressure from the Reagan administration to kick him out.

"I want that man back in India, where he belongs, never to be heard of again," Meese was rumoured to have said, while Bhagwan was being deported. Whether Meese said it or not, this policy objective was vigorously pursued by the US government wherever the mystic went.

One incident that interested me, as a UK citizen:

On 6 March 1986, Bhagwan was deported from Greece when his tourist visa was abruptly cancelled. He'd been staying on the island of Crete, at a villa near Aghia Nikalaos, giving daily discourses. Within days, hundreds of sannyasins had started arriving and hotels closed for the tourist off-season were opening up to welcome them when the local bishop of the Greek Orthodox Church freaked out and threatened to dynamite Bhagwan's house.

Simultaneously, every newspaper in Athens received an envelope filled with US newspaper clippings detailing the Oregon saga and all the accusations made against Bhagwan (apparently, Mossad, the Israeli secret service, admitted responsibility for this, returning a favour to the CIA). And that's when the Crete police raided Bhagwan's house, arrested him and – after threatening to dump him on the first India-bound ship in Heraklion harbour – escorted him to Athens airport.

Airborne in a chartered jet, Bhagwan's sannyasins had a problem: where to take him next? They tried Spain, France, Switzerland and Sweden . . . no one allowed him in. Late that evening, their jet landed at London's Heathrow Airport and a stop was now mandatory to permit their pilots to sleep. But Bhagwan was not allowed to pass the night in Heathrow's first-class transit lounge.

"You don't have first-class tickets," stonewalled an official.

So they bought first-class tickets, simply in order to rest in the lounge. But the officials were adamant: the only way Bhagwan and his non-UK disciples could spend the night at Heathrow was in the airport lock-up, behind bars. The order came from senior officials in the Home Office, who presumably had received specific instructions from Downing Street. Margaret Thatcher, arguably Ronald Reagan's greatest fan, wasn't about to pass up an opportunity to impress her political ally across the Atlantic.

One of Bhagwan's male disciples recalls sitting on a bunk bed in jail at Heathrow, feeling completely distraught. Bhagwan smiled at him and said, "When in prison, behave like a prisoner," then lay down and went to sleep.

Welcome Home

In the end, Bhagwan had no choice but to fly back to India, which he did on 30 July 1986. Landing in Mumbai, he stayed for six months in a disciple's house in the Juhu Beach area of the city, where, once again, he started giving discourses. He didn't want to go back to Pune. He was still hoping to create a new commune, somewhere else in India, but it was the same old story: everybody knew the trouble he would bring and nobody wanted the headache.

Staying indefinitely in a small city bungalow wasn't an option either, since hundreds of sannyasins, arriving from around the world, were obliged to wait weeks just to be able to sit with him for a single evening discourse in the bungalow's modest-sized living room, so in the end Bhagwan had no choice. On 4 January, 1987, he returned to his old Pune ashram.

In October that year, once it was clear that Bhagwan had stopped travelling, I also returned. Rajneesh sannyasins were being denied visas at Indian embassies, but when we dropped the red clothes and malas, and said we were tourists heading for Goa, there really wasn't much the Indian government could do – nor did they try very hard.

To their credit, I don't think India's leaders enjoyed being pressured by the Reagan administration. One sympathetic government official even showed us a memo from the US Embassy that instructed: "Don't make Rajneesh's stay comfortable."

And you know India. There are always ways around everything. So when a team of labourers armed with sledgehammers showed up at the front gate with orders from higher-ups to smash the ashram's marble-floored meditation hall, hastily proffered trays of freshly baked cookies and a generous amount of *baksheesh* soon changed their minds.

Pune's Police Commissioner hated Bhagwan, but the mayor loved him. Somehow, in the struggle between the two, the ashram survived and gradually Koregaon Park's long-suffering residents got used to the idea that Bhagwan was back. I'm sure some of the local landlords didn't mind. As I mentioned earlier, the ashram's illegal structures had been torn down when Bhagwan left for the US and accommodation was now restricted to the original buildings, so the demand for renting nearby rooms sky-rocketed.

I was looking forward to walking in the gate after so many years, but was surprised at how powerful the experience turned out to be. Entering the ashram's energy field was like Jake Scully slipping into the body of his avatar and stepping into the magical world of Pandora, in James Cameron's epic movie. The impact was much stronger than on the Big Muddy. It was as if I'd been suffering from some kind of spiritual vitamin deficiency. My body soaked up the energy like a sponge and it was then that I realised how "dry" I'd become, even living in a comfortable place like Marin County.

But it wasn't just Bhagwan. It felt bigger than that, and I recalled his explanation that India carries a special vibe, created over centuries by all those who'd become enlightened in this country. It is this vibe that pulls spiritual seekers from all over the world and makes it such an easy place to meditate. Certainly, in that moment, I could feel the truth of it.

That was the first surprise. The second came when I was sitting in the auditorium, waiting for Bhagwan to give his evening discourse. My mind was chattering away, busy with the logistics of arriving in Pune: finding a place to live, buying household stuff, meeting old friends, catching up on gossip . . .

Bhagwan walked in and my mind stopped. Without even trying, without any intention, or effort on my part, I found myself slipping into a deep, silent, empty space of meditation. It was a remembrance of something I'd always known: in those precious moments when the mind stops distracting us, we find ourselves relaxed and at home, in our innermost being, in our blissful buddha nature.

For me, this was also a moment of understanding. No matter what had happened, no matter what errors might have been made, Bhagwan's basic mission had always been the same: to give people a taste of this silent space of meditation and encourage them to find the source within themselves.

It was good to re-experience it and to realise that beyond morality, beyond legality, beyond conventional spirituality and ultimately beyond duality, there was a space of pure consciousness where he and I could meet, merge and disappear into oneness, godliness . . . or whatever you want to call it. This had always been the bond between us and probably always would be.

When I saw him, walking into the auditorium in his trademark robe and hat, he looked the same as he always did. No real difference, or so I thought. But the next morning, I was strolling through the ashram and spotted a photo of Bhagwan in the bookstore, in which he was standing, smiling at the camera, without his hat. I was shocked. He looked at least ten years older than I remembered him on the Ranch. His hair was thinner, his face was less round, with the forehead and cheek bones more exposed, as if he'd lost a good deal of weight. It was almost, although not quite, the face of an old man.

It suddenly occurred to me that Bhagwan might not be around much longer. My welcome home contained a warning: I was back in India with my favourite mystic and my spiritual journey with him was continuing, but it wouldn't be forever – at least, not on the physical plane.

Love Letters

My return to Pune would not have been complete without an exchange of "love letters" between myself and Bhagwan.

Really, it was quite predictable. Even though I was delighted to be back in India, and happy to see him again, I couldn't leave the Ranch behind without writing to Bhagwan, saying he'd made a mess of our stay in Oregon by allowing Sheela to remain in power too long. I wrote, in capital letters:

"YOU FUCKED UP, BHAGWAN!"

He sent a message back, saying he didn't want negative disciples like me around anymore, and if I couldn't change my attitude I should leave. I stayed away from the ashram for a few days, hanging out in a room I'd rented in a new housing complex at the back of Koregaon Park.

Soon, I felt my behaviour was absurd. I'd come all this way to see Bhagwan and yet the first thing I did was to create a situation that pushed me away from him again. I wrote a heartfelt letter of apology and gave it to my Austrian girlfriend to hand in. When Bhagwan got it, he chuckled and immediately sent me to work with Hasya in the press office.

So far so good. Then I requested a photoshoot with Bhagwan and his newly acquired stretch Rolls-Royce limo, complete with built-in cocktail cabinet and television set. After all, just because he'd walked away from 93 of them in the States, we didn't want the world thinking he was driving around in a Ford.

The shoot happened one evening, outside his car porch, at the back of Lao Tzu House. When Bhagwan walked out, one of the carefully erected lighting towers blew a fuse. Clearly, there was more than one kind of electricity in the air. Although he obligingly posed with the car, the feeling I got from Bhagwan was different than on previous occasions. This time, I sensed him as an intensely private man who loved nothing better than being alone and in silence. It was as if being around people had become an effort.

That was the last time I saw him, up close, face to face.

But we had one more exchange. Early in 1989, after staying for about a year in Pune, I went back to California to make money, which I did as a ghost writer, working with the well-known Tantra teacher, Margot Anand, on her classic, soon to be best-selling Tantra manual, *The Art of Sexual Ecstasy*. At the same time, I managed to get a free hernia operation, paid for by Marin County, repairing an injury I'd suffered during my stint there as a gardener.

Meanwhile, back in Pune, my dear colleague in the press office, Krishna Prem, was getting into trouble. His arrogance was irritating everyone. During one of Bhagwan's evening talks a question was read aloud, stating that an old sannyasin was walking around the ashram declaring, "I don't exaggerate, I lie, like my Master." The questioner invited Bhagwan to comment.

He replied: "I can only imagine two persons who could have made that statement. One is Subhuti, who is not here, and the other is Krishna Prem, who is sitting here. Both are ex-journalists, and although they have been with me and they love me, they cannot drop their old orientation." He then explained the difference between the "lies" of an enlightened being, who knows that truth cannot be said but nevertheless tries to convey it, and the lies of a journalistic mind that deals only in sensational rubbish and is incapable of perceiving truth.

In a moment of high drama, Bhagwan made Krishna Prem stand up, in the middle of his discourse, and asked him if he'd said it. When the stunned fellow nodded in affirmation, he continued:

"There is no need to have an apology for me because I love you – you can say anything. But you have to apologise to all the sannyasins. You have hurt them badly. Fold your hands and go round."

Krishna Prem humbly raised his hands in a Namaste, turned slowly around in a circle, and sat down. Then Bhagwan shifted his focus to the absent Subhuti:

"The same was the case with Subhuti. Twice before he left the commune. Again he came and said, 'I have changed completely, I will not bring my journalist mind in. Please allow me in.' Twice I allowed him. Again, he did the same. Now I have told him, 'The doors are closed. You have closed them yourself.'"

News of this event travelled at light speed to Mill Valley, CA, where I was recovering from my operation. Soon, a videotape of the discourse arrived, together with a letter from Hasya. After watching the video, I opened the letter. Hasya told me that after the discourse, in which Bhagwan had "closed the doors" on me, she'd explained to him that I hadn't left the commune. In fact, I'd been helping her with some press work in the US and needed time to recover from my operation before returning to Pune.

He chuckled and said, "I just wanted to make sure he wasn't up to his old tricks." Presto! The closed doors were magically reopened.

I then wrote to Bhagwan, explaining my medical problem and then adding a PS about Krishna Prem and myself:

"PS I have a confession to make: Krishna Prem's arrogant attitudes have been irritating me for years and I've been waiting patiently for you to hit him on this very point. Finally, you do it, but then you spoil the whole thing by hitting me as well!"

A short while later, Hasya wrote to me saying: "He enjoyed the PS."

The Hitler Salute

You'd have thought that, after doing jail time in the US and being hounded from country to country, Bhagwan would have liked nothing better than to retire quietly to his Pune ashram and cease causing trouble and provoking people.

Not one bit. His basic prescription as a mystical doctor never changed and always included a strong medicinal dose of confrontation, intended as an antidote to spiritual sleep, but also causing severe side-effects such as shock, disturbance and anger.

B.K.S. Iyengar, Pune's most prestigious yoga teacher, found out the hard way. Sometime in 1988, Bhagwan's sannyasins in Germany wanted to participate in a New Age conference to be held in Munich. But, for all the usual reasons, they were banned. When Bhagwan heard that Iyengar – author of *Light on Yoga* – had already been invited as a special guest and was scheduled to speak at the conference, he told his secretary to write to the organisers, saying that Iyengar would be representing him as well.

To anyone who knew them, this was absurd. They were poles apart. Iyengar had great respect for India's traditions, whereas Bhagwan wanted to destroy all traditions. Iyengar considered Bhagwan to be a fraud, while Bhagwan considered Iyengar to be a fossil. But I guess the festival organisers didn't know, because as soon as they received our letter Iyengar was also banned!

The yogacharya was enraged, which leads me to speculate that his mastery of spiritual discipline had yet to raise him above the level of human emotion.

Then India's Buddhists got upset because Bhagwan declared that Gautam Siddhartha had returned after 25 centuries – as the long-awaited Maitreya – and had requested permission to dwell in our Master's physical form. Bhagwan generously agreed and for a few days the two seemed to get along fine.

I wasn't sure if this had really happened, like some esoteric marriage of twin souls, or whether Bhagwan was just being provocative, or if the mystic was truly beginning to lose his mind, but anyway we began to address the two-in-one mystic as "Rajneesh Maitreya Zorba the Buddha". The underlying message, I gathered, was that Buddha had somehow recognised the folly of urging spiritual seekers to renounce the world and had returned to set the record straight. Since Bhagwan was doing this anyway, it seemed to me an unnecessary duplication of effort.

However, just as Pune's angry Buddhists were getting ready to march on our ashram, Gautama vacated our mystic's physical form and conveniently left town, having objected to the "luxury" of Bhagwan's bathroom Jacuzzi.

My favourite rumpus, though, was the night of the Hitler Salute, which happened in March 1988. I guess you had to be an insider to appreciate it. You really had to know Niskriya, Bhagwan's bald, bullet-headed, German cameraman. You had to witness the friendly teasing Bhagwan aimed at this fellow, night after night.

Niskriya was the guy who made all the videos of Bhagwan's discourses from 1987 onwards. He was so focused on his work that once, while doing a shoot in Bhagwan's private chambers, he turned off the AC – the cold air was interfering with his video equipment. He didn't think of Bhagwan, who commented afterwards that "this fellow will kill me".

Niskriya thought only of his camera. That's how he got his reputation as "Stonehead" Niskriya – nicknamed after a famous Zen Master in Japan. He went through a succession of girlfriends very fast because they soon realised he loved his camera more than he did them. In short, Niskriya was a likeable, single-minded, thick-headed German. And that's the excuse Bhagwan gave as a reason to give a Nazi salute in discourse.

"I was just trying to wake him up," explained the mystic, saying that laughing at our past frees us from its grip.

However, it may not have been entirely coincidence that, on that very same night, two journalists from *Bunte* magazine were sitting in the front row. Hilmar Pabel was the photographer, Inge Byhan was the writer. They were in Pune to do a photo-feature for the popular German mag.

The day following Bhagwan's salute, Pabel sent in a discourse question, asking about the significance of the "gesture" he'd made. In his reply, Bhagwan said the question was from both Pabel and Byhan together. That's when poor Inge Byhan got really upset – at being included in the question without her permission, as well as by the salute itself – and almost stood up and screamed with fury in the middle of his discourse.

Personally, I wished she'd done it. Instead, she sat like an unexploded bomb until discourse was over, then unloaded all her emotional baggage on Turiya, Princess of Hanover, who was her escort.

"She could not see the joke," reported Turiya, in a letter to Bhagwan. "She was totally enraged. She said what you were doing was a terrible insult to humanity – she was screaming afterwards."

As you can see, Bhagwan wasn't too concerned about making a good impression on visiting journalists. But this was his way of getting publicity. "All these idiots have made me a world celebrity," he commented afterwards, "and I am just an ordinary man."

Around this time, we heard that citizens in The Dalles, Oregon, were thinking of building a "Rajneesh Museum" in their town, showcasing memorabilia from the days of our saga. It gave me an idea for an unusual press release.

"No, no, no! That is *soooo* sick! You can't possibly send that!" I was told by everyone in the office.

"Send it in to Bhagwan, I have a feeling he'll like it," I countered.

And so it proved to be.

What was it? Well, I quoted Bhagwan as saying that, after his death, he would be happy to donate his stuffed, poisoned body to the museum as a reminder of what the Reagan administration had done to him – with the help and support of the people of Oregon.

The story was published in one of The Dalles' newspapers. The museum was never built.

Historical note: about 25 years after our saga ended, a small museum was opened in Antelope by a retired couple, featuring the whole of the town's history, from initial pioneering days to modern times, including, of course, the Rajneesh chapter.

Transition Time

In late October 1989, the citizens of the German Democratic Republic began to stream out of their country via Hungary and Czechoslovakia, heading for West Germany. The political landscape in eastern Europe was changing rapidly. The Iron Curtain was lifting.

German sannyasins in Pune were excitedly following every step.

"Looks like East Germany will soon be empty," joked one.

"That's good. It can become Bhagwan's new commune," said another and we all laughed, because ever since the Pune ashram had begun, some 15 years earlier, we'd been talking about "the new commune" – whenever and wherever it might happen.

That joke gave me an idea for a press release, so I wrote it up and sent it in for Bhagwan's approval. He gave it the go-ahead. Minutes later, we were faxing it to the DPA news agency in Delhi, and next morning it was all over the German media:

"Bhagwan says East Germany can be his new commune!"

This was a typical example of how we used the media to keep Bhagwan in the public's mind: find a topical event, put a novel spin on it – everybody wants to leave East Germany but we want to go and live there – and get his name in the papers.

But, unbeknown to us, the game wouldn't go on much longer. Bhagwan's body was getting weaker and weaker, sicker and sicker, and he was preparing to check out.

We all have PhDs in hindsight, as they say, but looking back, the signs were obvious. One year before his death, Bhagwan appointed an "Inner Circle" of 21 sannyasins to run the ashram and oversee worldwide publication of his books. He stopped giving discourses and introduced a "White Robe Brotherhood" evening gathering, where we sat in silence together with him for a few minutes, then, after he left, watched a video of one of his earlier discourses.

He built his own memorial. Saying he wanted a new, grander bedroom, he asked us to convert an open-air auditorium into an exquisitely designed enclosed space. It had pure white Italian marble flooring, tinted glass panels from floor to ceiling and breathtakingly cold AC. When it was ready, he lived in it for two weeks, then went back to his old bedroom, saying we could use the new chamber for meditation.

A visiting journalist from *Wien*, an Austrian magazine, was shown the new room, immediately understood its true purpose, then returned to Vienna and wrote the headline, "Bhagwan has built his own Mausoleum." We all howled in protest but that was exactly the case.

He also changed his name from Bhagwan Shree Rajneesh to "Osho". We'd already been introduced to this term, as a Japanese form of address, since it was used in the Zen sutras on which the mystic had commented in some of his last discourses. "Osho" was a loving and respectful term, used by disciples when speaking to their Zen masters. The mystic also said he liked the sound, which reminded him of the term "oceanic", sometimes used by meditators to describe the vastness of their spiritual experiences.

On 19 January 1990, sometime in the late afternoon, Osho died. I had the feeling he timed his departure right down to the last day, even to the last hour. Having done his best to set up a stable, functioning ashram that could continue without him, he more or less declared, "Okay, now I'm off." The official cause of his death was heart failure. The real reason, I believe, was his desire to be free of his ailing body. Maybe, too, Osho could see that he'd taken us as far as he could on our spiritual journey and now it was time for us to fend for ourselves.

Years later, a controversy erupted about whether the mystic was murdered by his closest aides, culminating in a book by an investigative Indian journalist, titled *Who Killed Osho?* To me this is implausible. When you look at how Osho set up everything to run without him, it's obvious he was intending to leave and that he was in charge until the end. He may have asked for an injection of a lethal drug to assist his departure from the physical plane, but, if so, it was given at his own request.

As instructed by Osho, we took his body to Buddha Hall for a short celebration, then to the nearby burning ghats by the Mula-Mutha River for cremation. We sang and danced all night around the fire. Two days later, his ashes were brought back and placed under a marble slab in his new "bedroom". It became his Samadhi, the name given to the tomb of a saint in India. Now it is simply called Chuang Tzu Auditorium.

Maybe I should mention here that Vivek had died one month earlier, apparently from an overdose of sleeping pills. I'm told that, two years beforehand, she had chosen to drop her role as the mystic's caretaker, having struggled with mood swings and depression. Osho asked for a picture of Vivek to be set into the wall of one of the ashram's buildings, using the name Nirvano, which she'd adopted since returning to India in 1986. On Osho's instructions, the inscription under the photo read: "In loving memory of Ma Prem Nirvano, who died an untimely death."

For me, it was a reminder that it doesn't matter how close one gets to a mystic physically, in daily life. What matters is the depth of meditation one achieves, using his presence as an encouragement and an inspiration.

When Osho died I was sad, of course, but also somehow excited. Living in synchronicity with an enlightened being for so long, I was eager to feel what it was like to be alone, steering my course through life without his guidance.

In fact, nothing much changed. The inner, spiritual navigation software that had brought me to Osho in the first place was still operating nicely – in fact, upgraded significantly during my time with him – and has guided me ever since.

In any case, it wasn't really goodbye, and for me, personally, I doubt if it ever will be. The space of meditation inside me and the quality of love in my heart will always carry his flavour, his fragrance, and that's just fine with me.

And still, sometimes, when I look back at everything that happened, I shake my head in wonder at the way Osho carried out his self-chosen mission to awaken those around him. Knowing all the trouble it would cause, knowing he would be misunderstood, knowing that he would be dismissed as a charlatan and a fraud . . . he did it anyway, and he did it with humour, style and a scattering of four-letter words.

"These were the cards I was dealt by existence," said the mystic, shortly before his departure. "I played the cards as best I could."

I'm glad I was around. It's been a privilege to ride the tiger, to have my eyes opened, to dance with a madman and live with a wild wild guru.

PART FIVE

Q&A

Religion or Racket?

"Is it a religion or is it a racket?"

We now fast-forward to the evening of 29 September 2010 in the UK, when BBC television is screening a documentary by John Sweeney, an investigative reporter probing the secrets of the Church of Scientology. I know nothing about Scientology, apart from the fact that Tom Cruise, John Travolta and a number of other Hollywood actors seem to like it. But Sweeney's question, directed to a former "cult member", is significant. How do you know whether a religious movement is genuine? How do you know whether your sincere desire to develop your spirituality is being exploited?

The bottom line is: you don't. Because anything can be justified from inside a religious organisation, seen through its own beliefs, and anything can be made to look sinister from the outside.

For example, one of Sweeney's chief criticisms of Scientology is that it "tears families apart". It sounds pretty damning, until you recall the words of Jesus, who warns that he has come not to bring peace, but with a sword to set fathers against sons, mothers against daughters. And we all know the Old Testament story of Abraham offering to sacrifice his own son by cutting his throat on a mountain altar, if Jehovah so much as gave him a nod.

In Tibetan Buddhism, there are tales of great enlightened beings who, as part of their initiation, were obliged to step over sick and dying old people, left bleeding on mountain paths, without feeling even a pang of pity or a flicker of a desire to help them.

Zen masters, as I've already said, often beat their disciples, and according to the holy scriptures of the Hindus, in the *Bhagavad Gita*, Krishna urged Arjuna to fight and kill his own cousins in the Mahabharata, the greatest war in Indian history.

In other words, there are no objective criteria for distinguishing between a religion, a cult and a racket. What seems heartless from the viewpoint of conventional morality can be regarded as the greatest virtue within the context of a spiritual mystic and his teachings. What does this mean? It means that the only person who can decide is you. Your own personal intelligence and the sensitivity of your own heart are the only means of knowing what is helpful and beneficial for your spiritual development. It may seem scary to be so alone; to be wholly and solely responsible for yourself and your actions. But it's also the dignity and freedom of each individual.

It also means that, when it comes to enlightenment, morality is irrelevant. Being a kind and good person doesn't have anything to do with waking up to your buddha nature. Of course, being a bad person doesn't either, so there's no need to get excited about Osho encouraging immoral or licentious behaviour.

And while getting involved with weird spiritual communities like the one founded by Charles Manson is clearly to be avoided, you will, without doubt, still find yourself outside the secure, comfortable folds of mainstream society. Why? Because society creates itself by imposing an identity on its members, while spiritual growth requires you to dissolve your identity. Society needs you to be somebody. Meditation needs you to be nobody.

In 1982, a team from *60 Minutes*, the CBS News television magazine, headed by Ed Bradley – one the of the programme's star investigative reporters – had come to the Ranch. Asked by a local rancher what he thought of the Rajneesh outfit, Bradley shrugged and said, "It's a good business."

Actually, it wasn't. The Ranch was always outspending whatever income was available. But Bradley can be forgiven for seeing us merely as a commercial enterprise, because religion has one peculiar trait that makes it impossible to view objectively: it is an invisible commodity.

This means that you can sell it without actually having it. And if you do happen to have it, you can't prove it, so maybe you can't even find one customer to buy your product.

People spend a lot of time arguing about who's got it and who hasn't, whether that's Billy Graham or Osho, but the only person who can decide is you, based on your personal experience.

Bradley, by the way, had heard that Osho was anti-Semitic, so he sent a written question, asking for the mystic's opinion on the spiritual status of three well-known people: the founder of Hasidic Judaism, Baal Shem Tov, Martin Luther King and Adolf Hitler.

Osho replied that Baal Shem Tov was an enlightened being; he said that Martin Luther King was a nice man, but not enlightened; he concluded, "And, of course, Adolf Hitler is not, and cannot be, enlightened."

It wasn't the answer Bradley was hoping for, so it didn't get aired on *60 Minutes*.

Journalists . . . aren't they wonderful?

Success or Failure?

If you are in the mood for another Zen-style koan (unanswerable question), similar to but distinct from the one offered earlier in this book, I can leave you with this:

"Was Osho's community in Oregon a success or a failure?"

On the one hand, it contained some interesting success stories:

- It was one of the earliest experiments in large-scale organic farming.
- We had extensive environmental projects, with numerous check dams to prevent erosion through rain water run-off.
- We came from all corners of the planet and lived in peace with each other.
- We created a society in which there was sexual freedom for both men and women.
- Women could walk alone at night in absolute safety.
- We had a highly effective AIDS prevention programme.
- As far as gender equality was concerned, we had women in charge of just about everything.

On the other hand:

- We upset our neighbours and made lots of enemies.
- We did not solve the world's oldest political problem, which is that when people gain power, they mutate into a ruling elite that puts its own self-interest before the general good.
- We were never economically self-sustaining.
- We tried to create a utopian community, which disintegrated after four and a half years.
- An enlightened mystic ended up in handcuffs and chains, looking like a criminal.

If someone asks me to meditate over this koan, I'll bear in mind two things:

First, according to my own understanding, the Ranch was designed by Osho as a human pressure cooker, to create an atmosphere of intensity and totality, and I don't think anyone can argue that it didn't work.

Second, given mankind's historical tendency to sanctify and even deify enlightened people, raising them so high above us that they become unreachable, Osho has guaranteed we will never be able to do that with him. He ain't no saint.

Moving beyond dualistic thinking, such as trying to decide between success and failure, good and bad, moral and immoral, the real value of a koan is experienced when its fundamental un-answerability creates so much tension in the mind that, at a certain point, thinking suddenly stops, giving way to a profound state of inner silence.

If this happens to you, or me, or anyone else, while meditating on this question, then of course the Ranch was a success.

Mystic or Charlatan?

Many distinguished and famous people have said complimentary things about Osho, including the Dalai Lama, who once observed: "Osho is an enlightened master who is working with all possibilities to help humanity overcome a difficult phase in developing consciousness."

Others include Paul Reps, author of *Zen Flesh, Zen Bones*, one of the first books on Zen to attract widespread interest in the West. Reps said: "Osho is a mystical giant, a flowering of a unique intelligence and one of those rare humans expressing himself with joy."

Violin maestro Yehudi Menuhin, New Age guru Deepak Chopra, former Indian Prime Minister Manmohan Singh, author Khushwant Singh, actor Tom Cruise and singer Madonna . . . they have all commented favourably.

But the one person who sticks out in my mind is the 16th Karmapa, Rangjung Rigpe Dorje, who, back in 1972, even before I'd heard the name Bhagwan Shree Rajneesh, responded with so much excitement and enthusiasm to one of Osho's sannyasins, at the Rumtek Monastery in Sikkim. I find the Karmapa deeply impressive, not because he praised Osho but because, when I examine his life and his utterances, he conveys the fragrance of an enlightened mystic, and this sets him in a category apart. Like they say, it takes one to know one. It's a great pity the Karmapa died in 1981 at the age of 57, because if he'd lived a little longer, he might well have made more insightful comments about his fellow mystic.

What we are left with are his remarks to Govind Siddharth at Rumtek, and his observation that Osho had passed through a great deal of training in previous lives – presumably in the Tibetan Buddhist tradition – to be able to incarnate in this life and help others on their spiritual journey.

Allow me to remind you: the Karmapa, who as I mentioned earlier possessed a reputation for recognising reincarnated monks and lamas, *took the locket of Bhagwan in his hand, and he touched it to his forehead, then he said about him: "He is the greatest incarnation since Buddha in India and is a living Buddha. Now in this life, Bhagwan has taken birth specially in order to help people spiritually – only for this purpose."*

There is no way to demonstrate the truth of this assertion. Religion, as I've said, is an invisible commodity. But if it is an accurate description of Osho's mission, then I am impressed by the revolution in spirituality the mystic has set in motion.

Mystics are rebellious people when they are alive, but as soon as they are dead the priesthood moves in and, with full cooperation from politicians, sets about transforming a mystic and his message into a tool for subduing and exploiting the masses. There is no better place to see this at work than in Christianity, where a firebrand mystic like Jesus has been safely converted into the figurehead of a system of oppression and manipulation that has been controlling human beings like sheep – literally calling them "sheep" with Jesus as their "shepherd" – for 2,000 years.

It is going to be extremely difficult to do the same thing with Osho. He has taken spirituality out of all moral systems, all traditional belief systems, all relationship with conventional religious attitudes such as asceticism, fasting, humility, humbleness, sacrifice, saintliness, charity, service to the poor and the needy. With Osho, it all goes down the drain.

He has presented himself as an ordinary, fallible human being with one significant difference: he has managed to awaken to his own inner, enlightened consciousness. He has shown the path we can take, if we are so minded, to discover the same core of consciousness in ourselves. He has explained the practical methods needed for doing so.

He has also presented himself as a man in love with the world, enjoying what life has to offer, destroying the long-held notion that spirituality and materialism cannot be embraced simultaneously. He has exposed conventional religion as a fake insurance policy, offering a passport to a heaven that doesn't exist, ruled over by a God who is nothing but a product of our childish need for a father-figure and a figment of our imagination.

I could go on, but these are the basics of Osho's revolution. To me, it is an awesome achievement, one that will have a deep and lasting impact on humanity's ideas about what it means to be spiritual.

To others, the opposite will be true: everything I have just said in Osho's favour can be used as proof that he was a charlatan.

You, dear reader, must make up your own mind.

Oh, and by the way, as you've probably figured by now, the only way you can really make up your mind is to drop it.

Tourism or Transformation?

Two years before he died, I was listening to Osho give his daily discourse at the Pune ashram, when he suddenly said: "The moment is rare when eternity penetrates time."

I think I must have been daydreaming, not really listening, probably absorbed with some mundane issue concerning my personal life. But when he said this, it sounded so intriguing that I suddenly found myself sitting up straight and paying full attention.

Osho explained that life has two dimensions: the horizontal and the vertical. In the horizontal dimension, time flows from the past through the present to the future – life is a series of events, with only one destination.

"Wherever you are going horizontally, with whatever speed, you will end up in some graveyard," said Osho. "Every moment our graves are coming closer to us – even if you don't move, your grave is moving towards you. The horizontal line of time is, in other words, the mortality of man."

Then he explained that the vertical dimension opens up through meditation. When the mind is silent, when your attention is fully focused here and now, in the present moment, you naturally shift from the horizontal into a vertical dimension of bliss, consciousness and eternity. He went on to say that the two lines of the Christian cross symbolise the moment when the vertical can penetrate the horizontal, adding that the cross was derived from the ancient Aryan symbol of the swastika, which carries the same meaning.

It got me thinking – in fact, I still think about it today – about how these two dimensions have played out in my life.

The horizontal line has certainly been a colourful and fascinating adventure: my life in London as a political journalist, my love affairs, my meeting in India with Osho and the rollercoaster ride that followed. After he died, I continued to spend most of my time in India, for the next two decades. Only in recent years have I shifted to the UK and Europe, while still spending two to three winter months in the Mystic East.

Work wise, I never really plugged back into the mainstream, choosing instead to earn a precarious but sufficient living as an occasional ghost writer and part-time meditation teacher. I've never been good at making money, never owned a house and rarely even a car, but somehow I've been capable of doing what I want with my life.

In the nineties, I branched out into showbusiness, writing and acting in a series of musicals staged in the Pune ashram, all of them comedies, all themed on spiritual growth. I wrote two plays, one based on the dramatic story of a friend of mine who was set up in a drug bust in Kathmandu, then had to get out of jail by creating a trap for the real villains. The other was a comedy based on Shakespeare's famous line "To be or not to be," reinventing the Bard's life and showing how the real answer, in spiritual terms, is "not to be." Then I wrote a book describing the challenges I faced when staging the play for the public in India.

I wrote one novel, about an English businessman who falls in love with a wealthy Indian woman and gets involved in a secret Tantric cult. The location? Naturally, Koregaon Park – it saved a lot of research, since I knew it like the back of my hand.

After the eight-year relationship with my Austrian friend ended, I never settled again in a long-term relationship, which I'm sure has something to do with living in communes. It's strange: all my life, I've never been convinced that Osho was right when he said that communes are the next evolutionary step for society. Yet, when I look back, I notice I've lived for the past 43 years in communes! I mention this because it seems to me that commune life supplies a degree of friendly intimacy and affection on a daily basis, which makes the need for a steady, one-to-one relationship so much less urgent than, for example, when living alone in a city.

I can be grateful for all of these experiences on the horizontal plane. But what about the vertical? This, after all, is the essence of what Osho was trying to convey to us. And here I have to say, quite honestly, that, so far, I have not been able to permanently reside in that space.

If, for a moment, I can portray enlightenment in terms of a country, then I have been at the most a visitor, a tourist, perhaps occasionally even a Green Card holder, but certainly not a permanent citizen, living and abiding in the ultimate state of human consciousness.

It has been a sobering experience. You may recall that when I started out on my spiritual search, I was labouring under a number of delusions. I believed, for example, along with Oscar Ichazo and his Arica doctrine, that it was just a question of climbing a number of esoteric steps, using special techniques, to arrive inside the temple of enlightenment. I also believed, on coming to Pune and meeting Osho, that I would become enlightened within a few months and soon have my own ashram and group of devoted followers.

Well, neither of these idealised outcomes has been actualised. I suppose one can call it a spiritual coming-of-age on my part that such fantasies no longer interest me.

What then has been achieved? Certainly, I feel more relaxed and at home in myself now than I ever did before. I am able to enjoy life, not so much because of any special event, or success, but simply because daily living continues to delight and surprise me. My mind, that ever-present companion, has also relaxed. It understands, I think, that thinking is mostly a waste of time and even occasionally enjoys with me the moments of silence and bliss that descend through meditation.

I meditate every day. I also listen to Osho on most days, not because I want to hear what he is saying – I really have heard it all before – but because sitting and listening to one of his discourses is a lazy man's way of meditating. I don't know how it happens, but happen it does: just sitting there, listening, takes me into meditation. It's that simple.

Enlightenment itself? Well, I have come to understand how rare it is and I know how momentous it is: as I have said before, it is an experience of oneself as pure consciousness, freed from the mind and body, beyond the grip of suffering, beyond even death. As Gautam Buddha once put it: *Suffering has no beginning, but it has an end. Enlightenment has a beginning, but it has no end.*

In itself, I don't think enlightenment is so difficult to achieve, for me or anyone else. The difficulty lies in letting go of attachments such as love affairs, wealth and social success – the usual "unholy trinity" that keeps us fascinated with the horizontal plane.

I know I have used a similar quote from the Tibetan mystic Tilopa before, but it's so significant that I feel it's worth repeating:

The appearances of the world are not the problem, it's clinging to them that causes suffering.

Enlightenment may happen in this lifetime. It may not. I can imagine that it would be wonderful to enter into the experience of death being able to watch the whole thing with awareness, knowing that it is not happening to me. But right now, that would not be possible, so I'm grateful for any extra time on the horizontal plane that existence cares to give me.

One of the problems about being an Osho sannyasin, I find, is that life becomes so enjoyable, day to day, that meditation frequently ends up at the bottom of my "to do" list. Maybe those Tibetan monks were on to something, when they voluntarily walled themselves into their tiny, one-man caves – without even a Wi-Fi connection – knowing they would never come out again. It must have focused their attention quite sharply on the essential task of living vertically.

But asceticism has never been part of Osho's vision and I'm happy to agree with him when he says that "Zorba the Buddha" is the future of religion, blending the pleasures of the material world with the bliss of a spiritual life.

Maybe I will leave you with my favourite quote from Chuang Tzu, "Easy is right." It may not be the whole truth, but, in the language of enlightenment, it's a lot closer than hard work. Here's the full quote from the Chinese mystic:

Easy is right. Begin right and you are easy. Continue easy and you are right. The right way to go easy is to forget the right way, and to forget that the going is easy.

This makes everything clear . . . right?

Royal Madness

Metaphors can be useful to explain the unexplainable, so here is one that may do the job. It is an old parable, coming from antiquity:

Once upon a time there was a small town in Rajasthan, with its own king and queen. Nothing remarkable happened until one day the town's well became poisoned and the entire population went mad. The only exceptions were the king and queen, who had their own private well in the palace. They were relieved and grateful to escape the madness that was affecting everyone else.

Pretty soon, however, a problem arose. A rumour started in the town that the king and queen had gone mad – naturally, because they were not behaving like the rest of the population. The rumour grew and grew until finally a crowd of people gathered together to discuss the situation and they decided to march on the palace.

The king and queen were afraid. They asked their wise prime minister, who also lived in the palace, what must be done.

The minister said: "It is simple. I will go quickly and get some water from the town well and you must drink it. Then you will be mad like your subjects and they will accept you back in their hearts."

The king and queen were reluctant, but the crowd was approaching and they felt they had no choice. So they agreed, drank the water and went out to meet the crowd. Everyone was happy.

"Look!" people said to each other. "The king and queen have overcome their madness. They are back with us again!"

To me, this story illustrates a significant truth about our so-called "normal" waking state. The fact is, it's only normal because we agree on it. Anyone who disagrees is going to be regarded as odd, strange, dangerous, or mad.

Planet of the Humans

A second parable: Remember an old sixties movie called *Planet of the Apes*? Charlton Heston, playing an astronaut, crash lands on a planet and discovers that it is run by apes. There are also humans on the planet, but they are dumb, wild creatures and not considered civilised. Heston teams up with a dumb, sexy, young female human – funny how that tends to happen in just about any action movie of that era – and seeks answers as to why the apes are running the show and the humans are not.

In the end he discovers the truth: the humans blew it. This is, in fact, Planet Earth. He has landed in the future, after mankind has destroyed itself. The apes took over because we self-destructed. Nice, thoughtful movie, sufficiently well received to spawn sequels: *Escape from the Planet of the Apes*, *Return to the Planet of the Apes*, etc.

Personally, I'd like to see a remake, with a Heston look-alike, titled *Planet of the Humans*. In this movie, Heston crash lands on a planet where the humans are running the show, but they are behaving like apes. For example, they are in such a primitive stage of social evolution that they worship power. They talk endlessly about who is going to be the next president, the next prime minister, the next chairman of the board. Even stranger: they choose somebody, give him their power, then kneel down before him and say: "Tell me what to do!"

They continually try to dominate each other. This even goes into sport, so when *my* team wins, I can feel like a warrior who is victorious in battle. I don't know anyone on *my* team, they don't know me, but, hey, *we* won and *you* lost!

This is not all. They spend all day cooped up in small offices, doing things they don't really want to do, just to earn money to survive. They love to be branded, wearing corporate logos on their clothes, which are regarded as far more important than their own uniqueness as individuals. Even in their spare time they don't really live. Instead, they watch actors on television doing the things they really want to do themselves.

I could go on . . . but I'm sure you get the picture.

Heston tries to convince the planet's inhabitants that this behaviour isn't really human. "You guys are behaving like a bunch of stupid apes!" he exclaims. "You're not being human at all!"

Guess what happens to Heston?

Oh yes . . . you got that right.

So now you know the story of Osho.

Epilogue
The House Where Nobody Lived

It is January 1986 and I am walking through thick snow up the driveway to Osho's private residence on the Ranch. The compound is completely silent and empty. This whole area of the commune is deserted. It is a ghost town.

I reach the car porch then veer left, walking across the garden to a pair of French windows. Gently, I slide one of them back. Taking off my snow-covered boots, I step inside on to wooden parquet flooring and find myself in an empty room. This is where Osho spent his daytime hours, sitting in this room, doing nothing.

Standing here, in this silence, I am overwhelmed by the feeling that nobody ever lived here. I am struck by the same experience I had when I set eyes on Osho for the very first time. The man himself was a profound absence; on some deep level he had disappeared and was now only a doorway for others to peer into a vast nothingness.

The words of a poem began forming in my mind, which I subsequently wrote down, and this is what I would like to leave you with. It is a reminder, beyond all the fuss, of what he meant to me and perhaps to many others. It is called:

The House Where Nobody Lived

This is the house where Nobody lived
Where Absence walked on sandalled feet
And Emptiness drank tea.
This is the place where Silence slept
Where Nothingness lay down his head
Where Laughter turned the whole world red
And Love rode out each day with Doubt
To wave at you and me.
This is the place where Mischief sat
With Ordinariness, and that
Is where that very fierce old cat
The Tiger prowled, whose growl
Could make a herd of camels howl
But also set them free.
Yes, this is the house where Mystery lived
And those, my dear, who linger here
Look at the snow and think of him
Once more, before, we softly close the sliding door
And walk away into the world
Wondering where and when
We'll ever see our lover, Mystery, again.

Postscript

So that's the story of my dance with a madman, my journey with a wild wild guru.

Everyone sees Osho in their own way, so naturally you, the reader, will have your own perspective. And the way you see Osho tends to reflect who you are, because, in the end, Osho is only a mirror.

Look deeply enough into the mirror and you will find your authentic self, or nobody, which turns out to be the same thing.

People continue to become Osho sannyasins and somehow this act of initiation still succeeds in turning their lives upside down.

So, if you decide to hook up with him, all I can say is:

Enjoy the ride and mind the bumps.

With love and best wishes,
Subhuti